AMAZING STAGES

Memories from a
British-Canadian actress

**Marye
Barton**

◆ FriesenPress

One Printers Way
Altona, MB R0G 0B0
Canada

www.friesenpress.com

ISBN
978-1-03-830341-7 (Hardcover)
978-1-03-830340-0 (Paperback)
978-1-03-830342-4 (eBook)

1. BIOGRAPHY & AUTOBIOGRAPHY, ENTERTAINMENT & PERFORMING ARTS

Distributed to the trade by The Ingram Book Company

Praise for Amazing Stages

"A truly marvelous ride. *Amazing Stages* is a multi-layered, very well written unfoldment of a wise and beautiful soul, an outstanding autobiography."
—Alan McKee, author of *Embracing Radiance*

"*Amazing Stages: Memories from a British-Canadian Actress* is a must-read for cultural historians documenting English-Canadian theatrical life from the Sixties and Seventies onward. Viewed through the prism of her own varied and highly successful acting career, Marye Barton's text connects us with the astonishing array of talent which flourished in Canada in the latter part of the twentieth century and into the present. Packed with anecdotes, personal detail and more than a few household names, this is both primary-source reading and an entertaining foray backstage and on-stage with a gifted actor."
—Carole Giangrande, author of *The Tender Birds* and *All That Is Solid Melts Into Air*

Contents

Part Three   215
1969–1983

Epilogue   395

Part One

1935-1957

"All the world's a stage…"
—**William Shakespeare**

"I regard the theatre as the greatest of all art forms,
the most immediate way in which a human being
can share with another the sense of what it is to be a
human being."
—**Oscar Wilde**

Chapter 1

Cyril and Dolly Barton

On the morning of my birth, during the middle years of the Great Depression, my mother hurried from her bed in Quinton, Birmingham.

"You were almost born down the lavatory," she used to tell me with a smile.

Constipation was the only lesson I received from her regarding anatomy.

My parents, Cyril and Dolly, were hard-working and conscientious in their parental responsibilities. They were cheery and ambitious, yet I can't recall any obvious sign of affection between them. I would have loved that. Not a greeting or goodnight peck on the cheek. Never a hug. You might understand this as "English reserve," a common label when describing natives of our Motherland. Yet Mum often liked to tell of how she could have married another fella: "He'd been a-courting me for longer than your father. But I chose your dad, because I loved him." And I believed her. She used to sing when Dad came home from work, and she always cooked him a separate meal from ours, which was "softer, to help him feel better," she'd say.

Times were hard. Times can seem hard during any period on earth, I know, but not long after I appeared, the world grew even more anxious. Rumours of an imminent second world war were gaining momentum. But by the spring of 1939, after our prime minister's promising agreement with the German Fuhrer that our two countries would never again fight each other, my father moved my hugely pregnant mother, my elder brother, and me from the Midlands southward to Britain's capital. A soft-spoken and intelligent person, Dad knew it was unlikely that he'd see any action behind enemy lines, due to his "dicky stomach and attacks of asthma." However, starting his new job as general manager for G. Beaton and Son—one of the country's major aircraft manufacturers—he would not only be creatively working at the heart of any world conflict but would also serve, if necessary, in the nation's Home Guard. So in Hanwell, a western suburb of London, Dad mortgaged a semi-detached brick house with front and back gardens where his children could play, and a garage to house a Ford motorcar.

Our previous life in Quinton, where my elder brother and I were born, had been idyllic, or so my mother claimed. Dolly, my mum, was a long-time worrier, so I imagine Dad worked hard to reassure her that the move was heaven-sent.

Officially known as Mr. Cyril Thomas Barton, Dad would have seen his new position as raising his engineering prospects, and that the large thriving city would give his children the chance for a more enriched education. That he might climb the hierarchical ladder from lower middle-class status was of lesser importance to my self-respecting father, who had turned down a chance for a university degree in order to work with his hands. According to Mum, "He didn't want to get above himself." I used to try to picture my father getting on top of his own shoulders and never could without giggling.

Cyril and Dolly Barton

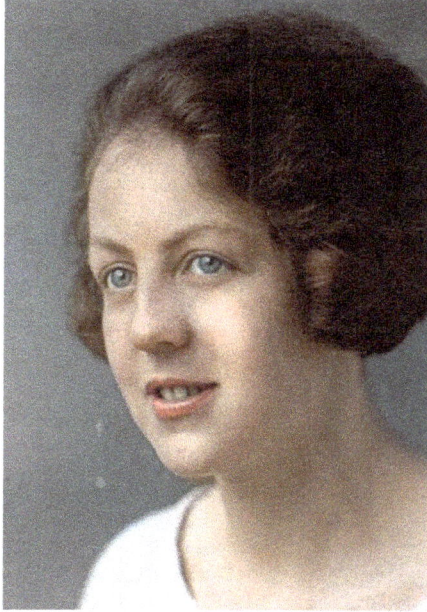

Dorothy Annie Barton ne Green

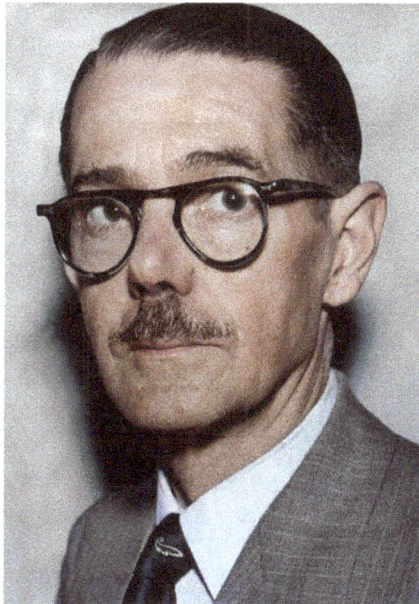

Cyril Thomas Barton

Amazing Stages

Mum and Dad with Grandma and Uncle Len in Birmingham

Mary aged 3, Birmingham, England

My handsome, dark-haired, five-foot-eleven father was more reserved, more subtle with his temper than my four-foot-ten, blue-eyed mother who, despite her height, could vocalize most effectively, even rant and roar like a Fury when roused. Shaped like a bouncing ball, my auburn-haired mum, of Irish-Scottish ancestry, was an erratic personality. We never knew when a frying pan might be seen in flames flying out the back door, her face the colour of an inferno. "Darn thing!" she would shout after it. Outbursts of her favourite curse word relieved her of much of her tensions, but a shoe or the back of a hair brush on her children's backsides was her first choice. When the storm of her rages subsided, everything turned golden. A calmness would descend with the sound of her singing, perhaps an aria from her favourites; *The Mikado or The Merry Widow.*

My father made caustic remarks when he heard divas singing on the wireless, making me wonder why he liked to hear Mum sing. Only later in life did it occur to me that he probably didn't. Every evening, she cooked his bland supper of a poached egg or a little steamed fish, often with a song. Then he'd have a glass of milk "to line the stomach" before the first beer went down. Years later, in my sixties, I read in the newspaper of a new discovery—the cause of peptic ulcers was not spicy foods but a viral disease—h. pylori—and easily cured. All that time! If only they had known.

In the front parlour of our Hanwell home, near the bay windows, sat a special table set aside for Dad's new inventions. It was a holy altar. One day as he sat there, he looked up to see me watching him.

"Think, Mary," he said, "how much the man is worth who invented the safety pin."

Hundreds of pounds, I imagined, and believed in him completely. In my young days, Dad gave me adoring attention, calling me his "Shirley Temple," after the popular child movie star. From his design desk he created and built, for my tap-dancing routines, a wondrous transportable wooden platform that would neatly fold into a bag. However, unlike a professional, I would only dance when in the mood, so when my aspirations turned from tapping toward singing and ballet, my great gift lay unused. He'd hoped to patent and make a "bundle" from at least one of his ideas, but unfortunately, fortune did not look favourably on him, or, perhaps like me, he too had a flexible heart. The sacred table vanished as the war wore on, never to be returned. Mum fretted over Dad's lack of faith in his artistic abilities, as more and more he preferred drinking beer in the evening with "riff raff," as she called his pub pals from the local White Hart.

The pair of dreaming lovers who created me in Birmingham must have soon discovered that raising a family, perhaps life itself, was a challenge almost too great to handle.

Chapter 2

Evacuations

My mother woke us that foggy morning with such a worried voice I thought the wolf was trying to blow our house down.

"He will, too, if you don't get a move on," she said.

After a cold porridge breakfast, Mum handed my big brother and me each a packed suitcase and our own lunch bag. Before she opened the front door, she pinned thick paper labels on our overcoats. Peter's read "Peter Barton" and mine "Mary Barton." Then, carrying my baby brother in a holder around her bosom, she took us from our house by bus and underground tube into the centre of London.

As we trudged alongside her, she nagged loudly over the noisy traffic, "Hurry! Pick up your feet. We can't be late. You're going somewhere special for a bit of a holiday."

Arriving at a big steam engine station called *Euston*—that smelled so bad I could hardly breathe—I looked agog at all the people. A throng, like Jesus had on a mountaintop, Mum said, except the people were all trying to make out a muffled voice coming through a loudspeaker. My brave mother, of very short stature, found a tall lady with a Red Cross sign on her arm and a clipboard in hand who should show us where to go.

Checking her papers and pointing over the heads of the crowd, the woman directed Mum. "Your two are on that far platform."

Mum hurried us on. There, Peter and I were jostled into a queue of children, all silently standing beside a trail of waiting carriages. I stared at the crowd. There were tall and little ones, fat and pushy ones, skinny and sour, red-faced and pimply, and many with boxes around their necks that I guessed held those gas masks Mum said scared her half to death. One couple carried buckets and spades and were giggling together as though off to the seaside. They all wore name tags, and I knew we weren't going anywhere happy. I watched as Peter followed a line of boys onto the train and disappeared. At that point I'd lost Mum's hand and was in a panic. Peter was seven. I was not quite four.

A man wearing a Home Guard helmet, like my father wore, ushered me along with girls who were boarding another carriage. Inside, against a window, I searched the platform for Mum, my nose against the glass. There. I found her between the crush of women. She was searching for me. The train jerked to a start. Everyone waved as she held my little brother close to her and he snuggled inside her arms. As the train picked up speed, carrying me onward, I tasted sickness upchucking from my stomach.

Days before Britain joined the Second Great War, in September 1939, all British parents and guardians were "strongly advised" by the current government to evacuate their charges from every main city to … where? Families had scant knowledge of addresses other than "the safe countryside." Even as the trains and buses left big cities all over the country, the accompanying official caretakers for the journey were still sorting and finalizing destinations. Four weeks later, when the current Conservative ministry declared the danger of attack "not imminent," we were all advised back to our homes.

"Were you a good girl?" Mum asked as she bustled around the kitchen.

My answer was a downcast stare. All I could remember were the nights in that giant building in the middle of nowhere, where I slept in a large room with lots of other girls in separate beds. We all had blankets, but I didn't have a pillow or a sheet because the uniformed lady in charge said there weren't enough to go around, and in the daytime, instead of playing in the girls' playground, I stayed near the boundary from the boys' side to try to glimpse Peter through the cracks in the fencing.

That excursion ended within a few weeks. Apparently, the British government had admitted that the imminent danger of Hitler attacking us had been an "unfortunate exaggeration." However, after war with Germany was officially declared, weeks later, Peter and I, with countless others, were dispatched again to out-of-town places, then we two were brought back again to London by Mum—because I'd pleaded for help so hard with God—only to be shipped out somewhere else after another scare. We were sent, always separated, to small-town boarding-houses, large country homes, or to our family's friends in the country. Once, for some unimaginable reason, we went to a temporary boarding school in Bournemouth on England's southern coast— opposite the German lines in Europe.

Mum tried to encourage us. "You both love the seaside. I wish I was going to smell the sea air."

I got used to the constant smell of seaweed rather soon, and the blustery wind, but the only sighting of water I captured was between the houses as my class of girls—tied together with rope for safety—were taken on walks along the back streets of the town.

Once, we were allowed to stop and look for ourselves, to see the distant English Channel. We stared. Laid out in strips, covering the pebbly beach, were large rolls of barbed wire. No buckets and spades or donkeys or ice cream carts. The cold wind across the channel made the vision even more foreboding. My tiny mind wondered what in the world we were doing there. Every morning, I made my wish as our line of girls passed a certain front garden that held in the centre of its lawn an artificial red structure with rope holding a bucket above a puddle. A real wishing well. It took loads of wishes, but Mum came and retrieved us ages later.

Back in Hanwell, Peter and I would attend St. Joseph's Primary, a mile's walk from our house—up and over steep Cuckoo Hill, with me trying to step exactly in the places that Peter placed his feet—until one morning we found the building little more than a charred pile of rubble. Bombs over London were increasing and would worsen still.

Mum and her children

After a bomb explosion brought down the house nearby plus our roof, Mum was in a right fighting fury. Dad ordered, "You take the kiddies and go to my relations in Wales. I can take care of here."

So Mum, in an unusual gesture, took his advice and left with us, while our father stayed behind to fix the roof, build our shelter, attend to his day job, follow Home Guard duties, and boil his eggs.

Due to his state of health, Dad had been refused conscription in the British Army. Since the enforced blackout had begun, for hours every evening after work, and his tea, our dad had worked with other volunteers to build Anderson shelters in neighbourhood gardens. I'd see him doff his uniform, boots, and helmet and be off to pound the streets, to check that no cracks of light were visible from any window, door, flashlight, fire, or automobile. At the sound of air raid sirens, I later learned from neighbours that he guided folk to shelters, rescued victims from bomb sites, retrieved piece of bodies for identification, consoled whomever he could, buried family pets, and sent whole bodies to the morgue. None of my father's experiences would he ever share at home.

I have no memory of our Wales trip, but within weeks of our arriving, Mum high-tailed us back to London, with the explanation that Dad's folk were worse than the Nazis. I saw my father patiently shake his head.

Between brothers

We spent many a night in our new and very tight Anderson shelter, although our dad never saw the inside after its completion with two bunk beds and a chair. Instead, he'd head upstairs, declaring to the universe, "The Germans won't get me out of *my* bed." And they never did. He was a proud but gallant man.

In my teens, I once asked Mum why we stayed in London during the Blitz.

"We didn't think it would last beyond Christmas," was all she offered.

Several years after the Great War ended, many parents publicly announced they would never again allow their children to be taken from them. "What in the world were we thinking?" a newspaper quoted. So far, the debate has never ended.

Chapter 3

Relations

The best times in those early years of the Great War occurred around noon of a bank holiday. There would come a knock on the front door followed by a loud rattling of the lid of the letter box and a familiar accent calling, "Anywoon 'ome?"

Amazingly, as if by way of wishing, what looked to be a horde of Mum's family would land on us, transported by automobile from the suburbs of Birmingham. Starting at daybreak, Uncle Les and his wife, Laura, in one car, Uncle Len and Auntie Nora, Mum's younger sister, and their son Keith in another, all would have driven six hours for an afternoon visit.

Doubly blessed we were if they brought our beloved little sharp-eyed Grandma. Always defending her husband's absences, helped off with her coat, she'd say, "He's sorry not to be here, my dears. Grandpa's now a policeman since the war began. He's right tired after defending us all."

"Ay!" Aunt Nora would add with a raised eyebrow. "Laid flat from his winnings on the greyhounds, more like."

My mother's face glowed as her eyes followed the visitors invading the house with gifts, food, flowers, and much "ooing" and "ahing" at how we children had grown or the newness of our hall wallpaper or the mounds of potato plants appearing in our front garden.

"Good trip?" Dad would ask.

"We found the petrol. There's always a way," Uncle Les would reply with a wink as he lifted a warm glass of Whitbread bitter. Then they'd discuss the advantages of the latest motorcars—a Ford versus a four-door or a two-door Lanchester.

Uncle Les was Mum's youngest brother, who, she said, had the same "Irish twinkle" as Grandpa Green. The Greens made up an assorted bunch. My favourite relation was Grandma, often the butt of loving teasing by her children, and who commanded her grandchildren to refer to her as "Grandma, not Gran." The only order she ever gave us.

Grandad in front of his air aid shelter

Grandma

On one of our too-rare visits to her wee, warm Brummagem home—with its two low-ceilinged rooms downstairs and one attic room, reached by a staircase that rose like a ladder from behind a door in her dining-room-living-room-parlour—there, on her central table, before supper, Grandma introduced me, aged six, to cutlery placement.

"The knives must always face inward and must never, ever be licked."

Vividly, I remember her hands—surprisingly strong for such a frail-looking lady. She had a queer way of pointing. Not with one finger as everyone else did, but with all of her hand, with her fingers stretched out like a bird's open wing. Once when I spilled salt in her kitchen, my father declared I'd have seven-years of bad luck. But Grandma ignored his remark, took a pinch of the spilled salt, and threw it over her left shoulder, then challenged me to replicate. I did, utterly bemused. When she told me I'd cancelled the spell, we both had a lovely laugh.

Whenever she came to our house, I danced up and down our stairs, each step a stage, and she watched every move. She never got distracted with people calling her. She was glorious.

My grandmother loved all her children. "Even the naughty ones," she once said.

Perhaps she was referring to Uncle Les. I remember on one of the visits he arrived alone in his car, and when Mum enquired about Aunt Laura, he smiled.

"She couldn't come today," he said. "I've locked her in the house."

That was the end of his story, at least in front of us giggling kiddies. But my imagination took off big-time, seeing his wife tied up and gagged. Aunt Laura always used to sit in our house with a glum expression on her face and rarely smiled. However, the following year, she surprised us with her presence, and in a high, squeaky voice spent the time berating Les for being useless. We wished Les would come and live with us because we thought him extremely useful. His sense of fun helped to change our lives from basic brown to rosy red.

Mum's eldest brother, Bill, who had a wooden leg after a motorcycle accident, rarely joined in family gatherings at our house. But one day, unexpectedly, after the war, he arrived at our door with his family—his wife and two daughters—to announce they were off to Australia as immigrants, so they couldn't stay long. That was the last we ever saw or heard from them.

Uncle Len, however, was my favourite and came the most often. He always appeared calm, gentle, steady, and was very handsome. Shorter by many inches than Dad, he wasn't a Green but married my mother's much younger sister, my jolly Aunt Nora, whom I looked up to as I might a movie star.

During those fabulous holiday afternoons, our house would be transformed into a veritable festive castle, smelling of roasting beef and potatoes, bubbling Yorkshire pudding, and ham glazed with brown sugar and mustard. Tables were laden with sponge cakes and little iced petit-fours. Set centre would be a vase of bright-coloured flowers that Mum laughingly called "mums," and always the aroma of beer and tobacco wafting through the rooms, topped with whiffs of lily-of-the-valley toilet water from the ladies as they passed by, to and fro. Surrounding all would be the sounds of music, stories, jokes, news, and laughter.

I remember one year enjoying our big family as we sat around in the parlour after dinner, seeing the grownups cajoling my mother into joining them in a "friendly fag." I saw her holding her burning cigarette far from her lips, squinting and trying to blink away tears from her eyes as she coughed out the smoke, emphatically calling, "I know how it's done." I think she'd been into the port wine.

Then, after more eating and drinking, when everyone had heard all the gossip, admired Peter's woodwork, and rescued John from an entanglement with his bigger cousin Keith, Uncle Len insisted I entertain them all.

"Coom on, our Mury! Give oos a shaw!"

Standing before them all, in a hushed silence, I became Carmen Miranda, the Latin-American movie star who was labelled the "Brazilian Bombshell." Dressed in a colourful, swishy flounced skirt and blouse—sewn by Mum—with a basket of tropical fruit on my head, made from scrunched up newspaper tied with string under my chin, thanks to Auntie Nora, with rhythmical rolling of hips and opening of exotic child's eyes, I began to sing: "*Ay, ay, ay, ay, ay, I like you veeeeery much … Ay, ay, ay, ay, ay, I think you're graaand …*" My first big hit from dancing class.

The roof-releasing applause afterwards was the day I first saw my desire for a life of show biz.

Both my parents encouraged and supported their children in any creative outlets they fancied, as were they by their parents, I came to realize later. For this I am supremely grateful to all.

After each visit, for the visitors to arrive home in the Midlands before the nightly blackout, Mum's relatives would set out around five o'clock.

My father always seemed to enjoy the atmosphere Mum's relations brought and quietly understood Mum's tears when they departed. The only member of his family I ever saw was his aloof yet kindly father when Dad, once or twice, took us to visit Grandpa Barton in a larger house than ours in the city of Rugby. He had a sister too, who lived "we don't know where exactly," Mum offered when Peter and I pestered for more information. Mouths were closed on that subject.

But on the topic of Dad, my mother could sometimes not be stopped. I remember one day hearing a revelation after a loud verbal fight between them, and my father had, in high frustration, returned to the pub.

"His mother ruined him!" Mum alleged with a sharp sniff. "Gave him everything he ever wanted, she did, and then left."

"She left Dad?"

We children were aghast.

"Did she go back to France?" Peter, the elder, asked, who knew more than I.

"No!" Mum frowned with annoyance. "She stayed and spoiled him to death is what she did, until he was twelve years old. Then down and died. So what can you expect?"

We expected anything she wanted to tell us. But no, that was that.

As time and the war dragged on, visitors from the Midlands became less frequent. Life returned for us to create our own brightness. Perhaps the tensions of the world, perhaps the atmosphere of death and danger looming around every corner, became too much at times, but my parents became less and less the happy homemakers.

Chapter 4

Killing Brother John

Three years into wartime, when I was grown to almost seven, Mum announced, "You're old enough to have a duty like big people, Mary. You can take John out for fresh air. It'll give me some peace and quiet for a while."

All I wanted was to practice my dancing but I saw quickly that grownups didn't practice anything very much of what they loved, and I had to learn to be like them. Oddly, it took me twenty years to discover John and I had not been bitter enemies.

Although I tried to look cheerful about it, back then, taking my little brother on walks meant less freedom time to dance or become an explorer across our open fields behind the house, pretending to ride horseback like the cowboys in Saturday morning pictures. On my first excursions as a nursemaid, I simply walked John's pram up and down our Greenford Avenue. One day after I'd been wandering further afield and had pushed him up a steep incline toward home, I stopped awhile at the corner of the main street to breathe and dream of climbing mountains as I gazed away from my burden. Even the noise of main street traffic didn't act as a warning. When I surfaced to the present, I saw that my two-year-old charge was not in his perambulator. He was crouched on top of the pram's open hood. With his left hand pressed down against a bent knee, he was reaching over and had a finger of his other hand on the bricks of a nearby garden wall. His little chubby body was stuck, straddled four feet above concrete paving. A voice inside me said, *Jerk the pram-handle hard. Just one tug'll do it. He'll crack his head open.* Shaking away the bad thought, I leapt forward, scooped him into the air, and dropped the enraged personage into the pram. I hurried home, assuring God, "I didn't actually *do* it!"

As John became an older toddler, my acceptance of my lot as keeper of my brother settled. I would take him in a new push-chair, this time down our main road to the big park over the river. Johnny could escape the buggy whenever he felt the urge and could plump himself back when tired. I liked the park, the air, the birds, the space, and I could skip and sing, pretend I was the heroine in a movie forced to babysit despite my royal personage. That is, until I passed a nasty man with his trousers down, emerging from doing nasty things in the bushes. He called out to me, but I grabbed Johnny and ran until my side hurt like Billy-o.

With our house one block from The White Hart, I often would see drunks singing or puking their way home from the pub. As Mum said, tramps and vagabond men were not unusual to see, what with so many injured or escaping the front line. But I didn't go back to the park for a long time.

As we grew, John and I kept up our sibling warfare. He'd ride his three-wheeler bike into the roadway so I'd have to run and save him, or he'd spoil my pretend games by jeering and laughing at me in my mum's shoes, with her lipstick glowing red on my face. Often we'd be in a fisticuff fight, rolling around the floor in dire hatred, and so repeatedly that I pretty well knew every bone in his body. Peter, the "peace-maker," as the neighbourhood named my elder brother, would glance at us fighting siblings and continue whittling wood or creating a new pattern for his stuffed animal creations.

By the time World War II finally ended, my admiration of Peter had grown even stronger and my fierce feelings for my younger brother softened. John became more independent and much stronger physically. Besides, I now had pets to care for: rabbits in cages in the garden—until they disappeared "for somebody's supper, most probably," my father said, but with such a super-sympathetic voice that you knew someone had eaten them. I also kept a pair of racing pigeons in a hut in the back yard. But they went the same way. Then an injured puppy I named Bobby—rescued from a car accident outside our house—whom I raised to doggy-hood. What a different feeling I had about these creatures! They all touched my heart with a tenderness I'd never felt for my little brother when he was my "job."

Perhaps it was Mum's love and care for us all that smoothed the way between John and me. In my teens, I remember defending John when Peter and Mum were planning for him to apprentice as a tailor, to follow in his elder brother's successful footsteps.

"No," I shouted, as we three stood in our kitchen. "John would never sit still for hours sewing suits like Peter. He needs to go to art school."

Well, he did that. Then John took up as a professional musician. His skiffle band practised in our front room, and Mum and I became his first of many jazz groupies.

Mary in Tarantella costume by Mum

Over the years, there has been much mentioned in the media about the camaraderie built between people during both Great Wars, but fear for one's life and those we love can either increase a need for companionship or destroy it. My most lasting sense of that time was of a terrible sadness in myself and a secret solitude. For many years afterwards, war movies, no matter how patriotic and hope-filled, were impossible for me to watch without my body clenching. The sound of planes overhead almost froze my blood. Perhaps a change to the old British dictum of yesteryear is valid: "Stay Calm and Carry On, and Keep Caring."

For years, I carried guilt for my misdirected rage toward John, especially after immigrating to Canada and entering psychotherapy. I wondered how I could make it up to my brother. I believed I'd missed a budding friendship with him through my sulkiness. In the spring of 1969, many years later, I made one of my infrequent visits back from Canada. John was still living at home, although engaged to be married. Enthusiastically, he invited Mum and me to a jam in Acton, to hear him play and sing with his jazz band, about a half hour's drive from home. I was thrilled. During his break in the pub, after setting down more beer and shandies on our reserved table near the stage, John gave us his full attention.

"I always looked up to my big sister," John proudly stated in his lovely lilting Cockney accent, as though to the world. Then he turned to me. "Remember?"

I only stared in shock.

"Yeh! Always did." He leaned back. "Remember that day when I came home crying to Mum and you asked me why. I said this kid had beaten me up at school; you grabbed me and marched me to his house, round the corner on Beresford Ave." At this point in the pub, John stood by the table. "You knocked on his door, and when he opened it, you punched him one big one, right in the chopper, and shouted, 'You touch my little brother again and I'll kill you.'"

"I never!" I said in astonishment.

He sat again, smiling. "You certainly did." His fingertip touched my nose. "You don't remember!"

Sadly, I missed John and Margaret's wedding. I hadn't the finances to return. But I have a photo of them all sent to me by Mum: the wedding party on a flight of steps outside a church or maybe an office building. The groom in a crumpled suit that Mum said he must have slept in after his bachelor party, and Margaret, his bride, with her flower bouquet wrapped in plastic, standing in the centre, both looking totally ecstatic. It is one of my guarded treasures.

John and Margaret's wedding picture

Chapter 5

What's in a Name?

"Mary, Mary, Quite Contrary" was often sung at me in so-called fun. You know the nursery rhyme—it goes on about gardens having "bells and cockle shells." My mother would merely smile and say, "Mary certainly is contrary."

For me, "contrary" meant difficult. But I knew I was lots more than that. My name was the same as God's mother, but she had a string of titles I heard repeated every Sunday—*Mary, Queen of Heaven*; *Mary, Mother of God*; *Mary Immaculate*—going on forever.

"Why do I only have one name?" I asked my mother, home from kindergarten one afternoon.

"One? You have two: Mary Barton."

"No, Mum. When Sister calls the register, there's Mary-Jane, Mary-Ann, and Mary-Margaret, and Mary-Louise too, but she's French."

My father tried to explain by saying Mum couldn't think of another. No help at all.

But my time came, or so I thought. We, the little kiddies of St Joseph's school, now having reached their seventh year and "the age of reason," would be confirmed in the Roman Catholic faith, as was the custom, and the Sacrament of Confirmation was conferred with a new name!

"Each of you can choose your own," Sister Josephine, Form One's teacher, explained. "By choosing a name, you honour that Saint, who will then look after you for the rest of your life."

My best friend at that time was Chrissy. We knew not to ever say the word "Christ" or we'd be punished, but *Christabel* sounded utterly beautiful. The bell on the steeple! I mouthed *"Mary Christabel"* all the way home, up and down Greenford Hill. One couldn't do better than God Himself plus His Mother!

That bright spring Saturday, the girls, dressed like tiny brides in white, lacy frocks and veils, handmade by our mothers, and the boys scrubbed to perfection, sporting new short-trousered suits and ties, were escorted into St. Joseph's Church. They— under orders to prove themselves reasonable, now they were seven—were seated to the left of the aisle, girls to the right. Behind were the families and relatives, all dressed in their very best. Facing us at the altar rail, in a large oak chair, sat a heavy-set, stern-looking gentleman, draped in long black and puce garments and a peaky hat.

"Do you agree to all that the Church professes?" the bishop called to the seated children.

As directed, in chorus, we all shouted, "Yes, we do."

For me, the joy of the day was not the prestige, or the gift from the Church, or even the strawberry jelly afterwards. It was the new name. Excitedly, after many chants and prayers and testing of catechism knowledge, our moments arrived. Each in turn, we walked to the bishop's chair, knelt, and kissed his big red ring. The beating inside my chest must have been heard by everyone as I moved up for my moment of grace. I concentrated on thanking Virgin Mary for letting me have her name all these years and hoped she wouldn't mind sharing it.

Unexpectedly, as soon as I knelt in front of the big man's chair, he leaned forward and muttered, "What's your name?"

He's forgotten his list.

"Mary Bar—" I began.

But before I could finish, he placed his open hand over my head and announced in a loud voice, "I now confirm you ... Mary," and waved me away.

I returned to my pew, a certified Mary Mary.

On the bus home, Mum tried to soften my misery by explaining that Confirmation names were not recorded. Not legal at all. But nothing eased me for several days.

* * *

Years later, at an extra-curricular class offered in 1989 by the late Spiritual Science Institute (another monumental influence on my life-long search for meaning and purpose), I decided to change my name. During a sound workshop—where I'd been fascinated by the experiments and discoveries of the instructor, whose name I've forgotten— the attendees explored vocal and non-vocal sounds. For one exercise, using our own titles we investigated and played with the vowels and consonants. I was astounded at the effects that emanated from me.

"The sound keeps dropping off at the end of MARY," I complained, when asked for feedback. "I can really get going with the first part but then I disappear."

I thought of the line from Shakespeare's Twelfth Night where Duke Orsino (extremely melancholic at the time) demands of his musician, "That strain again. It had a dying fall." In the exploration of my name, although in no way depressed, I'd seen my whole life's patterning before me: a constant fading away into nothingness.

"What sound would please you?" asked our instructor.

"MAREEEE," I cried. "MARY has that weak, unstressed, what's officially called "feminine," ending. It should end on a definite, strong note." (I hoped my life would not end on a nothingness).

However, the spelling of the popular version, M.a.r.i.e, looked cutesy to me. Nick Rowe, an inventive and quick-witted friend, suggested I change the i to y. From Marie I became Marye. I was too lazy to change it legally so it became my personal and "stage" name.

However, the change took energy to alert my contacts and associations. My family called me "Mary Hee Hee" until settling on my chosen version. When strangers inevitably said, "I've never seen that spelling before." "Oh, it's old English," I now tell people, for the 1000th time. It could be true.

A few years after my change, I found 'Marye' written in an autobiography by an American author, Laurel Elizabeth Keyes, who wrote of a friend of hers named Marye. Vindicated! Yes, until a friend informed me that the book's spelling was actually pronounced "Maaaarie." Yuk! Strangers to me usually presume I'm Mary with an 'e' (like Ann with an 'e' in Lucy Maud Montgomery's *Anne of Green Gables*). Life's one long problem. Still, I've been called worse in my long life. However, as William

Shakespeare writes in his play *Romeo and Juliet* "... a rose by any other name would smell just as sweet."

* * *

Advancing into Form Two at St. Joseph's (one night, in 1943, before the school was bombed by a direct hit), I tried my best to be a good and proper student who enjoyed the rules of school despite the terrifying black-encased nuns and their strap punishments. Truth was, I hated it all. Then one morning, to everyone's astonishment, my preschool teacher sent a special envoy to invite me back for a visit. Joy hurried me down the stairs to the large nursery classroom just below ground level.

Mrs. Trevor, a warm-hearted, bouncy lady, greeted me with her beaming smile that reminded me of the blissful hours in my earlier childhood.

"Hello, Mary. Welcome back. I've been telling the children how beautifully you recite. Please, honour us with something. Perhaps your powerful rendition of 'The Boy Stood on the Burning Deck.'"

I stood stuck at the door, transfixed. My beating heart seemed stopped altogether. Here I was in the safe space with its tall, high windows that poured light on everyone, the flickering large stone fireplace warming a long row of half-pint bottles of milk, one for each child at morning playtime. I looked at the mass of expectant little faces staring up at me from their miniature desks.

"Just the first verse will do, Mary," Mrs. Trevor said encouragingly.

My soul longed to be back amongst them, cozily drawing, singing or learning those lovely poems from my much-missed teacher. My mouth refused to open.

Mrs. Trevor, Mum, and the school nuns had multiple theories on what was to blame for my "sudden sullen incompetence," as described by witnesses. The war, problems at home, an unknown sickness perhaps causing my ivory-pale complexion. I worried about them worrying about me. Then, my unexpected lingering mood developed into a vocal problem. The following year, stammering began. Dad would follow a neighbour's advice and shout at me, 'Sing it, girl, sing it!" only forcing me to tears, annoying him all the more.

Mum came to my defence by saying we should look to our good King George VI.

"That man is an example to us all, Cyril," she said. "Look how he stutters on the radio, giving speeches, and everyone loves him!"

Amazingly practical, especially in emergencies, Mum was a smart lady. She read books and newspapers too. She knew that Britain in 1943 was fostering national pride by supporting cultural festivals and arts competitions. She put on her coat and her "best foot forward," just like she always told us to do. She took me around to festivals in the nearby borough of Ealing, and I entered recitation contests.

"We're on the way, Mary," she'd say as she ironed my Sunday dress, sending a warm aroma of hot cotton around the house as I practised my pieces.

Loving all the excitement, the challenge, the smiling new faces, to my audiences I would announce my entries clearly, with great aplomb, "'Milk for the Cat,' by Harold Monro" or "'Tarantella' by Hilaire Belloc.'"

Do you remember an Inn, Miranda?
Do you remember an inn
Where the fleas that teased in the high Pyrenees
And the wine that tasted of tar?...

Although I'd little understanding of the verses, I spoke with wondrous passion from the general sense of them and the delicious music and rhythms of the words. Few judges could resist the enthusiasm of this youngster. Mum wasn't surprised I was bringing home prizes. I got such kicks from the audience's responses that I was sure I'd found my niche in life. I got hooked on people loving me loving poetry. And I even enormously enjoyed my name when it was called out by the judges.

Chapter 6

VE Day

May 8, 1945, the Japanese nation had not yet surrendered, but Britain and Europe, although shattered and flattened, were brought to victorious life. A national holiday was announced via radio and newspapers. Vera Lynn could be heard singing over every loudspeaker in Britain, "There'll be bluebirds over/ the White Cliffs of Dover …" On Victory in Europe (VE) Day, we believed world peace was a breath away, and the blue mythical birds were materializing.

Every living person seemed to take to the streets. Although millions had died agonizing deaths or were crippled for life, our boys would be coming home. After six plus years of terror, most people were jubilant, even the "Black Marketeers" who had hoped for longer years of austerity. However, the profiteers need not have worried. Rationing of food and scarcity of goods would threaten us for years to come.

Around Buckingham Palace, crowds grew with loud shouting for the loyal Royals. Time and again the family appeared on the famous balcony until, stirred by the moment, the two young princesses—Elizabeth, destined to be our future Queen, and her younger sister, Margaret—descended and danced, unidentified, among the crowd.

Winston Churchill—Prime Minister for still a few more months—had spoken via radio that afternoon to congratulate us all, but also to warn everyone of a hard toil ahead to overcome the near tragedy we had avoided: life under Nazism. Most who heard probably pocketed his words until later. All traffic was stopped. Bus and train drivers were not to be outdone. On Greenford Avenue, I watched as people set out makeshift tables onto our main road, arranged them end to end, spread bedsheets for tablecloths, then placed food and drink gifted from every oven and pantry in the neighbourhood.

"We've got the bleedin' Gerries now!" I heard bellowed through microphones, followed by resounding cheers—whether or not mouths were full—from the folk seated around on an assortment of chairs. I saw people dancing on tables, kicking empty beer bottles onto the road, and I smelled more drunks than usual passing our house as they groped their way home, party after party.

On VE Day, our family seemed miraculously intact and well-prepared to move on. We'd been lucky. Yet I remember that as I sat on the concrete steps of our house studying the scene before me, my nine-year-old body felt strangely unsociable. Suddenly sad. Perhaps, like me, many children were in a similar mood, unnoticed in all the festivities.

* * *

By the summer of 1945, Dad had lost his position as an aircraft engineer. We were now in "peacetime." The industry in Britain that had developed so quickly and so well during the war was believed to be redundant. My father thankfully accepted a position in the British Army of Occupation in Berlin. The rank, he proudly announced, was "equal to that of an army major."

Dad in Berlin

Of course, Mum stood firm on English soil, not wanting "those Germans to get their hands on my children."

After Dad left for Berlin, Mum, in Hanwell, received a compensatory gift of a shiny black telephone—the most valuable modern invention. It lay on its own special table in the parlour that stood, curiously, exactly where my father's invention desk had been. This new apparatus enabled us all "to keep in touch," explained the installer-man. I saw the black arm in its black cradle playing dead most of the time. It sat silent until a sudden shriek would ring out, repeating again and again, screaming worse than a baby. "Blasted thing," Mum would say, straightening her

41

corsets, as was her habit when anything alarmed her. I wanted no part of it. I wanted Dad.

My father returned on leave twice, bringing with him new foreign toys, sweeties, and fascinating objects. A metal and fabric thing that when you pressed a knob opened, section by section, into an umbrella.

"Those wicked Germans have such clever stuff," Mum said, quickly pocketing the thing.

For Peter, there was a soldier's helmet with a spike on the top. Vicious yet super-glamorous. A "memento of war," Dad called it. Peter, gentler by nature, was more impressed with the abundance of toffees we now had, each wrapped in colourful, waxy paper. We all loved those. Dad also proudly showed us photographs taken of him in Berlin, where he seemed to be oh so happy. Here was a side to my dad that I rarely saw at home.

After eighteen months of "helping to rebuild Germany," my father's contract ended. Returning to London, he bitterly searched for employment alongside thousands of others in an England growing increasingly debt-ridden. He put enormous effort into trying to create a business of his own by showing old movies in church halls and private homes. But the lack of comfortable and glamorous venues soon destroyed the venture.

"They're rebuilding that bombed out Odeon Cinema in Greenford," he told Mum. "People will soon have a palace for their Cary Grants and Frankensteins."

Becoming quite deflated by his own and the nation's state of affairs, disbelieving the decline of the need for airplane construction, he looked overseas to continue his career in his original choice of work.

Perhaps the state of affairs in the world caused my parents to separate their beds. Who was I to know? Children knew better than to ask silly questions! I only knew that one night, ousted from my little "box room" high over the front door of our house, I had to sleep for the next everlasting forever in my parents' room, in the double bed with my mother. Gone were my private night times squeezed into my little windowsill, my secret escape to read books or watch the stars or imagine myself on a magic carpet, ignoring the drunks as they passed below.

One day, an offer came from across the North Atlantic Ocean. Not from the United States, "the land of milk and honey," where the streets were "lined with gold," as we all knew from Hollywood movies, but from a country called the Dominion of Canada, "Where the streets are lined with *nickel*," one of Dad's pals said. Silly man, I thought. "Linings" were inside women's skirts that Mum saw as "proof of good clothing." I was surprised that Canada, with all that snow and mountains, had streets at all.

This time, Mum put both feet down. He could go if he wanted. If Hitler couldn't make her move from England, her husband certainly couldn't. So began my parents' long separation.

Along with the monthly allowance and mortgage money, Dad occasionally sent care packages across the ocean. We, his children, wrote letters of thanks, dictated by my mother but viewed by us as forced labour. I mean, at first it felt like Christmas with a big package arriving from across the seas, but our excitement soon simmered when we found no deviation from the same salty pink baby shrimps, oysters in oil, and cans of sardine sandwich paste. Never chocolate or chewing gum. Neither, for Mum, did the allowance change. In those days, we didn't appreciate that the

Canadian dollar was worth a small fraction of the pound sterling. My father must have lived very frugally during his first years in the new country, but he supported us well at great expense to his health, I'm sure, and even after he began the gambling game on the stock market.

Our mum would complain to us, "The cost of living is going up every week, but his allowance never changes." Then she'd straighten her apron and mutter, "He's saving to come home, that's what's doing."

Mum was making herself happy; her children knew that. We could see the writing on the airmail letters, even if she couldn't. Over the years, we children took news of him like one did the weather forecast—rain soon forgotten in the busyness of life. We trusted Mum would solve grownup problems. Many of our friends were permanently fatherless and envied us having one alive at all—and one "near Hollywood yet." Neighbours said my mother was lucky her man even wrote at all, because so many husbands and children were leaving to be never heard from again.

Unfortunately, Dad's departure coincided with my move from Primary to Grammar School, when I was eleven. My unconscious fears of a life without him surfaced in the form of night terrors and lack of any interest in my education. Peter, my elder brother, now at fourteen and my father figure, was attending technical school, with little time for his sister, and Dad didn't come back even for a holiday for a very long time.

Chapter 7

Grammar School Dramas

I entered grammar school with a new uniform in blue, a fresh change from St. Joseph's dour brown. St. Anne's Convent School for Girls in West Ealing provided several lay female teachers who relieved the students' concern about only learning from flowing black convent bodies. I was allowed to choose my course of studies: Academic or Domestic. Mum preferred the former, but I shivered at the thought of higher mathematics and English grammar. However, the idea of reading loads of fascinating novels appealed much more than cooking and cleaning, so I opted for Academic. I'd won a government grant to attend and all seemed bright, yet my depression deepened.

At the school interview, I swear the headmistress winked at me. I stared back in wonder at Sister Mary Stanislaus—she who would prove to be a prodigious influence in my young life.

Surprisingly, a conscientious and keen young married lady on the staff, seeing my uneasiness heightening, invited me to her home for a week's holiday during the Easter break while her husband was working across seas. Pretty Mrs. Sealy took me under her wing. To my horror, the first morning in her bright cozy guest room, I woke in a sea of stinky pee.

My teacher's gentle lack of criticism eventually dried up my nightmares. Soon I woke to happier dawns and even began to chat. For seven days I enjoyed fresh air, countryside, village grocery shopping, conversation, my chores—brushing down the staircase every morning—by mid morning I was walking to the woods to watch and listen to the birds. There, near a little town called Leatherhead, no more than ten miles south of London, wearing a skirt over bare legs, no bug spray or sunscreen or even a hat, with only my fists at my eyes for binoculars, I'd wait for a chirp or a song, or the rustling of leaves, to catch glimpses of tiny winged creatures calling, preening, searching, or flying by: a thrush, robin, wren, chaffinch, woodpigeon, goldfinch.

On returning back to London, I was shocked to see my mother's place so shabby and disorganized compared with the bright neatness of my teacher's. I stood by the dining room table and couldn't hold back my erupting tears. But Mum let me cry. Very gently, she said she'd make a cup of tea and I could have an iced bun. My heart grew almost too big for my body for her not getting upset about it and just letting me cry. I loved her more and more for that.

Teachers can be life savers, but best friends are essential as one advances in puberty. In my second year at St. Anne's, I found my perfect pal—Super Sylvia Stokes, whose father, she said, was also "nowhere." Sylvia's ambition, she revealed, was to become a famous actress. Wow! To even admit it showed outrageous nerve.

"I want to be a teacher like Mrs. Sealy," I said, expecting high interest.

"She's so wifey."

My friend's out-spokenness confirmed her as my perfect pal. Because Sylvia lived in the direction of our house, we'd take long, wandering walks homeward—chatting, arguing, making up games, laughing at cuckoo sounds, or simply strolling. Sylvia and I bonded with powerful buddy-glue and advanced through the next school levels like a music hall act.

For Sylvia and me, Saturday Morning Drama Club became a haven from the world. My mother had discovered the club through a newspaper article. Holding up the paper one evening, she'd read out: "The club's mandate is to give the next generation firsthand experience in theatre arts, offering the benefits of social interaction and creativity. Miss Peggy Batchelor, our well-known local actress of stage and radio, is one of two lady instructors."

For Sylvia and me, this fit the playbill. The converted garage and main floor of the ladies' home in Ealing Broadway were given over to a dozen young people for three hours every Saturday, a fifteen-minute bus ride from home. Students enjoyed games, open discussions, writing, improvisations, and opportunities for back-stage or onstage activity in the most ancient art form known to humankind.

We began the following September, 1947. Sylvia took to the club immediately. Not me. I needed more reconnoitering. She and I were different in several ways. My best friend was growing tall, robust, and bumptious, a natural blonde with fair plaited hair who was destined to be a brilliant beauty. She was energetic and more sociable, while my confidence moved at a snail's pace. Even though I'd long since grown out of a stammer, Mum worried for my "lack of gogettedness," as Dad had quipped—forgetting her own extreme social discomfort.

On our first morning while Miss Leonard, the larger and gruffier of the two ladies, officiated over the eagle-eyed and cross-legged students on the hardwood floor of the house's living room, I was studying Miss Bachelor. She appeared the nicer, definitely the more petite of the two leaders. I was fascinated and shocked to notice that under her flowery dress and blue cardigan, she had no bosoms. Not even nipple points. Not a sign, while Miss Leonard, more heavy set, wore trousers and a big woolen jumper over a well-developed set of boobs—although not near the size of my mother's. The nuns at school you couldn't tell much what they had … but then Miss Batchelor spoke.

"Now that you're all officially welcomed, and you know where the bathrooms are and the rules, tell us something about yourselves," she said with a bright voice. "I want you to remember something that has happened, that got you excited. What might come to mind right now?"

God! My mind was on bosoms!

Sylvia shot up her arm as though she'd seen flames. "I can tell. I go to a Catholic school, even though I'm not one," she declared. "I won a scholarship, and the nuns will get a huge allowance for having me there."

Both ladies smiled. I sat in awe of my friend's enthusiasm, astounded at how quickly she became one of them. Then others had offers but I didn't much listen. But then Miss Leonard was looking straight into my eyes.

"Mary?" she called.

Pressure built in me. With my chin out, I growled, "Nothing ever happens to me!"

"Untrue!" Miss Leonard remarked, and then turned to the others, leaving me alone with my lie.

This fun club is a dumb club! Not like the poetry festivals I attended. I was welcome and fit in very well there.

Due to the ladies' expert approach to child education, slowly, at my own pace, I joined in the club's activities. Saturday mornings became a time for me to be serious or silly, true or false, angry or sad, and where, within the rules, we could express our own exciting selves, solo or together. The place became a splendidly enriching playground of learning where, eventually, I proved myself to be invaluable.

The occasion of my great advancement in self-esteem happened due, in great part, to the club's quandary over costuming for *The Two Mandarins*: a legend in one-act and our first major presentation. Costuming was usually handled by mothers who sewed, but with this production, we were faced with a daunting challenge.

"We can wear white school blouses for our tops," my friend Sylvia had cleverly suggested. But as I explained to my mother, "the problem is the Chinese bottoms."

"Yes, but who's going to make eight identical black trousers?" she answered. "Who has the money for all that material?"

I didn't even have to pray to St. Jude, because the answer was given at school the very next day. While picking spinach in the convent gardens—my duty for the day—I found not only a paradise of peacefulness among the trees and vegetable patches but lines and lines of nuns' laundry making flapping noises in the autumn breeze. I blinked up into the air. Behind the rows of sheets hung two lines filled with sisters' black pants. I flew like a crow, straight for Sister Stan's office and, breathless in front of her desk, poured forth my plea.

"Please help us, Sister," I blurted. "Our club's doing a Chinese play, and I need your knickers."

My headmistress's eyes widened. "Well, firstly, lunch!" she said, seeing an empty bucket in my hand. "Then we can discuss this more serious matter."

St Anne's was extraordinarily fortunate in the years that Sister Stanislaus led the school. Her insight into the advantages of art appreciation in any form showed itself in her endless organizing of operas, concerts, choirs, art exhibitions, and the hiring of staff who could encourage these talents. She was helped by the current approachable national government.

The following Friday afternoon, I took the bus home with the huge paper parcel tied with string that a laundry nun had handed me. After our "spectacular" weekend performance, I returned to the back door of the convent a rather smelly brown parcel. The idea of us putting the knickers in the wash had never occurred. We were actors!

Sister Stanislaus was not so kindly the following year when she discovered Sylvia and me playing hooky from field hockey. After the art-room space had been cleared of equipment and all signs of the week's classes, on Friday afternoons we'd been having a grand old time in our own "theatre," improvising made-up drama. Who wouldn't?

That weekend was a torture of worry and despair—our worst punishment, as it materialized. Clever Sister Stan! She'd simply ordered us to be at her desk first thing Monday morning, after prayers.

"You planned and executed deceit within these walls. Isn't that so?" the tiny, severe-looking nun questioned, that day.

We nodded, eyes on the floor.

"Are you special, different from other girls?"

We vigorously shook our heads.

"You've failed yourselves, my dears. And your class. Your team. Teamwork in life is essential, as is fresh air and exercise. But bald deception I will not tolerate."

She beat time with a pen on the old mahogany desk. Then she pushed back her chair, moved in front of her desk to parade in front of us.

"I'm saddened, ashamed of you, Patricia Stokes. I thought you more responsible. And as for Miss Barton. You are full of surprises."

She is about to cane me, just like the nuns at my primary school. Yet with a jingling of rosary beads at her side, Sister turned and resumed her seat. I sensed a wee bit of ease in the atmosphere, then more relief.

"Did you know, Miss Barton, that your entry in the last art examination won first place in the whole of Great Britain? I learned this morning that we must congratulate you. What a shame this good news has been so badly tarnished by your treachery. You have now placed me in a confounding position. I must hand you a punishment and a prize."

She sat silent. We stood, waiting to be sent home for the day or expelled forever.

"You will each write an essay on team spirit. And I want examples included. Hand them in tomorrow. To make amends for your sins, also as punishment, you will share your dramatic activities with every class in this school. We all want to see what you two girls risked so much for."

With that she dismissed us. Confusion set the room spinning in my head. If I were "full of surprises," Sister Stan was much more. What a wiz!

Because the school had not yet acquired a hall with full stage and auditorium, the following Monday, all day, up and down the school building, my partner in crime and I moved our homemade props and costumes from classroom to classroom. We figured that for safety's sake, we should give St Anne's what the students most enjoyed. Almost a dozen times, in front of each blackboard, instead of our favourite *Underworld Vampire*, we presented our fast-adapted version of Rachel Crompton's *Just William:* the half hour dramatized radio series that most English children turned their ears to after school. The effort paid off with hearty notoriety for at least two weeks. Sylvia and I were cheered theatre pioneers. Two years after I left, a large, fully-equipped stage was erected at St. Anne's. How canny Sister Stan had been and how craftily she brought her love of the arts to us.

My art prize was a gaily covered little booklet: *BOTTICELLI: World's Masters New Series,* containing the official label from the National Drawing Society, dated 1950. Despite my endless moves over the years, and having never taken up the visual arts, I still have kept and treasured that trophy.

The year before my best chum left school, Sylvia and I were chosen for something really big. At Easter-time, along with hundreds of other women, we were stoning Jesus as she made her way to Calvary, carrying her cross around the floor of the Royal Albert Hall. This was real theatre! That monumental event, the *Passion of Christ*, presented to an audience of five thousand and written and produced by the Grail Catholic Ladies' Movement, instilled in me more fervour. Not an enduring great passion for Jesus, but a need to seek out the galvanizing glow I experienced during those hours in the spotlight.

When lovely Jesus, beaten and burdened, almost falling under the terrible load, looked up and smiled directly at me—her soft face in the beaming lights from above radiating all the love and understanding Jesus must have exuded on that historic day, I knew. I understood precisely in which direction my future lay. That amazing afternoon, God seemed to say, "I've given you the gifts. Now go for it, Mary." So I have the Grail to blame for what happened.

After the second and last performance, Sylvia told me.

"I'm quitting school at the end of June. Mum says I'm old enough to start work. I know she can't afford for me to finish."

"You'll miss your O levels. What are you going to do?"

"I'd be good at personnel work. Mum thinks there are openings at Marks and Spencer's."

"What am I going to do without you?"

She smiled. "You'll probably be an actress, Mary."

Feeling like Stan Laurel without Oliver Hardy, I continued with work and no play at St. Anne's. I especially missed my friend at the greatest outing of the year—even greater than the school's outing to see Laurence Olivier's film *Henry V*, and that was mind-boggling. In the spring of 1953, the senior classes of our school had seating outside Buckingham Palace. In tiers constructed for the occasion around the Victoria Memorial fountain, we witnessed the grand parade that escorted Elizabeth Regina in her golden carriage to Westminster Abbey, there to be crowned Queen of the British Isles. I will always remember that day, the wave of her hand and her beautiful smile. How we cheered! We had no selfie cell phone cameras or streaming on television, so seeing pictures in the newspapers the next day of the millions of people forming a thick carpet up and down The Mall, I felt the tremendous power of crowds of unified people. And this was real life. No wonder writers needed to write great dramas about it, and when they did, I wanted to be part of parading it all. Theatre was my destiny.

"The life of an actress is too much of a challenge for a young Catholic girl," Sister Stan explained to my mother. "Noel Coward calls it a 'wicked stage,' and I think he should very well know. I suggest she try for a diploma from a well-established theatre school to teach dramatic arts, and apply for a London city grant. It's Mary's vocation."

"Dame Sybil Thorndyke trained at London's Guildhall School of Music and Drama," claimed Miss Batchelor, who herself had graduated from the school, years before. "There, Mary would enjoy the greatest years of her life."

From these discussions I heard only the words "drama school." Nothing else mattered.

Chapter 8

Guildhall Audition and Afterwards

Before my entrance examination for The Guildhall School of Music and Drama, I'd prepared nothing. I no longer had enthusiasm. The thought of studying what I loved most becoming ruined by dull teaching classes bothered me no end. However, as I physically approached Guildhall, on the appointed day, worry became mixed with excitement as my feet instinctively responded to the music I heard as I advanced on the building. My new high heels clicked rapidly on John Carpenter Street at the sound of a trumpet, then scales on a piano conflicting with an operatic soprano voice, all practising, practising, welcoming me, "Come play, come practise!"

As I sat waiting in the main hallway, I remembered, in horror, that my mother on my application had falsified my O level count. Five subjects were required for entry, but I'd only passed my final school exams in four. Math had been the bugaboo. I wasn't teacher material. Thoughts of these deceits had me seriously worrying. Here was I, oh so near, and yet so far from what really mattered. *You're not good enough for this course of learning, which you don't want in the first place.* I remembered the audition Mum escorted me to for the Royal Academy of Dramatic Art. I really wanted that. Two years earlier, I'd tried for a place at RADA: Britain's finest. I'd shown not a quiver of trepidation. After all, I was fifteen, a young woman. At the allotted time, with feet firmly on the ground and knees steady as boulders, I'd given the judges a well-rehearsed version of *King Lear* by William Shakespeare. My presentation was unexpectedly cut short. Apparently, all the speeches in Scene One, plus those of his three daughters, was a little too much for the judging.

"A pity they stopped me," I said to Mum, as we travelled home, "because I was just getting into it."

Afterwards, I decided Miss Bachelor was right with her audition analysis—my choice had been "a little strong." Anyhow, Mum said I was "best to finish schooling." So, I tried that again.

A strong male voice called my name from my dreaming. The meeting lasted a mere fifteen minutes. I left Guildhall convinced I'd blown it. The elderly admissions officer, from behind a large desk, had asked me several questions, but the one I dreaded came right at the beginning of our meeting.

"So, Miss Barton, you are applying for the Teachers' Course in Speech and Drama, yes?"

I stared back at the smiling man. The room was stifling. I tried to breathe.

"You prefer teaching, I gather?" the patient examiner continued.

I stared into his eyes in shock. Now was the time of reckoning. His supposition was incorrect, but I didn't know how or if to correct him. Instead, I returned him a silent smile, hoping he might read from my face a willingness to be a perfect pupil.

Referring to his papers, the man again lifted his head toward me. "You have won several prizes, I see, for recitations. Yes?" He waited in vain for any response. He tried again. "Do you think all children should be offered better communication skills, or only those with more natural aptitudes in speech?"

I managed a cough. "I think that's right," I said, almost vehemently.

My eyes widened as I stared at him. I'd hardly heard his question. "I really love theatre," I blurted, blood rushing to my cheeks. "I want more than anything to be involved, to learn from the very best." I felt my ears blocked, some pounding inside my chest, my mind trying to clear itself of muffled screams.

At my inquisitor's next request, I demonstrated some dramatic ability by standing and presenting a charming piece most fitting for my age. Waiting while he scribbled with his pen, I felt the room close in on me like a coffin.

"Thank you, Miss Barton," he eventually said. "I'm very glad to hear you love theatre."

Slowly, I left the halls of the dark old building and made my way, with blocked ears, back down John Carpenter Street, telling myself over and over exactly what I should have said and done, and what I didn't do. Before facing the tube and my journey home, I dawdled along the Thames Embankment, looking over the wide stretch of water, breathing in the non-judgemental, damp spring air as it blew across the great river. Why couldn't I do what I wanted to do? *When Guildhall rejects me, so will London County Council.* I dreaded applying all over again somewhere else. Feeling understood by the slow-moving river and forgiven by Mother Nature for my self-imposed misery, my heart opened and tears trickled down my cheeks. In operatic style, I imagined merging with the deep waters to become lost in the great sea beyond. No. Mum will want to know how the interview went.

* * *

Even though the postman had brought good news, I knew I was heading for failure even as my first term of the three-year teachers' training began. Misery of conscience can be crippling, yet also revealing. *You need to either knuckle down to teaching or 'fess up and leave with a smidgeon of honour.*

There was little difference between classes in the teaching and performing courses at Guildhall. The teacher training emphasized poetry analysis and diction, an expansion of the study I so much enjoyed with my past elocution teacher, Miss Peggy Bachelor. I recognized the subjects but with nothing like the excitement I felt when I performed poems myself.

Toward the end of the second semester came the day of my first practical class of teaching, and my decision to go another pathway toward my future. In an East End primary schoolroom, before thirty small boys staring with curiosity at me behind their single desks, I led the class in reciting lines together from John Masefield's "Sea-Fever." This was one of the recommended poems listed for clear articulation and fluctuating pitch. With their schoolmaster behind me holding his cane at the ready, the boys obediently echoed:

I must go down to the seas again, to the lonely sea and the sky,
And all I ask is a tall ship, and a star to steer her by ...

The sea of sad faces before me revealed what we all knew was the truth: parrots mimicking the lunacy they heard. These boys, I could see, were in longing not for the "lonely sea" but the busy streets outside, where they could be free to create their own lives. Standing that morning before inner-city children,

Mary begins Guildhall

instructing them to speak like the Queen, squeezed my stomach so tight I thought my breakfast would erupt. An acute attack of nerves overcame me again as I recalled my own severe primary schooling by harsh superiors. Barely finishing the hour-long speech class without collapsing on the floor, I left for home, filled with anger for what I saw as a complete charade, myself at the controls. Why belittle a boy's Cockney accent? What was so bad about a localized manner of speaking? English children were taught to converse in French and other foreign languages. Why not explore our own London sounds? Suddenly, this day became a triumph. I'd found my perfect reason to find some other way of building a career in theatre arts.

Before the close of the first year, I appealed in writing to the Corporation of the City of London—the organization who originally built Guildhall School—and to the London County Council, who paid my expenses. I claimed unsuitability for the present course of studies, declaring my heart was "elsewhere," careful not to criticize the school, the system, or my course of studies.

After I'd posted my request, I waited. Throughout the spring months of 1954, I wondered what new path I might take, but at the end of June I received a letter. It informed me that I could reapply with a further examination and audition: a team from the London County Council would question, hear, and judge me.

Amazingly, I answered their questions as honestly as possible. "No, I can find no fault in the teachers' course. The Guildhall School is flawless in its knowledge and training. It is I who am living a lie and should not continue toward a training I will never use. I am striving in a land unsuited to my core abilities, lost in a pretence of beliefs in a future other than my own."

My listeners were as one in their silence. The truth was, I disapproved heartily of the school's use of the teachers' course. But I continued the interview by presenting my audition piece with no hesitation and with well-controlled nerves, giving them a two-minute inspirational speech from Sophocles' *Antigone,* followed by my improvised line from *Henry V*: "God! Are you with me? Forward, toward the stage!"

With straight faces and steady voices, the committee wished me well. A week later, they granted me permission to transfer and with increased financial aid. Yeh, my forgiving God in Heaven, it was meant to be. I continued on at Guildhall—as a performer—for two more years. The Council, I subsequently learned from my mother, had quickly adjusted their rules to disallow any further student changes. Little did any of us know that one day I would have my own studio where I would successfully offer dramatic speech training for both actors and non-actors.

Chapter 9

First Guildhall Summer Break

The intermingling of students in various courses at Guildhall during my first difficult year had helped me to form a few joyous connections. Led by Trevor Ray, a clever and ambitious young wit, four students from the acting course developed the idea of a summer break performing troupe to go on tour with scenes from Shakespeare. Ray invited me to join, having seen me, he said, perform "very aptly" in a few study pieces. I was over the sun with excitement.

The following months, our band of six green teenage thespians, planned, built, rehearsed, and then travelled southeast England. We learned volumes about live theatre and how to cope with at least a few of life's turnarounds, and then how to laugh at all the catastrophes.

After someone's father finally loaned us a truck to push off for occasional weekend day-trips, the group took off. We created "showlets"—a term coined by Margery, our stage-manager—with homemade costumes and props, and there was research by all members as to where we might find audiences. Through the support of local councils, we entertained not large crowds but definitely gatherings of folk in parks, fields, halls, and, once, against the backdrop of Colchester Castle. That was an especially magical evening, with the audience seated on the grass surrounding the outer medieval walls, the setting sun providing colourful atmospheric lighting on Shakespeare's befuddled characters in *A Mid-Summer Night's Dream.*

To somewhere within driving distance of London, each working weekend we presented selected scenes, excerpts from England's greatest dramatist. We were happy as toddlers at the sea-side, travelling players like modern old-timers.

Once, the truck was held up on a main road with a blown tire. We didn't miss a showlet, even though that day we never reached our intended destination. Instead, we delivered our goods as a mini-Shakespeare in, around, and on our broken automobile, improvising *Henry VIII*—because everyone would know shocking stories of that king—with made-up characters wearing as many hats as we could muster at the time, presenting drunken scenes with gobble-dee-goo dialogue and blank-sounding verse in vague iambic pentameter. Passing a hat, we made a few pounds and arrived back home as pleased with ourselves as if we had just invented cheese.

Thinking that people would prefer the fun of Shakespeare's comedy—with its supernatural creatures, potions, and lovers in confusion—rather than his heart-wrenching tragedy, we shouldn't have been surprised to find audiences absorbed in our murder scene from *Othello,* where the deceived nobleman, the hero, in a jealous fit kills his innocent wife. When we presented this offering at an army barracks one Saturday evening, we were astounded at the impact.

On the afternoon of the play for the Forces, waiting to enter the temporary stage from a nearby room, we heard what sounded like bedlam coming from the audience in the large lounge-classroom-cum-meeting hall. "The Young Company from Guildhall" was announced through a megaphone but hardly heard in the uproar of soldiers offered an evening's entertainment. I decided interrupt by opening the door and entering, in character, as the young wife, Desdemona. That would hush them. Dressed in a white nightgown, moving across the stage, I imagined the audience expected a ghost story, but the raucous cacophony continued as fifty men fought for best seats in the back rows. I backed upstage, retreated, hoped to make a second, more dignified entrance. But just as I moved, a sergeant major joined me on our platform. He faced the men.

"Quiiiii-et!" he yelled over the heads of platoons of soldiers all moving in clumps of half-laughing bodies. Suddenly, complicit silence was enforced. All eyes turned to the front. I stared back at a houseful of men in khaki uniforms, standing and seated, their eyes wide.

The officer on stage raised a long arm and shouted, "These good people have come here tonight to give us some English *culchar*! So I don't wanna 'ear a bloody squeak out of any of ya! Now siddown!" With that said, he sat himself in the front row, crossing his arms assuredly. In a new, whispering quiet, I gently and courageously re-entered.

In the midst of attentive stillness, our lengthy scene proceeded through to the playwright's tragic end, followed by what sounded like a thunderous clapping of hands with rowdy cat-calls, yells, and whistles. They loved us! From that time on, our little troupe put about that we were "bringing *culchar* to the nation." Perhaps unbeknownst to us, many in that audience may have been genuinely moved by such a heinous act through jealousy and false facts. We chalked up the soldiers as being our Number One audience.

The uncanniest experience on our ventures happened in the countryside of Essex, performing to an empty "house." The seats in the auditorium were completely unoccupied. No host, no audience. We were being paid to do our thing on a small but fully equipped stage for nobody. The building holding the theatre appeared to be a very large mansion, but apart from a butler-type welcome from an elderly gentleman who showed us our shared dressing room, we heard or saw no one. No reason, we thought, to have special stage lighting. Our experience would seem more like a rehearsal. A most spooky one. On cue, at exactly the specified hour, with enormous uneasiness, we started our prepared scenes from *A Midsummer Night's Dream:* the fighting lovers in the forest, and me as the trouble-maker Puck following them around our improvised set of forest trees.

Margery instructed us, "move around the stage as usual," and she gave us our signal to start. Expressing ourselves for nobody but ourselves was impossible without holding on to each other in attempts to muffle uncontrollable giggles, convinced that we were being cleverly had. Obediently, like true troupers, we concluded our task. After Puck's final speech—given, of course, to complete silence—the open curtain remained in place. No applause. Nothing. We weren't foolish enough to give the empty space a curtain call. Feeling slightly more than jittery, we exited, in silence, into a hallway outside the auditorium.

The butler-gentleman appeared with a smiling face and hailed us. "You were splendid!" he called, with expended arms. Later, over tea and sandwiches, he told us that the audience, and there was one, couldn't see us but heard every line, had listened to our shuffling feet, and "especially enjoyed our laughter." They were patients in a tuberculosis sanitarium who were isolated in their beds, listening on earphones for the words of the Bard. A woman dressed as a nurse finally joined us and said the listeners were "deeply appreciative." Hearing this, we were humbled and much more empathic.

So ended our mid-summer adventures, having learned important acting lessons along the way: 1) The best rule is to make every performance vital, no matter the situation. 2) In any company, the actors are the last to know what's happening.

Chapter 10

Guildhall Acting and Alexander

As a second-year performing student of Guildhall, with experience already behind me, I learned quickly. Everyone enjoyed a laisse faire atmosphere. No attendance registry. No grades. We were "advised" by teachers to attend the scattered and limited formal classes on the curriculum, such as stage makeup (faces categorized as *buttons* or *horses*), Shakespeare and poetry analysis, mime (gesture through truth as opposed to ballet mime), body movement and period dance, fencing and stage combat (for both sexes), general knowledge of back-stage work, plus a weekly half-hour private session for poetry.

Most of us attended the infrequent classes but all were on time for scene study rehearsals and public performances. I learned that the student lounge was the best place to find the most useful stage tricks and the latest gossip. Also, not to expect to find teachers always present at class. This I discovered firsthand on arriving at Stage Lighting and Construction. I joined the crowd of twenty silent students crowded backstage in the school's grand theatre, waiting. A middle-aged, muscular man arrived very late, wearing work dungarees. He immediately leaped onto a nearby ladder.

"I'll say this once," he shouted above our heads. "You learn this work by *doing it*. So you *volunteer* on student shows! Right?"

He waved high a hardcover book. "Get the text. If you need to know about something technical, ask me. I'll tell you the page."

With that, he slid down the ladder, and left.

I didn't buy the book but rather spent my grant money on French's play scripts, or spaghetti dinners in the newfangled coffee shop on The Strand.

With its new and fascinating challenges, drama school continued, offering fun and freedom, ups and downs, and wonders of opportunity. My childhood education had many warnings against questioning. "Curiosity killed the cat" was the one I hated most. How liberating now to be instructed to do the exact opposite: to listen keenly and take note of what people said around us, to observe and recall how folk moved, their expressions, their tones of voice, their overall demeanours. This would be the substance of our art. Sitting on the Embankment of an afternoon, I would research people as they walked past, noticing which part of the body was leading the rest: the nose, the knees, the stomach, the forehead. Fascinated, I wondered at people's endless varieties of showing life. Then what a lift I got when I used these observations in class—the way a character moved or handled a glass, talked, or used a tone of voice, a jiggle of the head, and especially a cigarette. I soon had matches and a box of Matinees in my handbag. If the best learning came from experience, as the saying went, then I had no choice, did I? Adulthood loomed ever nearer.

Overall, our training at the school favoured the old Victorian Era. Improvisation was discouraged. Television was considered without culture and more redundant to a serious stage actor. Cinematographic motion pictures merely acceptable. Of course, we youngsters were intrigued by these modern technologies, especially film. The student grapevine was more influential than authority. When not lost in "the gods" (the highest auditorium balconies) of London theatres, we spent hours lounging in cinema houses. Rather than abhorred by "foreign wierdnesses," as international films were described by our elders, we sat awestruck by movies like *La Strada, East of Eden, The Bicycle Thief.* The classic, *Les Enfants Du Paradis,* featuring the great, enigmatic Jean Louis Barrault, I would watch over and over again—as one could, all day, in those days—just to enjoy the magic of that magnificent mime.

Mime gave me no worries. I relished expressing physically and specially creating laughter without words. In that class I could create action like a dancer but without the rules of that highly disciplined art form. Nor did I have to worry about my high voice with its low London accent. A well-developed, flexible voice was essential for a stage actress, and although I'd won the character prize in the annual student competition, I'd in truth aimed at the best actress award. After my presentation, and hearing stifling sounds of muffled laughter, one slightly empathic adjudicator told me that Juliet was written as a young woman of noble birth, unlikely to exhibit working-class twang.

"Also, Mary, unfortunately, you have a voice of such quaint, nasal quality that it drills fiercely through one's ear drums."

My private professor for poetry had more sympathy. He encouraged me to "use my lower register," although that often hurt my throat.

At Guildhall, basic breathing was discussed only in part, for singers. An actor either had a "good" voice or didn't. There were no classes to learn improvement. At that time, a true actor's tool-kit was hard to come by. His or her quality and power of speech depended solely on natural propensity and experience. Power was encouraged by directors shouting, "Aim for the back row." Hoarseness was considered lack of vigour.

The idea that I could understand and so improve my vocal sound came during my final year when I studied the Alexander Technique with Mrs. Margery Barlow, the niece of F. M. Alexander. This amazing actor/author was curing an assortment of ailments caused, he maintained, by ill-use of "postural habits." My grant money paid the fees. *Who needs body food when art is starving?*

Changes happened inside me beyond my dreams. The physical practice that affected the voice became a fascinating study. My ease with dance and mime led me to understand the natural connection between body, mind, and voice. As I continued twice-weekly classes with Mrs. Barlow, I felt uplifted in spirit as well as physique.

"It's all in the HOW, not in the GOAL," my cheery, lovely-looking teacher said.

I hardly understood her words, but the sense of it got through to me somehow.

"Firstly, stop! Think Alexander's directions," the lady would say. "Only by stopping firstly can we limit our learned faulty habits."

I liked her. She was gentle but very firm.

"Let go the tensions," she'd say, "then allow Nature to do it. It's a matter of *undoing* your usual ways. It's all in the thinking. Think about it."

Thinking rather than imagining was new to me. My imagination I used most hours of the day. But *to observe what one was thinking at the time of thinking*? One might think that was easy. But you think about it. After a thought, the mind always wants to automatically move on. Years later I learned more through discovering meditation.

These lessons were all very new, but my general enthusiasm for bodywork allowed me to quickly accept the odd approach. Besides, with this practice I could feel my spine growing permanently taller. At five-foot-two, I thought I could use some height. In the near future I was able to prove how helpful these classes were by successfully singing, with no full rehearsal, above a forty-piece orchestra.

Chapter 11

Losing innocence

Student days were passionate times and I was deeply, recklessly in love. The possibility of encountering my obsession in the flesh each school day became a torturous pleasure, until during poetry analysis one morning, when my closeted heart seemed to suddenly explode outward. Seated in individual wooden desks, in a poetry class, was already a reach back to infancy. Perhaps childhood overcame Tom Boyd that afternoon. The large, loud American music student's arm shot high in the air as his deep voice called from behind me to the teacher.

"Please, I have an example of inner rhyming. May I present it?"

He abruptly stood as though on parade. Then, in a strong mid-western accent, he announced, staccato-like, "Mery married a merry Emerican," then sat himself convulsed in giggles.

I stared into the top of my desk. Feeling the eyes of the whole class turned to me, a dreadful thought entered my head: *Did my desire for his attention work some kind of magic?* To secretly have that power was more than scary.

My ardent reaction to this wild, humorous, talented musician who was striding both the music and drama courses at Guildhall was, of course, not kept secret from my best of girl friends in the school. Jessica, then on a directorial course, merely smiled with raised eyebrows when I told her, and she made tea when

I stayed over again in her rented Chelsea room. Jessica Taylor and I shared everything. Or so I then thought. She it was who shared important fem advice, like, "Bras can be worn two or more days without washing, but each morning one should wear fresh knickers."

My attraction to this large though dainty personage began early in my second year as I saw her seated in an arch chair in the drama students' lounge, deep in the dungeons of Guildhall, painting her long, pointy fingernails a shocking shade of red. With a pretty, unpainted face topped with long, straight black hair and bangs, she dressed always in black, with a long full skirt. Jessica would listen to discussions and arguments, responding in a clipped, cultured, almost staccato voice, either with heat or humour, and always opinionated. She and I looked opposites yet had a lot in common with problem fathers and Catholic backgrounds, although my friend's mother was Jewish. I adored her. Our group—Tom Boyd, Stanley and Lionel Segal (Tom's friends from the music department who also were writing musical comedies), Jessica Taylor, and I—became a set within and without our school compound and an indelible influence on my development as an actress, entertainer, and as a person.

Jessica, Tom and Mary by Stanley Segal

* * *

Several months after the poetry class embarrassment, I lost my virginity. Of course. One welcomed all new experiences in one's final year. Tom was surprisingly gentle about it all. Or maybe he was nervous. We seldom had much to say to each other in private unless working on some project. Jessica lost hers too, I was later to discover, although not that night, and not with Tom.

My American wonder didn't exactly come on to me. We simply were magnets. I missed my last train home. Of course I did. I lingered until the guests and Jessica had all dispersed and Tom's apartment-mate was late back from waiting on tables. I looked around his rented Chelsea basement flat. Cigarette smoke hung in the air over empty wine bottles and blackened, stub-filled ashtrays. Tom's long-playing record turntable sat now motionless beside a futon couch squeezed beside the front door. A couple of long-playing albums still waited to be jacketed and reshelved, including *The Pajama Game* that he'd forced us all to enjoy until a smiling, young policeman had arrived at the door: "There's been a complaint."

I declined his first quiet invitation as we lay together. Late in the morning, I woke in his tiny bedroom bunkbed with daylight attacking my eyes through a flimsy curtained window, and Tom's big bulk half on top of me. The air was quiet. We were alone. Beyond him sat the neighbouring bed, its temporary occupant, a medical student who had answered Tom's ad to share, had already silently left, his place neat and clean. How impressive was that! Now we had some privacy. How hungrily I craved this adored body now rolled over against the wall. I wanted his total devotion. An immense need rose in me. I silently screamed, "Keep me! Make me yours forever."

Awake, he whispered soothingly, "How about now?"

"Yes! Yes!" I murmured, with only a tinge of hangover and grateful for Jessica's warning about fresh underwear.

Tom's arms enclosed me to him. The sensation of piercing lasted only a moment. Mostly, the action put me in place of a pillowcase being stuffed, his big body-flesh jamming harder and harder inside, with accelerating energy, wetter, then rougher and tougher as we rolled around and repeated. Oh, I liked it. Although I can't say I felt any ecstasy. Only lovely satisfaction. That familiar belittling yearning had vanished. Yes, this was good.

I did worry about the sheets, though, the surprising stain, but Tom assured me everything would be taken care of. I'd better get home. He knew best. He was four years older and had been in the army already.

As I walked back along busy King's Road toward The Strand tube station, I repeatedly felt clouds of pride surge through me. The act of walking, though, felt odd. The space between my legs, inside me, still felt full with the body-memory of his big, fat personal part. Experiencing a highflying sense of grown-up-ness that day, I imagined the sense of euphoria would remain for a lifetime. My Cheshire-cat smile lasted almost two hours.

My mother looked most put out when I eventually reached home that morning.

"Where've you been?"

"I missed the train," I answered, running upstairs to my little box bedroom.

"You might have phoned me," Mum called.

"There wasn't a phone," I lied. Surely, one had no choice but to lie. Suddenly, I felt dropped into icy water. *My mother is the last person I want to talk to.*

There should have been a fanfare. A rejoicing. A celebration with at least some sort of ritualist welcome to the adult world. I'd merely joined another club of secrecy.

Back at school, things looked rosier. Tom and I were a hot team. He wrote comic songs for me to sing with his accompaniment. Our duo became a hit. I can't remember any sexual intercourse between us after the initial love-making. We were a couple, and I must not expect anything more. After all, I was a

Catholic and had sinned and asked forgiveness. I was reaping undeserved benefits but mustn't push it. That much I knew.

As Tom's girlfriend, he took me to theatre openings and first-night parties. His easy connections with well-known people of the theatre astounded me. One night, through his current friendship with a student of the Royal Academy, we attended the opening of *Look Back in Anger,* where the soon-to-be famous Alan Bates (Tom's friend) was playing a role. While chain-smoking, my bow regularly passed the day with Royal Academy classmates Peter O'Toole, Albert Finney, Brian Bedford, or Diana Rigg.

Tom took great pleasure in relating tales of hilarity that high-lighted me, yet not always in the way I'd have liked. Once at a party after the opening of a revue at The Arts Club Theatre, Tom had introduced me to a tall woman dressed in almost topless scarlet, displaying a long cigarette holder.

"You remember Fenella Fielding, Mary?" he said as he intro-duced the woman.

I only stared at the unfamiliar face.

Tom helped, "She starred in *Jubilee Girl*, remember?"

"Oh, yes!" I said, remembering. "Wasn't it ghastly!"

The actress blew smoke toward me, then glided away, drawl-ing, "Dear girl!"

Tom related this whenever he could as the latest "Can you believe Mary?" that had to be told. I would have forgotten the social blunder. I enjoyed too much my inclusion in all these affairs. I was making an impression as "a big surprise in a small package."

I don't think even Jack Spratt and his wife in the nursery rhyme were as opposite as Tom and I. We differed on most levels, even our opinions on humour.

"You've seen nothing 'til you've seen *Duck Soup*," he told me, one afternoon, as we took off for the cinema. "Now *this* is *comedy*, so brace yourself."

Watching the wit and antics of the Marx Brothers, and especially Groucho, Tom rolled in his seat with laughter louder than the rest of the audience together. I sat staring at the screen in bewildered irritation. That is, until silent Harpo appeared. The thoughtful-looking man with his magical music and clever ability to neatly solve problems made me shake to the point of pain. When the movie finished, after the Pathe News, the announcement of the next feature was screened. I settled in. This I needed.

"It's French," Tom hissed in disgust, trying to pull me from my seat.

We stayed. We watched *Monsieur Hulot's Holiday.* For the first time I was able to see another classic, this time by the master of silence in sound screen: Jaques Tati. I laughed through every single slow-moving scene until the tears soaked my face: Tom beside me, rigid as a rock.

Life lessons as well as those in dramatic art were plentiful during my time at Guildhall yet I think the most precious to me, in both life and art, was my discovery of joyous laughter. Invited to add some humour to our Christmas concert on the main stage, in my final year, I discovered I had a wicked talent for comedy. Not able to remember well the jokes that I'd heard, I decided to write down a few from anyone who could supply me with suitable stories, and did a stand-up turn as a comic who mixed up the endings, while throwing in short pieces of my own. The audience's loud chorus of merriment became an addiction for me. *This has to be the best way of giving to others!* Yet it was not until my later years that I took this lesson to heart. I was still too vulnerable and reliant on others' support.

Chapter 12

Dad Visits

One morning, Mum opened a familiar blue letter-form, post-marked "Canada."

"He's coming back," she murmured. "He says he's coming 'to celebrate our Silver Wedding Anniversary.'"

As I scraped Marmite onto my lunch toast for school, I saw the fine paper float from her hand to the kitchen table and land on the edge of a dish of margarine.

Mum slowly sank onto the kitchen stool beside me. We'd seen three monarchs come and go since Dad left to seek his fortune. I was beginning my third year of drama school and was pretty used to Dad not being around these past eight years. Mum had given up watching the clock for me of an evening. I often arrived through the back door after she and my younger brother were asleep and my elder brother away doing his National Service. I'd sit at the cluttered kitchen table with my ear to the radio, catching romantic songs like Frank Sinatra's "What Is This Thing Called Love?" or Lady Day's "It Had to Be You." What will it be like to have a father checking up on me?

Mum interrupted my thoughts in a more urgent voice. "Oh Lord, Mary. I don't know what to do."

I picked up the form-letter and wiped some grease off onto my skirt. "Gosh!" Then she grabbed it back from me. "What does he mean *by chartered flight*?"

I shrugged.

Turning to a more active habit, Mum put the kettle on. She seemed to be smothering elation with panic, or visa-versa. I wasn't sure.

Mr. Cyril Thomas Barton, provider of our family, arrived within a few days of his letter. I don't recall any anniversary celebrations, only a rather growing gloom. One incident, however, remains vivid in my mind. I'd arrived home early from drama school and found Mum crying into the roller-towel that hung on the pantry door, calling, "Please, Cyril! Please, don't go back!"

Dad was standing, staring at her from the door to the hall, speechless.

While I stopped, horror riveting me in space, I remember wondering whether the cloth under Mum's grasp was going to give way. Her knees were weakening beneath her. My father and I stared as she slowly descended to the floor. Her hands must have burned as she dragged them down the hanging cloth, desperately holding on to some kind of stability, her voice pleading. "Have pity! Cyril! Please, please don't go!"

Dad stayed silent. He looked bothered at her making such a show. I wondered how he couldn't see the terrible stabbing in her heart, the anguish. Was he deaf to her despair as she clung to rags for comfort? I could only stand frozen, worthless.

Within days, Dad left for almost the last time. A strange kind of emptiness filled the house. My elder brother away in the army, and John in his last year at technical school, Mum's pleading in the kitchen, "Have pity," resonated over and over in my mind. How come I had no voice, couldn't help? *Blame tradition.* We children never knew what adults' disagreements were about. Usually something to do with money. But the non-verbal arguments affected us the worst; the tight, bleak, silent rage, especially from my father, had the riveting effect that bright lights have on the eyes of a rabbit.

"He came with a return ticket," Mum stated one morning soon after Dad left. She was scrubbing the kitchen floor. She always got more verbal doing housework. Yet I feared for my mother's sanity as she slowly recovered her place in the world. Years earlier, before my teens, I remembered her retiring to her bed one afternoon. When I investigated, I found her lying and looking at the ceiling. "What use am I now? You're all growing up and don't need me anymore."

"Of course you're useful, Mum." The thought of her feeling unnecessary had shaken even more my already unstable world. Yet more important than my fear was Mum becoming her strong self again.

"Oh Mum! Just think, you could say, 'What use are babies?'"

She had smiled a little at that, and then asked if we wanted dinner.

Knowing we all were missing Dad after he went back to Canada, she took me one evening to a concert in Ealing to hear the famous contralto, Kathleen Ferrier. The deep, rich singing lulled and soothed us both into a great sense of peace, especially with the English folk song, "Blow the Wind Southerly." The whole evening warmed us wonderfully with such beautiful suffering.

On the bus home, Mum said, "He may be gone now, but we had Dad all through the war years, Mary. We mustn't forget that. He's doing his very best for us as he did in those days."

"Doing his best" was not nearly good enough for me. Was there not work here now for men with Dad's skills? Did he still have to be away to look after us? Believing I would never come close to any answers, I turned to new rehearsal plans at school. There was much in the future there. I couldn't begin to sort my parents too.

* * *

Weeks after Dad's airflight back, Mum gave me more news. "His prospects are looking very good now. He really is doing very well. And he didn't forget you, you see. He left you something. I wasn't supposed to say until after he was gone. He's left you a gift certificate from Creeds of London Fur Company. He thought that for your birthday, you should choose your own fur coat."

Well! He must be doing very well! Why didn't he tell me himself? He hadn't the gall to face me! Disappeared, he did, like always to solve his problems. It used to be the local pub—now, I suppose, it's Canada. When I mentioned his gift and my grief about it to my Guildhall friends Jessica, Lionel, and Stanley, the two brothers leaped around in excitement.

"We'll come to Creeds and help you choose!"

"He can stuff his stupid fur!" I insisted.

I looked to Jessica but she demurred, saying she "didn't do furs."

A few days later, smiling, I met the two Scotsmen in the heart of London's fashion district. Without a pause at the entranceway of the large shop on the corner of Oxford Street, they pushed open wide the big glass doors and gave a swaggering bow as I passed through. True to form, inside they confused the assistants by behaving like boys in Santa's Village. Stanley immediately took down the full-length furs, right from the standing models on the salon floor. He paraded around in one after another, modeling the minks and the sables for me to compare. Lionel moved in another direction. He went directly into the Regent Street window display. He began feeling up the quality of coats on display, in turn dismissing each one of the styles and colours, calling loudly to us in the salon, "No! Too doggy! Too ratty ... too pricey."

After much hemming and hawing, I chose a simple, three-quarter-length brown beaver. *It's Canadian at least.* For the dumb-struck assistant I managed a smile. But why couldn't I have enjoyed the experience without my friends' help? After all, Dad must have cared somewhat. I only wished I could enjoy life the way the brothers did.

Despite my mother's attempts to defend him, I only felt disgust for my father. Back at home, however, I noticed a change in Mum. She seemed to get on better with everyday things. Then she accepted a job as a cook and nanny for two little girls and was to continue with them for years, until they were well into grammar school, when she took a full-time accounting position. With the girls, she seemed very proud of having work away from home. On the personal side, I noticed she and I fought less.

Mum had surprising ways of finding comfort and inspiration. To give encouragement in life to her own children, she always pointed us away from herself, toward activities and other people. She gave no value to her rich qualities of love and well-wishing, her generosity, inventiveness, or stoicism. She didn't see that she herself was such a grand gift. I was slow to see her ways of generosity.

Chapter 13

We're from Missouri

Towards the end of school in late June 1956, there was too much happening to worry about where everyone might go, or even where my romance was at. Tom and my friend Jessica were heavily into rehearsals. She was directing his splendid show, which was based on Mark Twain's novel *Tom Sawyer.* The whole company was made up of volunteers, mainly students from both the music and drama departments—the first time ever in the history of the school that both fields worked in collaboration. The Guildhall principal must have been charmed by Tom's salesmanship as well as his potential. We had the music arranger, conductor, and a forty-piece band of orchestral musicians all willing to spend time on "mere entertainment" that many in the faculty deemed "of far less discernment than the superior quality for which the world-renowned Guildhall School of Music was recognized."

Stanley and I were featured in the cast of *We're from Missouri.* To rehearse my solo number as the comedy soubrette, Tom plunked out an accompaniment on a practice room piano while coaching me in the traditional manner by shouting, again and again, "Louder! Louder!" Not at all the method I was privately studying with Alexander. Yet I didn't scream back in frustration, the way I so much wanted. Instead, with a smile inside, I opened my mouth and finally let out a powerful volume of sound, as though I were a horn high on a hill, welcoming the dawn, with Mrs. Barlow's voice reciting inside my head, "Allow the neck to be free." And, boy oh boy, the roof was raised!

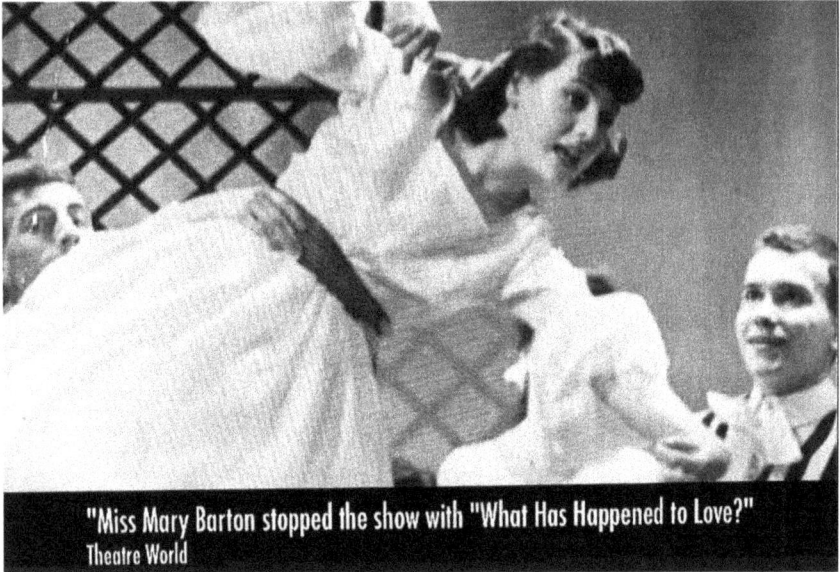

"Miss Mary Barton stopped the show with "What Has Happened to Love?"
Theatre World

Mary''s song in *We're From Missouri*

The musical ran for four very successful nights. However, after the opening night, while removing my makeup, I was amazed to see an irate-looking teacher from the Department of Voice and Microphone Technique march into the ladies' dressing room. While removing my makeup, in the wide mirror, I saw him head for my section. The man breathed in my ear.

"What games are you playing with us, Missy?" he hissed. "We do not appreciate being made fools of."

Before I could respond, the man exited, as though pursued by Shakespeare's bear in The Winter's Tale.

"Who was that?" my neighbour asked.

"Mr. Saunders, from Radio classes. He's the one who told me my voice wasn't right."

The Alexander Technique was finally introduced at Guildhall— two generations later.

Some weeks before the final days of Guildhall, a talent scout phoned the school with a message for me to call. I remember taking the note from the office and storing it somewhere. Later, I thought it might be in my purse or school bag. I wasn't sure where. Not to worry. It would turn up when needed. Then, before the opening night, on the street outside Guildhall, Tom and I had our last big verbal battle. He was bloated with fury at my refusal to go to a surprise garden party.

"Emile Littler will be there," Tom shouted. "You probably have no idea who he is. I bet you've never heard of him."

I knew he was some impresario, this Littler, but I had to get home to do my laundry. I felt so proud at having, at last, taken this chore from my mother. I might get to the tube station before another rain shower. As I turned away from him again, I heard Tom shout a kind of curse at me.

"You'll never be a success, Mary. You just don't have the right attitude!"

His voice echoing around the buildings up and down John Carpenter Street. Was he jinxing me? In the bright sunlight, we stared at each other for a few moments. Then my American turned and stalked away.

Suddenly, I knew with conviction that I wanted something even more than acting. To be a success on stage was one thing, but I wanted to be confident and happy all of my living life, everywhere I went. I wanted to like myself in between the acting.

I suddenly spoke to myself aloud. "You have to be a person first before you can be an actress. Yes, I'm going to be a person who is an actress."

What that was or what that meant exactly, I wasn't sure. On the train and bus home, I worried. Was I copping out? I knew how I envied Tom his popularity. Was I sulking again, trying to hurt him for wanting the best for me? Yet I knew my boyfriend had finally delivered an opinion he had held for some time. This was not a new thought. He resented my lack of "go-gettedness." He wanted me to be a star so he could claim me. I'd rebelled against my father wanting me to be his Shirley Temple. Back then, one learned quickly the weapon of the sulk. I didn't need that weapon now.

At that time, there were no graduation ceremonies like those in the Unites States. There were no raucous parties, no champagne fountains like we saw in American movies. We merely drifted away, focused on our future contacts, or began a search for some. I knew where a few friends were heading. Trevor Ray, a smart young man I enjoyed enormously, was joining the National Theatre Company; Mary Dalley, a gentle person and high-society debutante, already had an ongoing role in *Mrs. Dale's Diary,* a popular B.B.C. radio series; Frances Cuka was already on stage in London's West End. And yours truly had been handed a contract for professional summer stock.

Where was Jessica? I wondered. I'd not seen her. She wasn't around to talk things over, having strangely disappeared after the opening night of the musical. Her work with the show had finished—but friendships hadn't, and nobody I asked had seen her. Then a student told me he'd heard she'd left town. Never. Not without telling me.

When the curtain was finally down, when I'd wiped away all stage makeup for a while and changed my clothes that final night, I accompanied Mum and my younger brother back home. They had "very much enjoyed" Tom's musical, *We're from Missouri*, and I could tell from their faces it was true. John was beyond doubt happy to see the show's posters that he had designed displayed around the building.

"Tom has kept your original," I told my brother. "He says he's going to frame it."

I remembered that Tom had, at times, a gracious, gentlemanly way with him. This thought brought on an unexpected longing for the man again. But quickly stifling the panic of leaving behind familiar faces, a genuine excitement overcame me. The next morning, on the big bus westward for Cornwall, a sense of freedom filled me as I imagined myself being welcomed at the other end of my journey into the arms of fellow thespians who, for a whole summer, would enjoy theatre as much as I.

Chapter 14

From Perranporth to Where?

My time in Perranporth opened my eyes to how utterly alone one could feel even while working at one's dream job. Perhaps I may have rallied my spirits if the news of the Suez Crisis hadn't put a sudden end to the summer stock season. We were halfway through when one of the actors informed the troupe he was leaving and so were the other men. They'd been called up to defend their country.

I walked down to the village for a local newspaper. It was true. "Britain will lose power. Everyone must rally," I read. Egypt was nationalizing and claiming back dominion over the Suez Canal that linked us with major parts of the world. "All hands on deck," the local writer said, "no matter where or what that deck might be."

The women of the company tried to continue, the audiences fully understanding, but in those days, audiences weren't attracted by female detectives and all-female lovers. My aborted stage life would have to wait for another great opportunity.

Returning from the countryside, I found London as a foreigner might—a Babylon of chaotic business dealings. I had little idea how to continue on to become an experienced actress in "The Biz." Although a native of the great capital, I couldn't function like other actresses seemed to, with gilded resumes and glistening smiles, confidently knocking on London producers' doors. I tried.

With my hair swept up and pretty clips to hold permanent waves in place, I carefully outlined my eyes, blackened my lashes, and painted my nails, but my innards felt more like a stray dog's than those of an actress "at liberty." Nausea would overcome me at the thought of presenting myself before a talent agent's receptionist. I imagined her to be like a multi-headed Cerberus guarding the entranceway to Hades. Besides, she would demand a C.V. How did one write one? Our courses at Guildhall had focused only on artistic subjects.

Despite the shock of the city, I couldn't remain long at home in Hanwell after proving I could support myself, if only briefly. I headed for Chelsea, the area I knew best, and after a day or two of looking, found an attic cupboard space near the Embankment that held only a narrow bed and a side-table constructed from old *National Geographic* magazines. My clothes stayed in a suitcase under the bed. What more did I need? From there, after applying masses of face makeup in the common toilet area, wearing high heels and my father's suddenly useful gift of the beaver, I secured a waitressing job in one of the small, classy restaurants on King's Road. Ha! I was laughing! Most of the girls, I was told by one, were court debutantes working their way around the British Empire before settling down to married life and breeding with nobility. *I might try that, too.*

Transitions can be perilous, especially if one obstinately remains too optimistic. I imagined I would eat gourmet food, make loads of huge tips, and when I'd made enough would rest a while until I landed another satisfying acting gig.

The first evening, the loud-mouthed, foreign-speaking chef had hurled a knife across the hot kitchen to where it hung, quivering, in the wall just above my head. I'd stated in a loud voice, "Table seven wants more garlic!"—as a waitress might. Several young ladies passed by me, almost dancing, back and forth through the swinging doors. One young woman pointed out the garlic press in the tray of cutlery and ushered me back to the dining room, where I wafted the squeezer like a fairy wand over table seven's salad, receiving a high-pitched "Thiiink you" as the woman and her companion continued their conversation. I was already living in Canada when I discovered how to properly use the press.

My nerves finally got the better of me after I dropped water down a lady's backless dinner dress. I'd leaned over her right shoulder to pick up an empty cocktail glass, forgetting to remember that I had a finger bowl in my left hand that tilted as I moved. It was the scream that jolted me into dropping the piece of lemon along with the water. Leaping to her feet, the woman knocked everything from my hands onto the table. I was gone. I grabbed my fur coat and exited the back door before the manager arrived.

Extreme worry rose in me that evening as I wandered back to my attic room. I'd seen no close friends since leaving Guildhall. Ex-students I occasionally encountered in town had told me Tom Boyd, my drama school boyfriend, had returned to the United States. My insides ached with hurt. Jessica and the Segals were as elusive as the Scarlet Pimpernel. What had happened to the world?

One day, I met a colleague in Battersea, where I'd found even cheaper lodgings than Chelsea.

"You got a nice review in *Theatre World* magazine," the actor said.

"I did? When?"

"Didn't you know? Tom Boyd's musical. It said you "stopped the show." Remember me? I was in the chorus."

"Oh, yes." I nodded. But I didn't remember.

I had missed the news and more from moving out of town. As the familiar chap passed on, I suddenly remembered the talent scout who had left a message for me. Four months ago, it must have been. There was my chance. He could still be waiting.

We met at a posh city restaurant with white tablecloths, silverware, and a proper, professional male waiter. My luncheon appointment with the effusive, greasy-haired fellow proved I was in real trouble. Wearing my best summer dress, I sat in silence, facing him at a dining table. The skinny young man, in a grey business suit and tie, ate voraciously a three-course meal of soup, calf's liver, and apple pie. Between mouthfuls, he never seemed to stop asking questions. I could neither speak nor eat. I was not who he thought. Faking a feeling was a talent I had yet to develop. How could I bring back that bubbling-with-fun person he needed? Feeling only purple with rage at myself, I couldn't be what he wanted, not on demand. I wasn't his next brilliant big-bomb discovery. I could hardly hear his questions for the throbbing in my head, terrified my childhood stammer would come stumbling out to betray me. I couldn't even reach for the water glass, being sure to drop it.

"I saw your work in Tom Boyd's musical at Guildhall. How was that experience?" he asked, with growing exasperation with my lack of zest.

But the more he asked, the more frozen I became. I knew this interview could be more important even than the entrance exam for Guildhall. I had my wits about me then, but now, utterly useless.

The meeting ended with him rising, wiping his mouth, and slapping his napkin down on the table. With a final glance at me sitting like a wallflower in a dancehall, he walked out. I remember thinking he'd needed a good meal—and he did pay the bill. With no food in my stomach and an agonizing sense of nausea, I too left.

Still in shock at my increasing ineffectiveness, I returned to my latest bed-sit. I fell onto my mattress and did not rise. The darkness that overcame me took away any sense of time or place. The terror of moving my body an inch if I tried to rouse myself was worse than any stage fright I'd ever or could ever endure. I could only lie and try not to disturb anything. Sounds of ridicule deafened my ears, voices of worry and doom. Darkness again. I lay in a smelly bed for days as time came and passed in peaceful emptiness: a kind of open-ended abyss. Then, sudden panic. I heard a voice shout, "Explain yourself!" A nun stood over me holding up a cane. Her large, ugly eyes stared into my face. I awoke and longed for the emptiness again. If I lay very still, I might be all right. Still and dark.

Someone must have alerted my mother. Probably my landlady, who had insisted on a reference and phone number when I took the room. Mum must have called someone else. I don't know when or exactly how it happened. Jesus came to visit. I knew because I recognized her. She must have wafted me away, away somewhere into the countryside.

One morning I woke, as if I were Sleeping Beauty, from a long, long sleep. I felt a warm, soft bed, the sound of birds chirruping, sun filling the room as a woman drew open window curtains. The same woman brought me trays of refreshing food and took me for walks in a forest-like land. We talked about all kinds of things. She asked me no personal questions. I only recall a nice casualness that grew between us over several days. This tall, rather stout lady with a strong, square-shaped face slowly revealed herself to be Miss Hewitt, one of the women of the Grail Movement in England. I remembered her as a friend of the amazing goddess-like creature, Felicity Elwes—tall, beautiful, wavy-haired Felicity who had played Jesus in *The Passion of Christ* at the Royal Albert Hall, she whom I'd helped stone as she mimed her agonizing way to Calvary. My best friend and I, as teenaged schoolgirls, had stalked her during the post-show receptions, struck dumb with heavy juvenile crushes on the woman we had placed beyond humanity. I hadn't before realized how valuable that experience had been for me. Within a few days of my mental collapse, Miss Hewitt brought me through a serious episode of breakdown. She was my real live Jesus.

After I moved back home—at least for the weekends while keeping my room in Battersea—out of some brightening sky, Mum said, "I've had a letter from your father today. Why don't you try Canada, Mary? Dad says they're looking for young people out there. He'd like you to go."

What an idea! I was intrigued, flattered. Go to where Dad was? Go and see what he was seeing? Invited? I couldn't deny my excitement. Canada. All I knew about the place was that it was just north of "America." Yet according to the map, it was in North America. Very confusing. According to my history lessons at school, Canada had been loyal to the British and had stood its ground during a terrible war with the United States. Canada had remained separate, stubborn, like me. That I could identify with. Or better to see that Canada, out of loyalty and trust, had stayed connected to the Motherland. That was rather comforting. Was it a peaceful, joyous kind of country? All I knew for certain was that Canada had won my father to itself, and that had to be investigated. If I went, I could learn what it was he was now calling home.

I checked the flights to and from Toronto, Ontario. Impossible money-wise! On further study, I found if I emigrated rather than visited, the cost was far less expensive: only seventy-five-pound sterling. With my average earnings of ten pounds per week, I would never save enough. Then Mum offered to help.

"When you get work there, you can pay me back."

I hugged her. To make more money for the trip, I took a more dependable day job: filing for an insurance company plus supplementary usheretting evening shows at the London Palladium, and a calm waitressing weekend gig at a coffee shop near the Brompton Oratory in Knightsbridge. There I experienced the highlight of my waitressing career. I served he who was my pinnacle of theatrical supremacy. The demigod, Alec Guinness, was seated in my café, the young man who, in spite of him also failing his entrance audition for the Royal Academy of Dramatic Art, had become a radiant star of London's Old Vic theatre—the weak-looking young actor who amazed his army officers with the extensive size of his chest expansion, made possible by his theatrical breathing exercises. I knew all this from reading *Variety Magazine*. Only recently had I seen him on screen in that hysterically funny film, *The Lady Killers*. Heavens! There he sat, opposite a gentle-looking, ginger-haired boy—his son, for sure—both of them waiting for service, but not at my station.

"Please, please, let me serve!" I begged the other waitress.

She laughed. "You know the geezer? OK, but I want 'alf the tip."

Determined not to ogle, I stammered my usual, "May I help you?"

"Tea for two, with lemon, please," the great star stated.

I shall never forget those words. Floating back to the kitchen, I placed his order, and then onto his table I set a teapot, milk pitcher, sugar bowl, and two quaking cups and saucers, successfully stopping myself from kneeling to kiss his polished shoes.

If I'd known then that this great actor had recently returned from his starring role in the first production of the Stratford Shakespearian Theatre in Ontario, Canada, I would surely have "flipped my lid," as the saying went. But *Variety Magazine* never mentioned any foreign productions, even Commonwealth. On my celebrity's departure, Mr. Guinness bestowed on me a courteous nod with a glorious "Thank you" resounding from that deep, resonant voice of his. I took from his table, and to my breast, the cup that had touched his lips and found two sixpence pieces under his saucer. One I reluctantly gave to my fellow-waitress. The other, years later, was made into a ring.

Chapter 15

Emigration

Stanley frequently spoke of having tea at the Ritz, but when we met that afternoon outside London's Hyde Park Corner Underground Station, he walked me into the park.

With a twinkling eye he apologized. "The Ritz is doing some renovations. Can you believe it? We'll have to go another time."

He ushered me to a park bench near the Serpentine. We both relaxed, comfortable in each other's company. Knowing my friend as I did, and seeing his crumpled shirt and unshaven chin, I knew he knew his plan was but a wishful dream, yet I loved him more for dreaming it. Instead, we shared a thermos of cocoa he had brought along, and we sat and enjoyed the cool breeze beside the pond.

With an expression of a concerned parent, he asked, "Tell me. What is this I hear? You're trying Canada?" He grasped my hand. "Why? Mary, that's like looking for water in the Sahara. You're an actress!"

I listened. He didn't approve of my plans, but I loved him still—not only for his long appreciation of me, or his talents or Lord Byron looks, but for his innate kindness and love of my closest friend, Jessica.

"Where will you work in that God-forsaken country? Down a mine?"

"A mine?"

"Canada's stuccoed with mines. You'll go bonkers."

"No," I laughed. "I've already been bonkers. Now I want to go other places."

"Well, you may be right. I've always believed an actor should experience life completely. But do be careful, my wonderful lady."

"Don't worry. They're looking for people in Toronto, especially now they're starting television."

"Comediennes too? Mary, promise me you'll do comedy."

"I'll do everything." Suddenly, I knew our visit would be all too brief. "Tell me, Stanley, how's Jessica? I've not seen her for months."

Stanley Segal in actor mode

"She's in France, growing big with the baby in a loving atmosphere." He linked his arm in mine. "When she returns," he continued with much enthusiasm, "we're going to live together, in sin, until death do us part, in glorious happiness surrounded by mounds of children. You see, Jessica doesn't do marriage."

"I didn't think Jessica did children."

He unlinked his arm. "I don't think anyone really knows Jessica." He abruptly rose. He wandered to the edge of the pond and stood there gazing at the swan in the distance. The day was becoming chilly. Wrapping my coat more tightly around me, I joined him. Stanley spoke again, cheerily. "Have you heard from Tom?"

"Yes, a belated Christmas gift. But he's invited me to join him for a week in New York before getting my plane to Toronto."

"Oh, yes? I heard about that from the horse's mouth. He keeps in touch, you know. His show's going to be done professionally. Joan Littlewood's company wants to do *We're from Missouri*. Be a big thing."

"Really?" I felt sudden pangs of pain, paranoia, foolishness at choosing to leave.

"Lionel and I are working on a new script. You might come and see it next time you visit?"

"I will, Stanley, of course I will. Tell Jessica I miss her."

We parted with a warm hug and a jolly wave.

Apart from my father, I wondered what was drawing me to across the Atlantic. I only knew I couldn't hang around and wait for things to happen to me. I had to make them happen, where nobody knew how silly I felt inside. Perhaps in a foreign land I could become a new person, no longer avoiding go-getting.

Besides, if I found my father, perhaps I could find out more about him. If I found him, I might find more of me.

Back in my Hanwell bedroom, singing and bobbing to "Hot Diggity Dog Ziggity" on the downstairs radio, I began to sort necessities for my big crossing.

"There's a leather suitcase in the attic you can use, Mary."

I looked up to see my mother watching at my door. "Thanks, Mum." I laughed. "Funny! I never thought what to carry everything in."

She blinked away a creeping tear. "You will write your mother, won't you, once in a while?"

I stared for a moment, moved quickly to her, and we hugged the biggest hug that I could remember. Then to packing. Dad's fur coat gift will have to come. Apart from toiletries, pajamas, dressing gown, and a few blouses, I can think of nothing else essential. My feet are shod. I can wear all my heavier clothes. A list of Toronto contacts given me by a Canadian Guildhall student is secure in my violet-coloured handbag, along with ticket, passport, and saved cash. My violet beret and white gloves are waiting in the hall with my winter coat.

A neighbour of ours had informed my mother that Canada was "undeveloped territory." She'd added, "The Dominion of Canada is a largely untapped gold mine. Well, if not gold, then nickel, and that's worth more than most of anything in this post-war Britain."

My father, while visiting home, had amazed us with scraps of information. I could hardly imagine one country so wide that to cross it by train would takes days.

"You could drop the British Isles in one of its lakes," he'd said. "Canada is like an uneducated relative who needs help growing up."

Knowing nothing then of Canada's far different truth, I remember wondering if I could help too. But, then, all I wanted was to fly, explore New York City, find Tom Boyd and my father, and go on acting.

The future was one boarding pass away.

Part Two

1957–1968

"To look outside is to dream. To look inside—is to awaken."

—**Carl Jung**

Chapter 16

Arrival

Carrying a passport and an official visa for a short stay in the United States, I waited, hardly breathing, at Idlewild airport, for my old boyfriend to appear or a message to tell me "sorry." No, I heard a loud "Hi!" and saw his frantic wave. After dining on cheese and crackers the first evening in his rented room in Brooklyn, I was up and hurried out to the actors' Mecca: Broadway! Tom had contrived to buy the latest, hottest tickets to see the last night of Eugene O'Neill's sombre masterpiece *Long Day's Journey into Night*, with Frederic March and Jason Roberts Jr. leading the cast. Even with the time change after a nine-hour flight over the Atlantic in a BOAC airplane, I think I hardly missed a word of the almost four-hour drama, so fantastic was the production.

That was the beginning of my week, and so it went with every hour clocked in on Tom's typed-up agenda. New York City was "a gas," as the new saying went, as I basked in live theatre, ogled at skyscrapers, walked for hours, smelling pungent coffee on every city corner, danced in the fall leaves of Central Park, and lingered in the halls of the Cloisters. I was truly welcomed. Yet despite the attention and thrills, I felt a pull to follow my plans.

"Stay," Tom urged. He seemed to genuinely want me around. We'd made love the first night in New York, but we'd come to know each other that way as students in England. By this time,

I'd learned a little more about what I really needed. I was a good Catholic—of sorts—committed to promises and a waiting father. My time of high-flying in the city of glamour—whose roads were definitely not paved with gold—had to end.

* * *

On a clear, unusually warm day in October, I began my Canadian adventure. Through the window as the plane taxied toward its destination, I saw a long, low hut, like a toy model, on the horizon: Toronto's Malton Airport. This was it? The contrast with the city airports I'd left recently, was a jolt, yet as I excitedly descended from the plane and touched the black tarmac with my high heels, I stood a moment in wonder. The air felt different. Cleaner. The temperature sharper than in New York.

Seeing the other passengers moving ahead, with my vanity case and clutch-purse in one white-gloved hand, and holding in my other Dad's gift of the new beaver coat held tight from a sudden breeze, I followed toward the distant shed. Please, God, let him be there. What will he think of my sojourn in America? What other immigrant had a stopover for sex and theatre while pioneering?

Passing through a large doorway for both arrivals and departures, I spotted Dad at the rear of the crowded room. How could I miss that dark-mustached, distinguished-looking man, looking somewhat taller and thinner than the others around him, his stern face behind the familiar horn-rimmed spectacles. His dark hair showed greyer than when I'd last seen him a year earlier in England on that never-to-be forgotten cryptic visit when he returned but only to celebrate my parents' twenty-fifth wedding anniversary. What an anti-climax that had been! But now, he was here—my anchor in this unknown land. Now everything would be fine.

I knew Dad to be a man not given to effusive demonstrations, yet as he carried my suitcase from the Landed Immigrant enclosure his words stunned me.

"Did you have a row with your mother?" He marched me quickly across a large carpark. "Is that why you're here?"

What? Hadn't he told my mother this was the place for me?

He stopped, set down my suitcase, and looked at me directly. "You know, there's a plane going back to London right now, girlie. You should get on it."

I couldn't believe he was serious. "I only just got here!" I stammered.

Guessing I would stand my ground—knowing I was "a chip off the old block," as my family described me—without answering, my father loaded my case into the rear of a black, four-door automobile.

"Well, get in. And don't tell your mother I have a car. You have to have a car here. She wouldn't understand," my taciturn father added as he opened the door of what I took, at first, to be the driver's side. My first of many discombobulations as a newcomer.

Not understanding his reasoning for a car as necessary transportation, I obediently got in. Why was he in such a mood? Was he miffed at Mum about something, or at me because I had a holiday en route? Ah well, he'll come round. After all, one of the reasons I came was to get to know this wanderer. But things weren't boding well so far.

We sat in silence as he drove along a never-ending straight main street that showed no signs of the snow I'd been warned about. Even though the temperature was unexpectedly warm that October, I'd hoped to impress Dad by wearing the fur he had sent money for, but he wasn't commenting. The luxury item didn't exactly suit the carefree image I wanted as a daring young lass on an adventure. In the passenger seat, I began to feel hotter than my mother's worst temper, like a cheap Hollywood starlet without her makeup, and I started to blame my father for setting me up. Mum too. What was going on? I'd show them. If this country was crying out for newness, then I could bring new life. New countries must be filled with people wanting to start theatre companies.

Clutching my vanity box to my chest as though it were my only solace, I concentrated on the view ahead. Streams of wires stretched across from tall wooden poles on either side of the road. This pattern continued on one long line into infinity. What an eyesore! *Why aren't they hidden underground? Don't Canadians care?* At each set of traffic lights stood a church, a gas station, a bank, or a variety store—north, south, east, or west of the crossroads, then a stretch of stores on each side, one-storey buildings joined together in a long row, some of brick with tall wooden fronts. I was in a Western film waiting for the shooting action and the singing romance. But the picture was silent. The piano player hadn't shown. A sickening feeling slowly grew in my gut.

Dad pulled on the brake. I woke up to the present and saw he had parked on a wide avenue bordered by rather stately-looking buildings.

"This is Jarvis Street. I've booked you into the Westminster for the night."

Becoming more anxious, I followed him up the bare stone staircase of the hotel, into a corner room on the third floor. The linoleum floor smelled of cleaning fluid. He placed my suitcase on a mat beside a metal rail bed and a window overlooking rooftops.

"That faces south," Dad said. "That's Sears down there, a clothing factory. You might get work there. That's if you insist on staying."

I wasn't insisting on anything. Confusion continued to whirl around my brain. We had never been a talkative family, but this lack of communication was like a horror movie. I began to feel panic. Dad moved toward the door. We stared at each other: this scrawny-faced, unhappy man in his tweed suit, brown tie, and waistcoat, and I, embarrassed in my fluffy violet beret and hot beaver. My heart pounded. What was I doing in a hotel? Where was his home?

"How much money do you have?" Dad asked.

"Thirty dollars!" I was proud of my savings.

Dad reached into his pocket, took out his wallet, and thrust three small purple papers into my hand. "Well, there's another thirty. That should keep you another day." He turned his back, walked out of the door, and disappeared.

The ending of my journey was not happening as I'd imagined. This flight of fancy was becoming a really lurid trek!

The only sensation I remember then was that tiredness overcame me. I looked again at the bed. Its cover looked clean. No stains. I lay my head on the form of the solitary pillow and stretched out. The springs were working. If they could rebound like this, surely, I could bounce back from petty disappointments. I would not, ever again, let myself get as down as I'd been in London. Slowly, I began to doze.

* * *

Waking two hours later, the room looked dark, and my stomach growled. Anticipation of new discoveries surged through my nervous system. Newness always excited me. I opened the window overlooking the street and breathed warm air. Looking down below, I was tickled to see scantily dressed women standing in revealing poses under streetlights, some leaning into car windows, wagging their behinds like colourful, sequined terriers.

The hotel lobby seemed busier than when Dad had brought me through that afternoon.

"Our smorgasbord dinner closes at ten," the male receptionist told me. "There's places open round the corner." He indicated the direction with his head.

Outside in the balmy air, wearing only a light cardigan over my summer blouse, I passed two middle-aged women lounging against the hotel walls, calling to the men passing into the lobby. In case I should somehow become caught up in the business of hooking, I walked speedily down the street to the first corner. Turning right, I found a small coffee bar. I entered and sat on a high stool. Trying out my North American accent, I ordered tea and toast.

"Brown or white?" droned a weary-looking man behind the counter. He was clearly at the end of his shift.

116

I opted for white, giving up on accents. A metal pot with a teabag hanging on its side was placed before me, followed by two warm, mushy squares of dough clinging to brown crusts.

"Have you come far?" said a convivial voice near me.

Turning, I found a friendly, clean-shaven man leaning over from the adjacent stool. Evidently, he respected my new immigrant status, because the stranger was very interested in my plan to go down to the Canadian Broadcasting Corporation the following morning to see if I could find acting work. The CBC building wasn't far away. Perhaps my father had left me in what he thought was a convenient spot.

"What a coincidence! I have a friend works at CBC," the man offered.

Astounded, I silently thanked my guardian angel for the swiftness of her help.

"It's a bit difficult to talk in here," the man continued. "There's a more comfortable place along the road. Would you join me?"

How could I refuse my first request for company in Canada? Also, I considered the unexpected invitation could be an opportunity for acting research into humanity and dramatic incidents from which I could draw later. Cheerily I went along.

The guy's true intentions dawned on me slowly after I'd ordered, yes, why not, a zombie. That sounded a fun concoction. We were in a large, smoke-filled bar called the Brown Derby on the corner of Yonge (pronounced Young) and Dundas streets. I watched as my peculiar companion slowly changed from a helpful fellow-traveller into a vulgar creature, clearly with only sex on his mind. An escape plan was necessary. I contrived the perfect answer. For him to leave me, I would bore him to death. At top voice—in order to be heard above the loud piped-in country music in the crowded room of drinkers—with energetic enthusiasm, I began to describe the plot of the first play that Tom had taken me to see in New York: *Long Day's Journey into Night.*

"It's about this family, this famous family … well, the father is, or was famous, and he has two sons that are useless … well, everyone's useless, really, but terribly sad. The mother is addicted to morphine, and the youngest son is dying of TB … they're riddled with hurt …"

As I rattled on, I noticed the guy staring at me with disappearing interest. Then—my scheme worked—he stood and said he was "going for a leak." I knew he wasn't going to any bathroom. Ten minutes later, I passed him at the tavern entrance as he was re-entering with a laughing fake blonde on his arm. I giggled all the way back to the hotel, high on a strong, free nightcap. Acknowledging the hookers on the way in, I waved to the cats. *I'm not that much different from them.*

Chapter 17

Getting Grounded

With three days' sleep and rest in the Westminster Hotel, I gained energy and renewed enthusiasm to get going with my pioneering. I paid the hotel bill with the thirty dollars Dad had given me, with enough left over for a phone call to the local Young Women's Christian Association. There, from my meagre savings, I survived on a healthy diet of spinach and eggs for the following fortnight until I landed my first job in Canada. I tell a lie. Each Saturday, I bought a ten-cent candy bar for dessert, and one day a luscious, juice-dripping peach. Oh, I so recommend that as a reward for just existing.

In the evenings, with less stress, I would roam alone, up and down the sidewalks of Yonge Street, the central road that divides Toronto, east and west. The downtown area served as the main shopping and office strip by day, and in the evening was the hub of late entertainment. Store windows were stimulating at night, yet mystifying. Why was everything manufactured in England or the US? A display of elegant designer and hardy walking shoes had me wondering how a shoe store in Toronto could stay in business when everyone I'd met already had a pair?

Originally, Yonge Street was intended as a military trail leading to the northern Great Lakes. I learned all this from a history student at the Y. The long road began at the Lake Ontario docks, on the southern shores of Toronto, and in the late fifties, stretched all the way to Nipigon, where it joined the Trans-Canada Highway and was, according to this student, "the longest street in the world." As I walked along it, I knew it was the longest for me, as it led to Willowdale, where my father lived, or said he did, many bus stops northward—where I'd not been invited. The vibrancy and noise of traffic and people helped to keep me positive.

One morning, an angel appeared—as though from a story-book. I'd been sipping morning tea in an orange-painted restaurant, checking the want ads in a borrowed newspaper from the Y, underlining phone numbers with my fountain pen in my white-gloved hand. Seeing possibilities, I marked them before heading out to find a phone box. Waiting at the traffic lights on the corner of King and Yonge, I heard a male voice from nearby.

"You looking for a job?"

My eyes tried to take in this fortune teller.

"I saw you in the Honeydew!"

The lights changed. The well-dressed man held my elbow as we crossed the busy street and then stood with me on the other side. Perhaps because he wasn't smiling or trying to win me over with masculine charm, I wasn't fearful. I listened to his suggestion. He wrote down "Consumers' Gas" on a corner of my newspaper, and an address.

"It's just a few blocks on," he said, pointing eastward. "Tell them your uncle works there and that's how you know they're looking for clerks—in accounting."

"Accounting?"

"You can work an adding machine?" he asked.

As I shook my head, I expected my angel to evaporate.

"Listen up. Tell them yes, you can." He frowned a moment, then brightened. "They're looking for landed immigrants. You from England?"

I nodded.

"Perfect! They'll think you're very bright. If they test you on a machine, tell them you're used to pound sterling, it's the dollars that's getting you mixed up. Good luck, kid!" And he was gone.

At that time, Consumers' Gas Company was slowly advancing to computerized billing. I was hired for a six-month term to process gas bills by hand—with a decent Grade Three wage of $35.00 each week, less income tax, less $2.00 for union dues, non-negotiable. Still, a fortune! Now I could start to pay back my mother for my crossing. Surely every household in Toronto received a gas bill. This changeover could last years. Not that I intended to stay that long.

My Honeydew stranger appeared only once again—to my knowledge. Strolling south down University Avenue, about a year later, I heard a voice calling. Turning, I saw a man leaning out of the passenger seat of a car passing me, heading north. Throwing my arms skyward, I turned and waved, shouting, "Thank you again, whoever you aaaaare." My voice trailed off into the noise of the traffic as his car disappeared.

After landing a paid employment job in Toronto, the question of a decent home was urgent. Even if I wanted permanent residence at the Y, it was forbidden. Now was the time to explore one of the references given to me by a Canadian drama student at Guildhall.

Firstly, I met Les Rubie, the well-loved, wrinkled, and crackly-voiced character actor whom I soon located in the CBC canteen.

The gentle old man thought the actress Nonnie (Margaret) Griffin needed a flat-mate. She did. I remembered my father had once told me, with fervour, "It's not *what* you know in this life, girlie, but *who* you know."

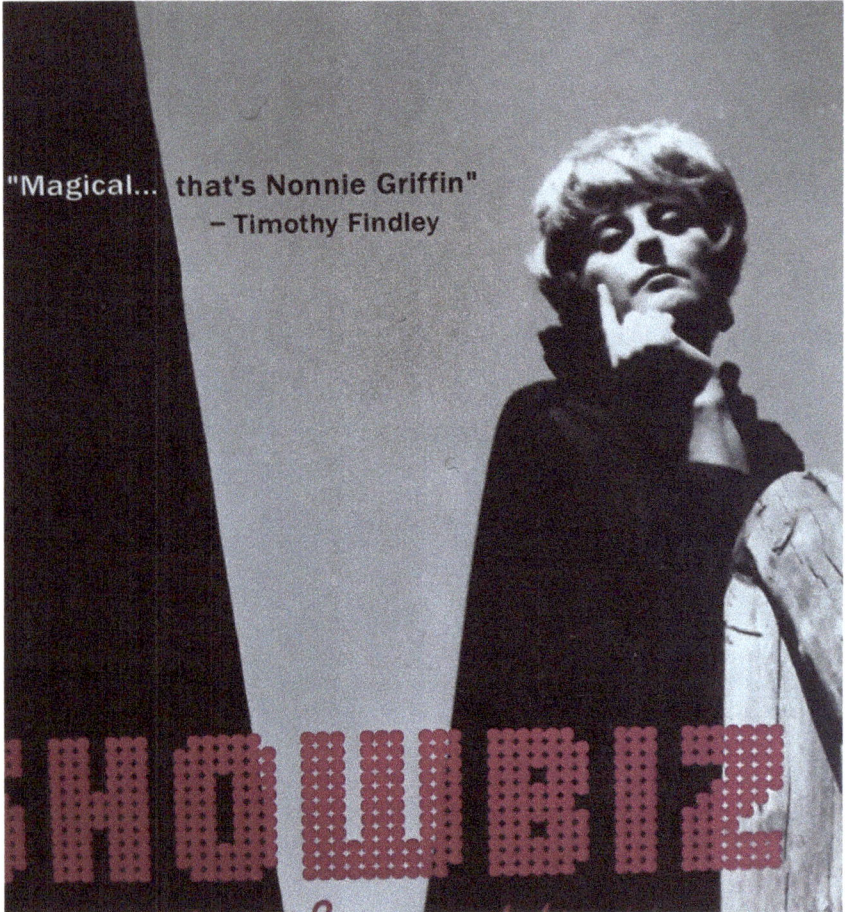

"Magical... that's Nonnie Griffin"
– Timothy Findley

SHOWBIZ

Detail of Nonnie Griffin by Laszio Szavassy

Like a poor relation with a battered suitcase, I was the fourth to share a three-bedroom apartment on Cumberland Avenue, the area of the city that was quickly becoming Hippy Kingdom.

One young occupant of our unit I rarely saw. To be married shortly, she was preparing to move out. Another, a grade-school teacher, I tried to avoid. When she first found me in the kitchen, I literally jumped. I'd been hypnotized by the frigid crispness of the refrigerator, the power of the tall, white, humming cupboard. I wasn't "dawdling," as she claimed. I'd never met a refrigerator before. Terribly North American. *Did the inside light turn itself off?*

"Close the door! Don't hold it open like that!"

Hearing the sharpness in her voice, I immediately complied. Best not to rock unfamiliar boats.

Fortunately, Nonnie and I shared a room with twin beds and two chests of drawers. She and I balanced each other well. Short little me, small-featured and flat chested, contrasted with lovely Miss Griffin, who exuded buxom beauty. Nonnie was as much a star as one could be in Canada, with the country having no star system. Photos of her were often displayed on magazine covers, but I knew from some of the things she said that her sexual appeal she found a "heavy burden." Well-known in the CBC TV series *General Motors Presents* and a very early TV series of *Anne of Green Gables*, Nonnie also excelled on stage and in CBC radio dramas. Her gravelly laugh reminded me of a barroom, yet she read poetry with amazing perception and eloquent inflections that rang like the music of Mozart. I couldn't have asked for a more generous or fun roommate.

Through Nonnie's introductions, I met people in the entertainment business, where partygoing helped let go of stress and seriousness. Inevitably, Nonnie could be found in the host's kitchen, sitting on the counter-top, singing with her ukulele to an entranced crowd. Returning home around two, in our kitchen she'd butter toast for us "to soak up the alcohol," then make sure our bedroom window was open a crack to "let in the cold."

"We beauties have to stay tough," she'd say.

At the sound of the morning alarm to wake for the office, I would roll myself, shivering, onto the floor, leaving my star to sleep 'til noon—like I knew all great actresses should. My images of blissful living as a successful actress were slowly beginning to fade.

* * *

My salary was my main incentive to endure the tedium of sitting all day in a roomful of rows and rows of office workers, all checking gas bills. Yet I preferred playing with my clever adding machine than listening to the guys at break periods.

They talked endlessly as though in a foreign tongue. Sometimes I made out a sentence like, "The Dodge? Jeez, the Packard or the Buick Century … your Chrysler New Yorker can't stroke the Royal 500, if you're talking convertible." No, I preferred my numbers. However, my second incentive was more creative. Consumers' Gas offices were situated mere blocks from the Canadian Broadcasting Corporation's radio and TV studios.

CBC in 1957 was pretty much the only organization that offered professional acting opportunities, so at noon hours, I shot from my desk like a Jill-in-a-Box to walk a few blocks to Jarvis Street, to the desk of a producer's assistant, hoping for a role on live television. If I were a handsome, smarmy dude, I would have sat myself on the secretary's desk and charmed her into letting me appear in any idly-piddly role. Casting for extras (background) was a secretarial duty in those far-off days.

"Anything going for me?" I'd ask, almost bowing.

"Too English!" was the usual answer. Slowly realizing the relevance of this fact, I was happy to play in crowd scenes to be on the inside of a TV studio. After I finally landed one, I rushed home immediately to see if my den-mates had caught me, but arrived back to an empty apartment. Poor me. Filming was very disappointing.

One day I landed an agent, Kay Griffin, who sent me for a television commercial audition. The director, who needed a happy housewife, patiently encouraged me, "No. Don't act! Just be yourself!"

Be myself? If I were truly myself, I would endanger everyone. I was likely to explode! These directors knew nothing of realism. I didn't win that jolly role, but I eventually made a few commercials. Hey ho! As Samuel Beckett says in *The Unnamable*, "I can't go on. I'll go on."

Chapter 18

Prudhommes Garden Centre Theatre

Sitting in Bassel's restaurant on Yonge Street one lunch hour from my day-job, I discovered a helpful grapevine of showbiz information.

"Near St. Catharines, just an hour away. Every year they look for apprentices," a friendly actor told me.

Apprentices? I was a graduate from London's second-best drama school, plus a half-finished season of summer stock—in England, no less! Yet if I could swallow a bit of pride, could start pioneering, I'd show them what brilliance lay within a mere apprentice! I sent in my résumé. I landed a position, but on the bottom rung of the snakes and ladders of showbusiness.

My C.V. meant nothing to Mike Anderson, the American producer of Prudhommes Garden Centre Theatre. He wanted manual labour. Among my many go-getting jobs in the heat of July, I joined another apprentice in painting the outside walls of the large, wood-framed theatre a deep green. Not once but twice. "Because," I swear, as my partner explained, "Mrs. Anderson wanted a brighter green."

Situated beside Highway 401 in Vineland, Ontario, this popular holiday complex offered many forms of entertainment: miniature golf, horseback riding, gifts stores and services, the distant undeveloped shoreline of Lake Ontario. Hollywood stars, appearing live at the theatre, were the main attraction for most holidaymakers. Each week throughout the summer, Anderson brought in one of a variety of movie personalities—usually on the way down the ladder of success—who were going the rounds of summer theatres in a play of the star's choosing. The cast was enhanced by a few Canadian actors to play supporting roles, while the celebrity was inserted into the action the moment before the first curtain rose—all reminiscent of nineteenth-century theatre.

Still tainted with the idea that if one was around famous people something of their good fortune could rub off, I was more fascinated by artistry than stardom. Lillian Roth, the renowned actress for her brave, agonizing autobiographic film *I'll Cry Tomorrow*, showed tragedy in her very bones when I met her at Prudhommes, as though a puff of wind might blow away her slight, fragile body. This lonely artist showed me vulnerability and compassion in the world of high competition, and a quality of true stardom. She took it on herself to befriend me, "a poor young beginner," she thought. She invited me to her motel room and offered me two summer dresses from her stacked wardrobe. The rather drab one I gave to Goodwill but happily wore the bright one for years.

After the last show each Saturday, I joined the crew to take off like missiles for fun, freedom, and relaxation. Eight of us climbed into a Chrysler Dodge and left dry Ontario, singing our way toward legal drinking in New York State. At the border crossing, Canadian-born visitors could pass straight through, but the hours that landed immigrants had to wait for their green light delayed everyone's precious drinking time.

"Where were you born?" a voice would demand as a bright flashlight was directed into each set of eyes inside the car.

Sounding desperately tired and bored, I'd successfully drawl, "Taranna!"

The officers weren't fooled, I'm sure, but those were the days, and the heavy hangovers we suffered the next morning proved our good times.

My age-old longing for an audience's laughter was revitalized, for a moment, that early summer. Following Lillian Roth, the next week's star to land with us was Arthur Treacher, Hollywood's famous English butler in an Agatha Christie mystery. On opening night, during the first intermission, the paintbrush I was then cleaning in the dimming sunlight was seized. I was quickly ushered backstage to take over prompting. *Is this my golden opportunity toward the second rung?* The stage manager stuffed me below a scenery window with the book of the play opened at Act Two. The curtain rose.

Treacher, as I viewed him through a crack in the scenery, was taller although stouter than I remembered him in films. Restraining my curiosity, I turned my eyes to the script and could make out a little of the dialogue, but I'd little light to see the printing clearly. I heard his heavy plodding around the set of an English mansion, his voice spouting lines. These stars never needed prompting. Wait! I heard nothing. Where are we? The sound of creaking floor boards brought footsteps up to my window and stopped. More silence. I reached up to the sill and, with my head almost in view, called a random line of the script. This was answered by feet marching away toward the front of the stage.

Treacher's voice bellowed out. "I can't hear a damn word the girl's saying!"

A wave of laughter from the audience—then applause! The prompter's book was seized from my hand, and I fell back to first rung.

At night, in the otherwise empty sleeping hut, my loneliness deepened. I missed Tom, my ex-boyfriend. He'd had little me on a pedestal. Withering in spirit one night, I hit on a solution to my misery: a novena. Repeating a decade of the rosary each night for nine consecutive nights would surely bring Tom here. He'd liberate me. Kneeling by my bed, fingering my beads that I always kept in my purse, I prayed a whole Sorrowful Mystery. On the ninth night—the magical night—my fingers shook. Would Tom suddenly appear at the door? He'd be furious I'd disturbed him. I suddenly thought: *He would interfere with my new life.* I pushed the beads away and stood. No. Tom can stay in his U.S. of A. I'll do bloody well all right on my own. Wow! *My prayer is already answered.*

Well, another miracle occurred a week later. But not before six of us crew were locked in St. Catharine's jail.

"On no condition do you stop anywhere," Anderson had shouted his instructions one noon hour as we stood to attention on the grounds of Prudhommes. "Until five o'clock, your afternoon task is to advertise the next show in and around St. Catharines. And no stopping!"

On top of a trailer towed by a pickup truck, we were to make general whoopee with dancing and banners while the driver blared through a loudspeaker, "Come to Prudhommes for fun and entertainment ..." On such a blistering hot day, who would trust us not to stop, just for two minutes, our throats sore from shouting, to try out the recommended "Best Ice Cream Ever"?

Returning to the hot truck, slurping our dripping cones, we found a cop studying the license plate he'd found lying in the back of the trailer.

"If this is your vehicle, you can all follow me to the station!"

A higher force was giving this order. We laughed. Anderson was wanted for illegally importing automobiles across the US border. But we grew increasingly worried behind classic iron bars as the time grew closer to our half hour call. We would be needed. Not surprisingly, our producer presented himself. He preferred jail to the loss of one night's take at the box office.

Out on bail a day later, Anderson appeared only slightly bothered. The shows never went dark—that is, until after I left. Nonnie Griffin had called me to ask if I would join her at Simcoe's Red Barn Theatre. I was gone the very next day.

Prudhommes Garden Centre Theatre burnt to the ground that summer during the run of *Cat on a Hot Tin Roof,* I swear. Foul play was never proved.

Chapter 19

The Red Barn

The Red Barn Theatre at Jackson's Point, by Lake Simcoe, was a quite different operation from the one I'd left. Rather than one producer/director, each year a different company tried to make a go of this romantic setting, often to financial disaster, but Ontario's oldest summer theatre had supported many Judy-Garland-Mickey-Rooney-style dreams, and mine seemed to be materializing at last. This year, the Red Barn was run by Nan Stewart and her son Norman, two English-Canadians who were late starting up because of earlier financial difficulties. As assistant stage manager (ASM), I would also play supporting roles in three productions. How respectful to a recent graduate of a London drama school! With great earnestness, I immediately joined the rest of the cast and company, who were already willingly working. From the old movie-house seats now in the large barn's auditorium we cleaned off the old and new bird shit. Looking up, I could see half the barn roof was missing, accounting for the problem.

"They're putting up a vinyl sheeting tomorrow," one of the actors explained as he scrubbed. "But we'll probably have no audience at all if the bats stay darting around when the lights go out."

Sure enough, it happened during the seance scene of Noel Coward's *Blythe Spirit*. Fortunately, half the audience laughed at the splendid atmosphere as we kept our cool on stage and carried on. Only a few ran off, shrieking in terror, though, I must say, not from our acting.

I wrote home to Mum in England telling her of my good fortune and also wrote Dad in Willowdale. I was sure he'd be pleased. I'd seen him only once, almost a year earlier, for a drink at the Westminster Hotel where he'd set me up when I first arrived, but I didn't hold my breath on his coming. He'd told me then that he was "an industrial engineer supervisor on sections of the design of CF-105, known as the Avro Canada Arrow." He also said, very proudly, "It's a delta-wing aircraft, an interceptor built for home defence. The Arrow is the greatest technical and aerodynamic achievement in the world of aviation history. It easily outsmarts any American capabilities." However, the man omitted to tell any of his family what I later guessed: he'd invested every cent he owned in Avro stocks for a six-year aeronautical study of the Arrow. He was gladly gambling everything on its success.

In our first production, I played Elma in William Inge's *Bus Stop.* The southern speech of my character came easily for me. I was a good mimic and took as my model Vivian Leigh's accent in *Gone with the Wind*. The Toronto critic and the audiences believed the Red Barn had brought in a new American starlet.

Yet the pinnacle of my happiness came with a message from my father, who'd driven alone, for an hour and a half, from the city that rainy August night to park in the mud-squelching field that was our parking lot. I'd sent him a rave review by Herbert Whittaker in the *Globe and Mail* newspaper. He wanted to see his daughter on stage again—for the first time since I was as high as his elbow.

After the performance, I found him standing alone in the foyer in deep thought.

"That was well done," he said with the hint of a smile.

I smiled back, making a feast from his few words, although I could tell from his eyes that he felt proud of me. Honoured and very grateful to have a father who would drive here for me, I stood staring at the man, taking in as much of him as would last before I had his full attention again.

We walked in silence to his vehicle, where we found the wheels slightly sunken in the sodden ground. Before he managed to drive away, he handed me a twenty-dollar bill, nodded again, and was gone.

I didn't want his money—I wanted him. A hug was out of the question, but a squeeze of the hand—something to remember. But he'd come. I wish now I'd told him I didn't want him to leave. That might have made a difference. Wandering my way back to the theatre, I was torn between rapture and loneliness, not yet understanding love and hate as two necessary conflicting feelings.

In early September, we all departed for more or less adventurous ventures. Norman Stewart moved back to England for work in television. Nan, his mother, would follow. Nonnie had already moved on to star for other summer stock companies and then left for a TV series in Quebec. Unfortunately, she gave up the apartment we'd shared, so I needed a new address.

Chapter 20

Back in Toronto

A new rooming house and a role in a University of Toronto production of *A Phoenix Too Frequent* by Christopher Fry saw me on the boards again. I'd seen the original production with Paul Schofield in London from "the gods" (the highest balcony seats in a theatre) half a decade back and was delighted with the chance to play in this brilliant poetic comedy.

Then, my first school tour took me around Ontario for four weeks. I played Audrey in Shakespeare's comedy *As You Like It*.

"We're educating the Ontario backwoods—a cultural desert of the Canadian school system," Mr. Grey, of Earle Grey Players, informed us at rehearsals. His wife, in her late fifties (surely), played the romantic heroine. I felt pity for her, in her red satin tights, as the school teachers yelled.

"Quiet! Quit that whistling! Keep in your OWN SEATS!"

During the quieter speeches, we all tried, unsuccessfully, to ignore the sound of Coke bottles rolled up and down the aisles. However, nothing could bring down my spirits. By joining the company, I'd signed the contract to become a fully unionized member of the Actors' Equity Association. I was a contracted "professional."

Back in the city, after a day's job hunting, joy awaited me—a blue airmail letter from Mum.

March 04, 1959
Dear Mary,

Received your money and new address with thanks. I enjoyed your last letter and am so happy that you are getting along well. Mrs. Malcolm says she never hears from her daughter who married that Yankee. Remember Mrs. Malcolm? I met her in Baxter's yesterday and felt very sorry for her. Peter and Lily have a little girl. Did your father tell you? Her name is Tracy. Peter has promised to bring her when he's in London next time, but heaven knows when that will be. It's a long trip from the Isle of Wight. John is away a lot with his band. Never home now. I've been asked to work permanently at Brillo, not typing but book-keeping. It's a long time since I've done it but they're very pleased and so am I. Write soon.

Lots of love, Mum XXX

I hadn't told her about my new boyfriend. One is never quite sure how long these things will last. Brian was gorgeous! I'd met him at a party entertaining with guitar and folk songs. The young musician glowed in a radiant rainbow of glamour that shot goosebumps through me whenever he directed his black eyes downward toward me as I sat mesmerized at his feet. He seemed so beautifully melancholic. After several more party dates where he sang and I ogled, he invited me to meet his parents. Inheriting his mother's slight build and dark East Indian beauty, unlike his large, exuberant Scottish father, Brian Beaton was scrumptious!

If I introduced him to Dad, my father might get to know more about me, I figured. But marriage was not in my mind. I heeded well my mother's words and never wanted to be caught like her. Boyfriend yes, even if it meant no passion, no heat, no sex. I could do without that if I had this good Catholic wonder-guy liking, wanting me.

I phoned Dad after his workday at Avro.

"I'd like you to meet a boyfriend of mine," I said with pride. "Would that be OK?"

"No, girlie."

I gasped. "Why?"

"I'm not interested, Mary."

What was wrong with the man? The shock of yet another cold shoulder intensified my bitterness toward him. My longing for Brian increased. Resistance, more than distance, makes the heart grow fonder. But like most other entertainers, my handsome new friend accepted music gigs more often out-of-town than in. What else could I do but find more acting to distract me from wanting men. Surprise! I discovered radio.

Chapter 21

Radio

Radio drama became my second love. With months between opportunities for theatre work, I found the art of the spoken word highly celebrated at the Canadian Broadcasting Corporation. I took to the medium like my soul had found home. My English accent, high, girlish voice, and credentials made me a shoo-in. Immediately cast in adapted works of Wilde, Dickens, Shaw, and even Medieval English, over those early years I performed in more than thirty broadcasts.

When I began, Andrew Allan, the internationally renowned pioneer of Anglo-Canadian culture and the former National Drama Supervisor for the CBC, had recently moved on to the developing medium of television, but in radio, his mixture of classics and original social dramas with series like *Stage* and *Wednesday Night* had become favourites throughout Canada and the United States. He "brought soul to radio," one producer told me. Canadian radio drama had reached its highest pinnacle and was enjoyed around the world. My friendship with the renowned Allan began with his return to live stage after his exit from CBC television.

Radio is a hot, creative medium for both artist and listener. Although contracts were offered sporadically to me, I quickly gained confidence from working alongside the best creators in the field: producers and writers such as Esse W. Ljung, Alan

King, and James Anderson; and actors like John Drainie, Martha Henry, Moya Fenwick, Timothy Findley, and many others.

I came to radio after the *Jake and the Kid* series had cemented Drainie's popularity. Aside from his masterly use of voice, John Drainie's radio scripts were works of art. I saw a typed copy covered with underlinings, slashes, crosses, dots, and circles: black markings as codes for interpretation, inflection, emphasis, expression, rhythm, and phrasing. He read with tremendous animation while listening intently to his fellow performers, sounding so natural that every listener was transfixed. No wonder Orson Welles considered Drainie "the greatest radio actor in the world."

Like TV at that time, radio was live. The work was demanding. One needed strong focus and concentration—and nerves in steady control. The rewards were awesome and mistakes were legendary. I heard of one actor who, thinking he was finished, left the studio to hear on his car radio another voice improvising the final scene. I didn't learn if he was hired again.

Radio drama was allowed only short rehearsal time to discuss the mood, style, rhythm, and wishes of the producer, usually immediately before the actual broadcast. At the allotted time, we assembled around one central microphone in a padded studio. Performers and announcer would begin with a signal from the producer, who sat with the technicians behind a glass barrier. The sound-effects man (I never saw a female), with his own marked-up script, was positioned to one side with a separate mic and paraphernalia: bells, wood blocks, whistles, coconut shells, sandpaper, balls of newspaper, a bucket of water, or anything else of his invention. At times, the CBC Studio Orchestra assembled with us. Then we worked in a larger recording studio and listened while they played between scenes—at those times I was lifted above heaven.

Pretty soon, I'd enough credits to join the Association of Canadian Television and Radio Artists (ACTRA). My self-assurance grew. I was even learning to be savvy—a North American term for the British word "cocky." Changes in my personality must have shown in my voice when, one day, Alan King, a radio producer-writer, stunned me with his request.

"Please, Miss Barton, give us more of your innocence."

While I became more desirable as an artist, my achievements increased my anxiety. I feared not so much the work but the camaraderie that abounds around the collaborative art form. The bridge between work and social exchange was one I found almost impossible to cope with. On lunch breaks, when invited to join a group, I'd gladly accept but sit like a new child at school, always anxious that I might be asked a question and not have the words to reply. A memory from my childhood, no doubt, but a fear I couldn't seem to overcome. I would always search for excuses to remove myself from these situations.

On a couple of occasions, I worked in radio with an actor whose name I believe was Graham Bell. (He claimed relationship to the great Alexander Bell, credited with the invention of the telephone.) I was shocked and full of admiration for the burly young man. Throughout rehearsals and again during breaks, he struggled with a bad stammer. Remembering my own childhood speech challenges, I admired him all the more and sympathized with his attraction to acting. The tall guy, displaying thick, curly, red hair as well as beard, was well known in the community, I discovered, and was well appreciated for his talents and courage.

The moment his cue arrived when we were "live," he had not the slightest falter, speaking his lines every inch an expert. What did it matter what chaos brought us to the microphone? What mattered was the result.

One afternoon a few years into my time of radio, after recorded programs were introduced, Moya Fenwick, a vivacious, red-headed actress, as much a fan of the Maple Leaf hockey team as she was of the CBC, said, "Esse, I hope we're not going to take too long," as rehearsals began.

Our producer, Mr. Esse Ljung, would rehearse before taping the scenes from George Bernard Shaw's *Mrs. Warren's Profession*. In one section of the play, Moya's Mrs. Warren talks for several pages. This very lengthy speech was cut slightly for radio purposes. I was to read Vivie, the daughter with whom Mrs. Warren is in conflict. I had merely a few lines.

Mr. Ljung suggested we first read through the script without interruption while he took notes. We did. With little to say, and it merely a rehearsal, my nerves were pretty steady, as was my reading, if not a little too relaxed. I was worrying about that when Mr. Ljung came out to join us from the recording booth.

"You'll be home well in time for the game, Moya. That was excellent."

He had recorded the rehearsal. That day, I learned again why an actor must *always* give of her very best.

Chapter 22

Canadian Grail and Dad

"After mass, the Grail Ladies will meet in room B."

Hearing the words from the pulpit of St. Basil's Church one Sunday morning, I sat stupefied. Did the priest say "the Grail"? *My* Grail? The ladies who saved my sanity in London before I left England? Who'd organized the great pageant years earlier at the Royal Albert Hall? I could hardly wait to investigate. If this same Grail was in Toronto, I would be at mass every Sunday.

After searching for room B, I arrived only in time to find the brief meeting already adjourning. I waylaid a young woman as she was putting on her coat.

"Sorry to interrupt, but d'you know if the Grail ladies are from England?"

She frowned as though I were asking about the North Pole. "We know nothing about England, but come and meet some Canadians."

To my bliss, I was given a phone number.

In my mid-twenties, I became a devotee of the Grail International Women's Movement in Canada. The audacious feminine, avant-garde approach to Catholicism I found inspiring. The most thrilling in Toronto at that time was attending mass in a room over a barber's shop on Wellesley Street on a weekday evening. The ritual took place as though we truly were at a meal, and rather than in Latin, as was the world-wide custom, one of the women gave the liturgical responses in Canadian-sounding English. I'd found a sister movement of the English Grail, with the familiar invigorating spirit and humour.

"You and I and all members of the Church are priests of Christ," a fair-haired, friendly Grail lady called Leona Chartrand explained to me one day. "The Sacrament of Confession, for example. Grace can be conferred by any lay person if the need is there and the intention is right. Sometimes there just isn't an ordained priest around."

Leona amazed me with her practical outlook. This generally serene woman could wail in anguish over the treatment of the female, not only in the Church but around the world—cases of which I knew little. This gentle French-Canadian, ten years my senior, gave me hope that I might be super-useful to somebody someday. She loved contemporary art and design and almost single-handedly ran the Grail art and bookstore on Bathurst Street. When I made plans to learn more about what sparked the spirit of these women, Leona was my best ally.

"The source for us lies at the Grail Centre in Ohio. The nucleus in North America was established there about thirty years ago. The place is called Grailville."

A four-month course of relevant Christian study was offered. But I could no way finance that. I'd nothing saved and little prospect of a loan or lucrative acting work.

"Ask your father," Leona said, smiling with soft blue eyes.

I heaved a sigh. "He refused to meet a boyfriend of mine a while ago. I never imagined I'd be asking him for money! I always thought I could be independent."

Leona Chartrand

Leona smiled broadly at me and nodded.

What induced Dad to drive to this lady's flat a few evenings later, in the rain, in the west end of Toronto, could only be guessed. He knew only that something of great importance was to be learned.

I was happy to relate that our hostess was not an actress. "Leona is a registered nurse," I explained after he'd seated himself on the edge of an armchair. *He probably thinks I'm pregnant.* Then Leona offered him a beer, and he, with a genuine smile and a glass of London Pride, settled back.

Leona chatted, in that straight manner of hers, about football, aeronautics, and the coming warm weather. I sat opposite, empty-handed—too nervous to hold anything. As they talked, I stared at an extraordinary framed etching that hung on Leona's wall—the only picture I ever saw of a laughing Jesus.

"The Grail?" Dad frowned.

Leona smiled. "Yes. But we don't call ourselves the *Holy* Grail!"

He lit a cigarette. The room filled with the aromas I remembered of my father. "As long as she's not becoming a nun!"

"No," she assured him, handing him a large ashtray. "We celebrate the sanctity of our lives in the world, wherever we are, whatever we do."

Dad was no fool. "If they're all like you, Miss Leona, they'll go far."

But my father remained aloof. He hardly listened to our reason for the visit. Perhaps he didn't like me going to such trouble to ask him for a loan. I understood only a little of my father's occupation and less of his private life.

About a month later, cross-eyed from office filing, I heard my landlady call up to me to come downstairs and take the telephone. It was Dad.

"I'm going back to England. Will you come with me? I'll pay your fare; don't worry about that."

I was dumbstruck.

"There's nothing here for us now, girlie. I'm leaving in a couple of days."

I hesitated. "I've started to make friends, Dad."

"Well, don't say I didn't ask you." The line cut.

My father had joined the unemployed again. The government had ordered the cancellation and the destruction of the great Avro Arrow aircraft—the Canadian wonder in aeronautics. Dad joined what newspapers called "Canada's brain drain." Thousands exited back to Britain that year or moved on to the United States.

"His spirit is broken," my mother wrote me in her ecstasy at his return.

I guessed he'd gambled all his savings on that great Canadian wonder of the air. I could only wish him a safe trip home.

After rigorous savings from salaries and generous help from Grail friends, I too left Canada—although only temporarily. I willingly offered up—for the good of the world—my most prized talent. Figuring I'd win more grace points if I sacrificed selfish interests in order to save lost souls, I threw into the garbage all my scripts, books of plays, even all phone contact numbers. Determined to prove useful to God, at last my purpose was clear. One way or another, I was going to Grailville to be a missionary!

Chapter 23

Grailville

Taking cheese sandwiches and a suitcase of necessities, one September morning I joined three other young women to travel to Grailville in the southern Ohio district of ... Loveland! I swear! Father Ted, a country pastor from north of Toronto and a long-time supporter of the Grail women, made a habit of driving people in his station wagon to the American centre.

Wearing our best buttoned-up blouses, tightly-belted flared skirts, and black high-heeled shoes, we girls were off for a long study of modern Catholic theology, history, and practices. We passed the hours by singing and storytelling, or enjoying Father Ted's ancient jokes.

"People are dying to get in there!" he'd repeat as we drove past every graveyard on route, always, of course, followed by our groans and hearty laughter. Father Thomas Mahoney gave the impression of a professional wrestler, not the wry, introspective parish cleric we knew. In the ideals and activities of the Grail, I believe he saw himself supporting biblical women rejoicing from the tomb of Christ.

During one Coke stop on the trip, the dear man confided, "When I retire, I'm going to be a priest."

The night air felt cool as our vehicle headed up a long driveway to the lights from a large, Victorian-style house heralding a turret, pointing like a finger to the heavens. Set within three hundred acres of land that contained many renovated farm buildings, the House of Joy stood as the main dining and reception area, also the residence for visiting lecturers, clerics, and theologians. And there were many. The inside shone with polished, hand-made furniture.

There in the large communal dining room, we sat at one of a dozen long wooden tables. As I stared through cathedral windows at nearby trees visible in the darkness outside, all was quiet. My senses calmed to the gentle clinking of spoons in bowls of hot vegetable soup and the occasional soft flapping of slippered feet. That night, I lay my head on the top bunk in a renovated hen house, my suitcase placed quietly at the door. Loud snores assured me I'd not disturbed the three other occupants. Closing my eyes, I prayed I would be worthy for the work ahead.

* * *

Inevitably, my three months at Grailville extended longer. There was much to discover by so many, and although slow to learn, I was always quick to sense. Very soon I knew the undeniable truth: some paths lead us back to forsaken ones. Catherine Leahy, a dynamic, effervescent lover of drama, gave my missionary idealism practical focus. I wasn't allowed to disappear into my dream world of martyrdom and sacrifice. These smart women knew better than to colour everyone in the same shade.

"Your talents are needed here now, Mary, not far away in missionary land," she said.

She invited me to study Christian drama and to direct dramatic readings. This, I admit, gave me a rigorous boost as I went about the myriad daily chores that helped the upkeep and development of the community.

"You're more practical than you think you are," said one woman, assigned as head cook, who put me to work for the communal breakfast, boiling two hundred eggs— "without bringing them to a boil." One lets them sit in baskets in recently boiled water for four to five minutes. I could do that—who'd hardly boiled water before.

"Listen to the lectures," we were told. "You will be giving them next year."

The place was truly a United Nations of international exchange, with students of many shapes and colours. The movement had been formed in Holland early in the 1920s, initiated by a priest and six young lay women (who had made no promises to any religious order), each of who took off for a different continent. They vowed to carry with them the message of Christ's grace in every member of the Church, not only the clergy or the nuns within bishops' jurisdictions.

At Grailville we listened to many stirring stories of foreign women's groups and organizations creating help and vision in the lives of local people. The Ohio Centre and the many Grail centres in various cities in America were developing educational and inspirational industries: the design and printing of Christmas cards with religious themes—unheard of at the time—artistic banners with motivating messages, translations of the complete liturgical calendar and biblical psalms into the vernacular, publications, modern design in religious pottery and woodwork, long-playing folk music recordings—all alongside meetings, discussions, and lectures from lay people and supportive clergy from around the world.

Although the mission preached goodness versus evil, and salvation by a Redeemer, scruples were not encouraged.

"If you must smoke cigarettes, enjoy the experience!" was the message handed down. "If you're not appreciating anything—rethink."

But I found little time to think apart from how little I knew and how little time there was to think. Woken before dawn by a voice outside each room singing, "Alleluia!" we would work for half an hour before celebrating the new day with Lauds, then breakfast in silence. During meals we listened to daily passages read to us from the writings of Dietrich Bonhoeffer, Paul Tillich, or Teilhard de Chardin—all directing us into new ways of experiencing spirituality rather than religiosity. I loved the idea that we were all free to spiral upward toward a perfect justice for all, as de Chardin wrote. Yet I wondered, as we set off to work, why, if God is so forgiving, do we have to keep asking Him for mercy over and over again. Is He very ornery or just plain deaf? My badness was leaking, I thought, to even think such things. I had a lot to learn.

Breakfast was followed by work until a silent noonday meal. I recall many legume lunches with homegrown cabbage. Plain and wholesome food was plentiful. I grew fat with wholesomeness. In the afternoons there would be workshops, lectures, meetings, or seminars taking place in various buildings, or even in open fields on bright days. Then there would be more chores before a little free time. At supper, general talking was allowed, except during the six weeks of Lent, when we ate less and talked not at all. That,

I preferred. I was never one for "idle chatter." I didn't see how people could laugh and joke about their day's work when we were all here to solve serious problems. I came to help change our world, not for a holiday. There was too much laughter. Perhaps a nun's life might have suited me better. Either my scruples were beginning to show or I was diving into the deep end of this new world of Catholicism. I might drown here.

Each day followed a reassuring liturgical calendar that was new to most Catholics, who only knew the Bible through antique versions or children's bedtime stories. I enjoyed best our comforting Compline prayers each night before bed. Exhaustion usually brought immediate sleep. Before bed, for some weeks, Eva Fleishner, a Jewish convert and intellectual, read stories to us in a loft strewn with bodies propped on pillows or wrapped in blankets, all in p.js. I especially remember listening to her favoured translation of *Viper's Tangle* by Francois Mauriac. I visualized the terrible tension between the old man in the story and his wife—the suspicions of both, their silent longing. I recognized in the story the excruciating, unexpressed pressures during my childhood between my own parents. To be able to write such graphic insights seemed to me miraculous.

Everyone sang at Grailville, and joining the community choir, I discovered that I wasn't too bad as a chorister. The discipline of Gregorian chant provided a means of rich vocal expression and a whole new art form to study. I was amazed to find printed books of liturgical music, previously read only by the men of the Church. Sadly, these new manuscripts went out of print after Vatican Council II.

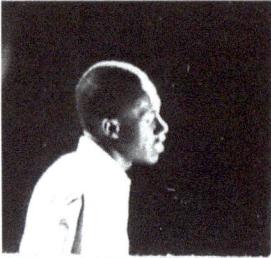

Grailville Oratory designed by William Schickel
Insert of Fr. Clarence Rufus Joseph Rivers, Jr.

When our choir leader was shipped to Ghana's Grail Centre, I learned much from young Lynn Malley, who took over the task. This lively teenage tomboy was often seen sitting on a stone fence between the fields, absorbed in her guitar, her mane of black hair sweeping her face. I saw Lynn bounce back from endless faux pas, in and out of choir. She would simply thumb her nose at misfortune and go on. I so admired this ability.

One October Sunday, a spritely parish priest from nearby Cincinnati—a cleric with no "dog-collar"—came to say mass. Father Rivers was a frequent celebrant at Grailville in the newly renovated oratory. This magnificently designed barn, by Schickel Design, sat on the outskirts of the property. Although still breezy inside, with floral wreaths and colourful felt banners decorating the farm-smelling walls, the renewed building delighted the eyes of visitors, friends, and curious local folk.

Our choir, seated on folding chairs like the rest of the congregation, were gathered to the side of the beautifully handcrafted wooden altar. The climax of the ritual—the transformation of the bread and wine into the Body and Blood of Christ—is normally signalled by an altar boy ringing a bell as the people kneel at the raising of the Host and then the chalice by the celebrant. Because we were advocating women's place in the Church, our choir director took on the significant task of the handbell ringing.

One Sunday as Lynn began directing her choir in the oratory, I saw her look around anxiously. "Where's the bell?"

No one knew. The climactic moment came. Father Rivers genuflected, then raised, firstly, the Host.

I saw Lynn swallow, then in a high, ringing tone, call, "Ting-a-ling!"

Father Rivers didn't flicker. Then as he raised the chalice, we heard again, "Ting—" But poor Lynn couldn't finish for the snorting of muffled hysterics that rippled through the choir, heaving in pain.

After the final hymn, when the friendly priest reappeared after disrobing his vestments, Father Rivers called, "You all sounded great—especially the bells!"

Lynn rushed to him. "Father, I'm so sorry about the ding-a-ling thing," and they both exited the barn laughing loudly together.

I thought if it had been me, I would be in South America by now.

During the summer breaks from Grailville, I kept myself from debt by babysitting in New York and staying on a friend's couch in Toronto while I returned there to renew my visa. While in Canada, I visited Brian, my Catholic folk-singing boyfriend, at the Stratford Shakespeare Festival to see him in the chorus of *The Pirates of Penzance*. But we argued. He was adamant that Gilbert and Sullivan didn't write send-ups.

"Their musicals are satires," I insisted.

We also disagreed over the singer Bob Dylan, who Brian thought was no folk singer.

"He's going electric!"

Nonetheless, Brian continued as irresistibly handsome, and I stayed entranced with his music. In the fall of 1962, Brian took his guitar on a cruise ship and entertained out at sea, while I travelled back to the Grail in Ohio, excited for more inspiration.

One evening in the House of Joy, after I'd read a poem at dinner, I was asked to meet a tall and imposing figure: none other than Lydwine van Kersbergen, the great Dutch woman who had established the American Grail many years earlier. This serene senior lady seldom stayed at Grailville but travelled a great deal. I imagined her already close to sainthood. As the fair-haired Lydwine took my hand, beaming at me through her clear spectacles, I was so affected by the softness of her skin I thought I might cry. She complimented me on my reading, then said, "I understand you've been presenting dramas. Claudia tells me you brought her out of the cow shed to play a role in *The Bespoke Overcoat."*

"Well, she was the best person for that part."

"She says she will remember it to her dying day."

I remembered the girl from Arkansas' terror when I suggested she do it. But she had seemed to dive right into the character and impressed me immensely with her presentation. Was there a problem I missed?

"Are you planning more performances?" Lydwine asked.

"I don't know."

I'd also directed Henri Gheon's *Christmas in the Market Place,* and later a drama by Paul Claudel. These had seemed popular with the community audiences. Directing gave me a great sense of wellbeing. But self-persecution had continued to haunt me with bouts of unexplained depression. To help sort myself, that spring I'd been ordered to the bakery. There I discovered solace in bread-making. The sweet smell of rising yeast from leavened, wholesome dough brought me in physical touch with growing life within my hands. Boy, did I make contact! I mixed and pounded, stroked and pounded, waited and pounded, sang, laughed, cried, and pounded. Working for seven days alone in the little, lone-standing barn, sweating by a hot woodstove, I revived. After a week, I re-entered the community—calm and attentive.

Lydwine was smiling down at me. I connected again with her.

"I hope you will enjoy a rich life in the Grail," she said, placing her hand gently on my cheek before she turned away.

The grand lady wanted me to stay, to take vows of celibacy and adhere to the movement as a core member for the rest of my life. A privilege, yes, that would be.

When Brian's long-distance call came, he sounded like a voice from another life. I rarely thought about him in Loveland.

"Mary, I'm going to be Manager of Entertainment for the Cunard Cruise Ships," he said with some anxiety. "I'm going to have my own office in England. I want you to marry me, Mary, and come to live in England with me."

I couldn't focus. My head ached from not having the answer. I felt nothing but more worry. I promised I would call him back.

The United States offered many advantages. The American Grail had been involved in the first translation of the book of Psalms into English. Its women had published new religious music and treatises; initiated the production of religious Christmas cards, crèches, and religious art; and had also produced a long-playing record of folk songs (a favourite with Max Ferguson, Canada's popular CBC radio host).

"Go after what makes you happy, Mary," one of my choir members at rehearsal advised.

Suddenly, clearly, I knew the answer. I allowed myself to feel the excitement of going toward what turned me on. I was going back to acting. The proposal, like a kiss from a prince, had woken me from a trance. I could be a good person by being a good actress. I could try. I will marry my art, I told myself. I'll journey onward with the Grail in Canada and answer the call to my vocation.

I was sorry to hurt Brian, but, thankfully, he found an English Catholic wife within the year. Then, only then, did I notice the guy's omission. Not once had he mentioned love.

Chapter 24

Toronto Grail, Andrew Allan

The Canadian Grail Centre, a narrow townhouse at Bathurst and Bloor, became my new oasis. (The buildings were expropriated two years later for the erection of Bathurst Subway Station.) On the top floor, across from the grey stone church of St. Peter's, I shared a room with Anne Otterson, also recently returned from Grailville. Anne quickly found work as a secretary with the CBC. She and I were somewhat like Jack Spratt and his wife: opposites in appearance and ability, but we could always count on each other to enjoy some disaster that had befallen us, although men, other than celibates, were never discussed.

The permanent residents at the Toronto Centre were a handful of devoted women, led by the round-faced, soft-spoken American Dorothy Rasenberger. Many women who gave a great deal of time and effort to the Grail Movement lived at home in various parts of the city, and a few Torontonians were serving their God in foreign lands: Olga Kolisnik, a nurse in Africa, and Ann Somerville, a teacher, whose sister, Janet, I'd so much enjoyed at Grailville. Across the street from the centre, Leona Chartrand, the woman who had gained my father's admiration, organized The Grail store, which offered new religious books, arts, and crafts. Using her keen eye and intuition, she dealt with many painters, including William Kurelek in his early fine art days.

* * *

Catholic teachers at that time were scarce. Substitute teaching for the Toronto Catholic School Board, I guessed, would be an easy and sure-fire means of income. With no training or even introduction, my association with the Grail made me a shoo-in to a Catholic school mere steps south from the centre. However, this stopgap work I found horrifying.

I met my class on the first morning of work: twenty-five tiny Grade Ones who guessed very well I knew nothing. I soon tired of the pretense of teaching the three essential R disciplines. The class was quickly erupting into bedlam. I turned to my only skill: drama. I devised ensemble activities in which we re-created Bible scenes (I planned to continue with fairy and modern tales). All in their desks, I had the class become waves of rushes on the banks of the river, or make wind sounds and motions of clouds. Some were gushing or swirling waters, and others made sounds of birds, rain, or even thunder claps—all depicting the early life of Moses.

Unfortunately, the principal came by. She reprimanded me for not following the curriculum, so I lost interest. Chaos took charge again until I found, in the teacher's desk, a thick leather strap. I held it out, and a hush came over the children. I ordered a scape-goat to stand out front. Then, in silence, as though witnessing a guillotine, the youngsters watched me strike a terrified child on the palm of his tiny, pale hand. A sensual thrill surged up through my body. Horrified, I promptly returned the instrument to the desk and resolved never again to ever hit a child. I also never again applied for supply teaching. I wanted my sense of power and excitement to come from a struggle with art, not little children. So I turned again to patience and trust in the unknown. I remained silent and found more filing jobs and never mentioned the sickening strapping incident to anyone.

Longing to be part of a simple band of performing players, I scoured the city for union acting gigs, joining, in spirit, the age-old gold diggers of Yukon Territory. Finally, I landed a role in a children's Christmas play directed by Jean Roberts, then a producer at CBC. Roberts and her two partners, Marigold Charlesworth and Keith Green, had recently arrived from England.

Beauty and the Beast, by the British playwright Nicholas Stuart Gray, was a sellout success in the now long-gone theatre in Toronto Central Reference Library on College Street. Through that production I made a warm connection with Jean, and a rather distant one with Marigold, whose direction would test my patience in later years.

* * *

One never knows when one is helping to make outstanding theatrical history. One can only hope. Yet in 1963, we did. Nonnie Griffin, my actress friend, phoned me one day to say she was about to take part in a most exciting new venture.

"I've spoken to Mr. Allan about you," she said, "and how you wowed everyone at the Red Barn a few years ago. He wants to see you."

Soon after, I was interviewed by the elderly, baldheaded gentleman and artistic director of this new venture. We had a good chat before I presented my best audition piece. For four weeks that summer, I joined the company for its first production with mainly English and Irish-Canadian thespians. On the second floor of the courthouse of tiny, insignificant Niagara-on-the-Lake, an hour's drive from Toronto, we took up temporary quarters where wooden risers were erected for audience seating, curtains separated dressing rooms, and the cast and company entered backstage via the side emergency fire escape. Playing young Dolly Clandon, sister of Philip, played by Roy Wordsworth, in *You Never Can Tell*, I delivered the first "professional" line for what has now become the world-renowned Shaw Festival, Ontario.

Prior to that time, Mr. Allan had left radio and television "in order to read and write a little," he told me. But George Bernard Shaw's astute showmanship seemed like dessert within Andrew's usual diet of heavy thinkers. Years later, through reading his autobiography and hearing from his colleagues, I learned of an intense despair in the man who had long longed to be a writer. Then, I only knew him as a wise old guy who cherished his privacy.

Following the Shaw season in Niagara-on-the-Lake, my friendship grew with Andrew. "Friendship" doesn't accurately describe my relationship with this internationally esteemed giant of arts, radio, theatre, and Canadian culture, because back in Toronto, I merely became company for his evening dining. "A bright escort" was how he described me, as he did other women, I was sure. He didn't mean the term "escort" in any indelicate sense. Andrew was of refined Scottish ancestry and always, for me, a perfect gentleman.

Dinner engagements were most often held in the elegant dining area of the Celebrity Club, a few blocks north of the CBC studios. Surrounded by other dining nobilities of the entertainment world, he would stand while waiting for me to be seated by an elderly waiter who flipped his white napkin over his shoulder before holding my chair for me to be seated at a candlelit table glistening with wine-glasses and crisp, clean table settings. Andrew charmingly suggested aperitifs and ordered both our meal choices.

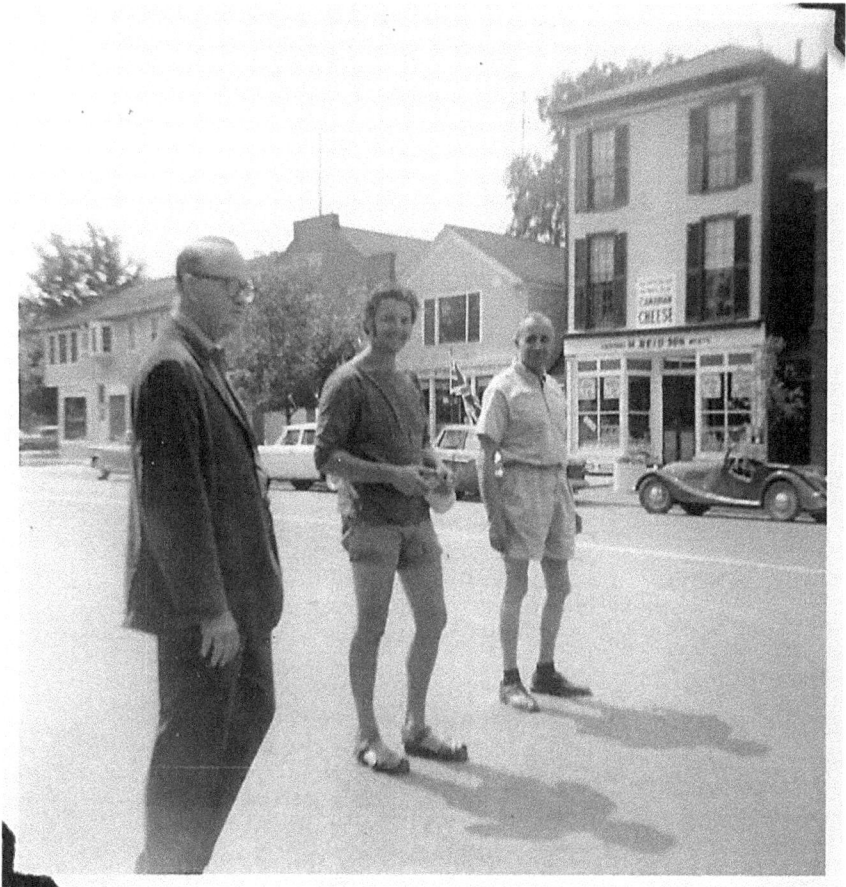

Break from Shaw rehearsals, 1963.
Andrew Alan AD, James Beggs, Alfred Gallagher.

Dinners involved long, one-sided philosophical conversations into which I would interject occasional comments. Andrew spoke, and I listened with intent fascination. With some humour, he would occasionally speak of his ex-wives. I was proud to be his current intellectual companion. We rarely discussed people, only reveled in ideas. We were both lonely. That I could appreciate.

With elegant dignity, Andrew would rise when I would excuse myself to visit the powder room, always offering a slight bow as I passed. On my return, he would stand again to support my chair, saying such words as, "I felt a great void, Mary, while you were gone," spoken with convincing sincerity.

Never having been spoken to in this manner by any person, my spirits would immediately lift like dandelion seeds sent sailing on a breeze. To my hungry soul, his tall stature, stately head, and large bespectacled eyes appeared always distant yet supremely caring.

The man became an austere yet uplifting father figure for me, and I gave him a pretty face to gaze on. The evenings were enchanting, always nutritious, and inevitably intoxicating, yet I always arrived home glad to be in my simple lodgings, wondering if I should accept another invitation, secretly wishing I had a real and regular boyfriend.

During that time, I was still living with a half-dozen women at The Grail Centre. Thinking I should repay Andrew for his generosity to me, on an impulse, I invited him to have dinner with us at the Centre. Perhaps the following week? I figured he could meet my folk, and he and I might expand our field of connection together. Our secluded meetings would be shared with the world.

Enthusiastically, with Dorothy Rasenberger, our gentle warrior chief at the Centre, I arranged the date and gave all the relevant information to Frances, the cheery lass from Scotland who served as our cook and general housekeeper. Frances made up a menu of simple but fresh local fare. "Perfect," I said, "For a grand Scottish gentleman."

Dinner was set at seven, and Frances happily prepared a grand lamb stew and homemade bread. By eight o'clock, Andrew had not arrived. I walked to the telephone and called him. He casually enquired how I was doing. I knew immediately that I'd interrupted him from one of his favourite authors. I didn't care.

"Where are you?" I said, sounding much like a frustrated spouse. "Everyone's waiting for dinner!"

Quietly he replied, "Mary, I said I thought it a good idea. There was no confirmation on either side."

My mind replayed our recent conversation. He was right. Anger at my stupidity swelled. He had to come and put my embarrassment to rights. "But we're all sitting at table; we're all here."

"Please don't put yourselves out on my account," the courteous man said, probably feeling almost as badly as I.

So that was it? I would have to tell everyone I fucked up, there was no date at all. Instead of shattering like broken glass, I must have heard that great guardian angel of mine. Quick off the mark, I decided there had to be a solution for this horrible disorder. Think! Miraculously, it came!

In a bright voice, I asked, "Andrew, have you eaten yet?"

"Uhm … no."

"Well, why not come? Now?"

After a pause, he agreed. What a guy!

"Give me half an hour," he said.

This great Canadian pioneer of international Canadian drama arrived by cab at eight-thirty, and the meal lasted until my eyes blurred and my ears hurt. He and the women discoursed into the wee hours, listening and asking many questions.

On that most difficult of evenings, I think I may have heftily helped Mr. Allan as well as myself. That was the last of his invitations to dinner. I felt free. Two years passed before he invited me back again to play at the Shaw Festival.

Chapter 25

First Visit Home

March 17, 1964
Dear Mary:

Thank you for your letter which I enjoyed very much. I'm having to get a separate address book especially for you and your moves. Your father found himself a job but it didn't last long. I think he thought it wasn't quite right for him. He never speaks about you, I'm afraid. He says he doesn't have a daughter when I mention you. You keep well. I've had a raise from Brillo, a nice one so I must be doing something right.

Love, Mum XXXX

Seven years after emigration, I was flying back over the Atlantic by way of another of life's miracles. As I sat in the ear-shattering plane, remembering Mum's letter, I wondered how Dad would greet me. I was my father's daughter and could keep up a standoff as long as he. *If he wonders how I paid for the trip, I'll tell him the truth: a stranger gave me the money. Totally out of the blue.*

Sitting listening to the drone of the plane's engine, I remembered leaving St. Peter's Church after mass, together with other Grail women, one Sunday when a stranger had spoken behind me in a thick Gaelic accent.

"Immigrants never appreciate their new country until they've returned at least once."

The voice brought my head around to see a roughly-shaven, little guy, wearing a rather drab, scruffy suit. I simply gave him a polite smile.

"You're with the Grail, aren't you?" he said. "Have you been back yet."

I shook my head and smiled companionably. Right there and then, reaching into his jacket, he took out a chequebook and handed me a slip of paper worth a thousand dollars—the fare for a twenty-one-day return ticket on a chartered flight. An astonishing sum. Why did he choose me? Did I look that needy? I'd never suffered from homesickness that I could remember. His reasoning he never explained, only that he wanted no returns. I never saw him again. Another angel. Like the guy seven years earlier, who'd led me to my first job in Toronto, who also disappeared.

Seated in the large Boeing, looking down over the clouds, I was unsure what greeting I would get at home. Straightening things out with my father should take five minutes. For Mum, I was repeating Dad's agonizing trip for their wedding anniversary. How would I handle three weeks in our house? After hugs and greets and all the "How you doing?" what in the world will I do? My drama school buddies had all disappeared in multiple directions.

As we prepared to land at Heathrow that September afternoon, my body began to jitter with excitement. I was now carrying not one but two union cards: ACTRA for Canadian film and radio, and Actors' Equity for North American stage. Surely that should please everyone.

Our Greenford Avenue Home, Hanwell

From the airport by bus into the city, my eyes lapped in the scenery, although dimly lit through grey clouds. Everything seemed tiny—cars, trains, and buildings looked like Dinky toys. The people seemed weary but cheery. Oh, how marvelous to be back! With my suitcase clenched between the calves of my legs, my eyelids drooped as the little red Piccadilly underground train snaked through a million stops until it reached Northfields in the western suburbs of London. I climbed the station stairs to look in vain for a double-decker bus to take me the final stretch. My luck held out. A man's head appeared from a baker's van standing nearby, calling, "Going Greenford way?"

"Yes! Oh, thank you!"

I fell onto a front passenger seat. All the way, the driver chatted in a Cockney accent, heartening my soul with familiar cadences. He stopped at the far bottom of our hill, and I waved goodbye, thanking him for his kindness.

Checking I had everything—purse, suitcase, my purple beret at the right angle and hair tucked around correctly—I headed through a gateway, up a tiny path, and ascended three concrete steps to the front door of the semi-detached. Ordinarily, our family used the shared alleyway to the back door. But this was an extraordinary day. Or was I taking the front because I was no longer family? The back door suddenly seemed an unearned privilege. Shaking off the negativity, my excitement returned. I quickly thrust my hand through the letterbox to pull out the familiar string that held the key. Finding nothing there, I pressed the doorbell, now feeling like a travelling salesman. A shadow appeared on the pane of the door's thick frosted glass—much too short to be my father's. I breathed more easily. The door opened and Mum came into view. I looked at the round, wrinkled, oh so familiar face.

"Hi, Mum!"

Her pale blue eyes stared as though at an electorate on a campaign trail. "Hello!" Then, straightening her apron with great vigour, Mum stepped back, allowing me to move inside. Quickly turning, she headed down the narrow hallway, calling back with forced cheer, "I'll put the kettle on."

The woman's nervous, distant manner was also all too familiar. From the kitchen radio at the end of the short hall, the sound of an orchestra filled the air. Why did I not reach out to give her a hug, a kiss on the cheek? An aroma of fresh housepaint told me I'd been awaited with some honour. Years ago, the place had held a pervasive smell of coal-fire smoke, burnt lard, and/or pine scented cleaning fluid.

Leaving my bags in the hall, I entered the small dining room and seated myself where memories of our lives together collided inside my head. The sound of music suddenly ceased. Only the patter of her slippered feet filled the silence as Mum joined me to sit herself the far end of the bare dining room table. The air descended around me in a kind of flatness.

"A bakery driver gave me a lift right from the Underground to the door," I said with enthusiasm. I remembered how a policeman in the fog, when I was a girl, had guided me home from school, walking his bicycle, showing me the way with a flashlight. Londoners are still the friendliest.

"Did you tip him?" my mother asked.

"I forgot," I lied. The thought hadn't even occurred. A sickness in my gut took me back to my childhood, to how thoughtless I could be.

This mighty-mouse Mum, with honey-coloured hair and the softest body anyone could be wrapped inside, could suddenly speak and it would be like a firework in my face. My stomach took on a kind of nauseous knot. I'd returned just as I'd left: a useless waste-of-time.

Mum stood and left the room. I became aware of my suitcase by the front door, waiting for directions. I didn't move. When I heard from the next room a clattering of tea things, I joined Mum in the hot, cramped kitchen where she sat, wiping her eyes. I began an apology—only to learn how even more severely how I'd disappointed her.

She cried, "You didn't even bring chocolates!"

I stood silently, helpless. After blowing her nose on the inside of her apron, she discretely folded and patted in place the soiled section of material. "Even your father brought flowers or *something*."

Thoughtless, yes, and I might have tried harder to be the conquering heroine returning in triumph, but I could never give her the celebration she longed for—to be lifted up into the world of her daydreams, into her past elations when her siblings, all the way from Birmingham, would unexpectedly arrive at our house.

I so wanted to please my strong, vulnerable mum. I was forever searching for freedom, but I could only succeed in stretching out some kind of bungee cord between us. Holding on, neither of us were able to let go, until, stretched too far, we headed fast back to the inevitable crash. Not at all how I'd hoped.

Back at the dining table, soothed by milky Typhoo tea and the promise of food, I ventured on a slightly less emotional topic.

"How's Dad?"

"As miserable as ever."

"Working?"

"No, upstairs in bed. He never moves from there these days. The doctor can't find anything wrong with him."

I saw the lids of her eyes relax. She was clearly glad to have an ear to bend. She patted in place her fading auburn hair. "One of his pals from the pub came by yesterday," she said, "and he threw a bottle at him."

"At Dad?"

"No, your dad did! The man brought him beer, you see, and he only drinks rum now. Has for years!"

Mysteriously bed-ridden with unexplained leg pains, Dad now lay in the front bedroom. Up the wooden stairs Mum carried a cooked meal twice a day and supervised a visiting day nurse. Her disappointment when I arrived was probably a reflection of the charm having worn off from having him home.

"How can I help?" I asked the weary woman.

"Probably best if you keep out of his way. Your father didn't like it when I told him you were coming." She opened a biscuit bin and placed half the contents on a plate. "But he asks me every day if you've arrived yet. Seems funny when he insists he doesn't know you. Says you owe him money or something. I can't make it out at all."

I wished my head would clear about that money problem that Mum had written me about. I was sure the thirty dollars he gave me when I first arrived in Canada was a gift. How wretched can one get? I must have failed him somehow when we both were in Canada. Or did I break some sacred rule? The thought of staying for weeks in this house of memories began a panic in me. Taking a moment to swallow, I breathed deeply, then told Mum my plan.

"I'd like to take a trip up north ... while I'm here ... to see some shows at the Edinburgh Festival. You don't mind, do you?"

"No, no. Go where you like. You always have."

She gently slid the base of her teacup across the edge of its saucer to prevent any stray drips from soiling her front. I knew I'd hurt her again but dreaded a long stay of unspoken misery, and the new festival would be grand to see. The Edinburgh Grail Centre would surely put me up for a few nights. Their phone number was in my bag.

"Can I come too?" Mum said. Her eyes, wide open, fixed on me as though I were Santa Claus in Autumn. "I'll pay my way," Mum said, her teacup hovering an inch from her lips, the saucer shaking under it. "Brillo owes me more holidays. I could leave your dad with the day nurse, just for a few days. He wouldn't notice I was gone."

I stood from the table and moved into the hall to find my purse. I could have wept with rage.

Chapter 26

Edinburgh and Dad Again

My last-minute escape plan to Scotland was foiled. With my mother in tow, I'd get no freedom at all on my holiday. Yet how could I refuse? She who was sitting now opposite me in our old home had changed from the icy personage who had opened the front door into a mirror reflecting my own needy, forlorn state. I couldn't deliberately leave behind such unhappiness. Taking a deep breath, I put on a smile.

"Yes. Why don't we go together."

Mum's face lit up like a struck matchstick, and mine brightened a little too.

"The Edinburgh Grail Centre will put us up. They won't mind if a member brings along her mum. Can I use your phone to check it out?"

"Be my guest," Mum said, gathering the dishes in double time. "Would you like me to make you some beans on toast?"

"Lovely!"

On the train to Edinburgh, I remembered happier childhood times, when she and I would take off to a movie together after dark, leaving Dad and my two brothers at home. Singing quietly, my weary mother would skip a little, stick my arm through hers, and say, "Tuck your leg in bed!" and together we would head for the bus stop. As it did in those days, my heart warmed to her again on that trip. During those few days, like a schoolgirl let out of a long detention, she sparkled with delight at every moment of liberty, and the mood was contagious.

We found only one snag. My mother falls asleep as she gets into bed but snores louder than a fire alarm. At the Grail Centre in downtown Edinburgh, we shared a double bed. However, I was young, guiltfree for once, and soon slept. The next day, because she preferred shopping to theatre-going, after breakfast Mum took her leave with a satisfied smile and a queenly hand-wave, while I headed in another direction: the grounds of the new Festival.

"Did you have a good afternoon, Mum?" I asked when we met up later.

"Yes," she offered, her chin lifting slightly, "I visited Woolworths."

I imagined her moseying around this cheap penny store. "Couldn't you do better than Woolworths?"

She was not belittled. "I like to compare them all. Edinburgh's is excellent."

She didn't let on, but I knew well she had also found a little corner in a fine restaurant, perhaps in the Cally Hotel, or one as prestigious and elegant, and had sat for an hour or so, gazing up at the great castle on the mountain while ordering tea with salmon and cucumber sandwiches—made with soft white bread cut in little squares, with no crusts—and, I hoped, some cream cake.

While my mother retired early, I returned to view the astounding talents of the Festival. Especially, I was amazed at the power of Joan Plowright in Shaw's *Saint Joan,* directed by Laurence Olivier. I became convinced that my choice of career was as brilliant. Oh, how I wanted to speak inspiring words that could marshal an army and bring on sainthood! Equally stirring but far more baffling was the afternoon symposium I attended: *Modern Drama and the Absurd*, held in the Great Hall of Edinburgh University. Very keen to understand more about a style I knew only as people talking nonsense for hours, I was thrilled to learn that a panel of five knowledgeable theatre folk would include the well-known playwright, Eugene Ionesco. The panel sat behind a long table on a large wooden stage opposite an audience holding its large breath.

After introductions, Ionesco rose and began a discourse on theatrical theory. But the hall lights began to flicker, then strange, loud noises were heard—as though made by rude clowns. The audience's eyes were drawn to a man's face staring in from one of the immensely high windows up above the stage. Too high! Then, from the central skylight in the roof, a body descended on a rope, followed by naked actors streaking across the stage in front of the panel of speakers. All the while, the discourse continued, undisturbed, for another half hour—with the audience in an uproar. I sat in total confusion, wondering if I should demand my money back.

From the next morning's newspaper, I learned I'd participated in a slice of modern theatre. Allan Kaprow, a pioneer in performance art, had been asked by the panel to set up one of his "happenings": arranged incidents that were quickly becoming popular ways of confronting traditional theatre, particularly its use of the proscenium or "fourth wall" that delineated the stage area from the audience—an anathema to Absurdist Theatre (Samual Beckett's classic play *Waiting for Godot* is a prime example of this style of playwrighting, for it appears to be ridiculously comical but has an underlying serious message.)

"The line between art and life should be kept as fluid, and perhaps indistinct, as possible," Kaprow was quoted.

Although I could neither agree nor disagree with Kaprow, because I understood as much of what he said as I did the absurdists—almost zilch—I've remembered that event as though it were a turning point in my life. Kaprow's statement echoed in my mind. Should my life be fluidly easing into my art? What art? I so rarely was able to work at it. Something had touched a long-hidden conflict within me and whipped it to the surface. I wanted to be modern, to be up on the latest developments in theatre. So why was I returning to culture-conflicted Canada? I only knew the taste of Canada had left me wanting more of it. Was acting really an art? Did life end when art began? Are they separate? I decided these were excellent questions, although they returned below surface again for many years.

Finishing our little vacation with a luxurious side trip to see Loch Ness, Mum and I took the coach back to London, with her telling everyone we met that her daughter had given her the "best holiday" she'd ever had. With great gusto she returned to her house, her chores, and carting upstairs her husband's bland and dismal diet for ulcers.

The day after our return, setting down his tray, she said, "He wants to see you."

"Me?"

"Just this minute, he said he'll 'have a word' with you."

I mounted the stairs. My knock at Dad's door was answered by a short growl. Entering, I found a double bed almost filling the sunny room that Dad now shared with nobody. There were paperback mystery books with orange covers scattered on a side table among several bottles and various-sized drinking glasses, but no sign of an ashtray. That was promising. The sun-filled room was stiflingly hot. Dad lay with his grey-haired head propped above pillows against a worn wooden headboard. He averted his eyes and sniffed.

Settling myself on a straight-back chair at the end of his bed, I could see him clearly sweating and in need of a shave. I sat in stillness, waiting.

Dad turned his dark eyes on me. "You owe me two hundred dollars I loaned you to go off to the US!"

"Not that I know of." I met his challenge. Our brown eyes clinched.

"It's not the money, girl, no. It's owning up to what I did for you."

"Listen, Dad," I said, "I remember asking you for money. I remember my friend hosting us at her place. Now, if you could believe that I have forgotten—that it's completely disappeared from my head that you actually gave me that cash, could you understand that? I can't remember it, Dad, and that's the truth. It's not that I'm lying to you, saying no, you never did lend me anything."

Dad turned and focused through the windows on the far side.

I wondered how this frail man could have once been admired by and have influenced so many people, how vainly I'd spent my life longing for him to show some warm affection toward any one of my family. Was he not an honorable man? Everyone used to think so. A long silence followed.

"I'll tell you what, girlie," he finally said, his eyes fixed on the shop opposite. "You know those earmuffs they wear in Canada? Those fuzzy things with the metal spring band over—"

"Yes, I know."

"I can't stand the blasted noise around here. If you send me a pair of those, I'll forget the whole thing."

Tears filled my eyes as I softened toward the wretched man. "I promise, Dad."

He picked up a book then and I left, quietly closing his door. We spoke few words ever again.

I headed back to my land of complexity, carrying still a paradoxical sense of achievement and loss. My next visit to England would be made nine years later, for a very fleeting and much more energetic trip, not directly from Canada but from Europe, when Dad nodded a greeting as though I'd gone out for milk. But even his grunts I accepted with a sense of peace. After sending him earmuffs, my father had reclaimed me.

* * *

Several months after I returned to Canada, Mum amazed me perhaps even more than had my father. Alone, she crossed the ocean to visit me, the Grail Centre where I was living—and the Toronto Woolworth stores. Again, she left Dad with visiting nurses. But the biggest shock happened on another trip together.

A few days after her arrival, as we sat in the Centre's living room, my mother pleaded, "Couldn't we take a couple of days and pop down to New York?"

"Pop down? Do you know how long a pop-down would take?"

Perhaps her natural impulsiveness and sense of adventure had been pent up for too many years and was now sprouting. She'd arrived from Toronto Airport in a terrible state of frenzy, worried that she had left my father with no supper. Regretting her reckless move, she would eat nothing at the evening meal set out for us by Frances McLaughlin. The six Grail resident women were very solicitous. Anne Otterson, my roommate, agreed to bunk in elsewhere so Mum could sleep with me, but my poor mum saw only that she was upsetting everyone. Sly and brilliant Francis asked for Dad's telephone number and then left the dining room, declaring in her Scottish lilt, "We'll check with the man himself!"

"Cyril, are you all right?" my mother eventually shouted into the receiver.

"Dol?"

"Yes, it's Dolly. I'm so worried, Cyril. Did you eat?"

"Of course I damn well ate … and slept … 'til now! It's three in the morning!"

We'd all forgotten the time change. After the call, Mum ate her dinner plus a second helping, and charmed my five housemates so utterly they envied me my mother.

The next day, we journeyed to the Big Apple by bus and stayed for a couple of nights at the Brooklyn Centre. In our double bed, I lay awake listening to her heavy night-time snoring, hating her for her simple company to the city of dreams where her wishes were primary, while I was sure to be inundated with nostalgic memories of lost love and past thrilling theatrical adventures. The opportunity for me to see New York for a second time had become a huge drag.

"Let's see *Beyond the Fringe*," Mum suggested, surprising me that evening as we walked around downtown. Curious that she'd be interested in hot English comics while visiting Broadway, I answered, "I'd love to … but wouldn't you rather see something American?"

Mum and Mary outside the Toronto Grail Centre

"No!" The little woman laughingly explained. "You see, then I could tell them back at Brillo—I missed '*the Fringe*' in London but picked it up in New York."

We got gallery seats and laughed all the way through—even in our bed. Yet the greatest eye-opener came the following morning.

I descended late to find a gathering of women around the glassed front door, staring at a black, shiny limousine parked outside the Centre.

"I'm being lunched at the main office," Mum said, casually drawing on her coat.

Before driving away, a uniformed chauffeur assisted my mother from the front door into a luxurious-looking vehicle.

"I know nothing!" I told the questioning women, my eyes as wide as theirs.

Was this the reason she visited me? No wonder she wanted to come to New York! How and when did she arrange this? Years later, my younger brother, John, told me that the manager of the London branch of Brillo had been so grateful to her for pulling them out of the red, he promised to leave her £10,000 in his will. Perhaps he'd died! He had.

"God knows where the money went," John later said.

In the National Gallery of Canada in Ottawa, I have stood before Andy Warhol's sculpture *Brillo Soap Pad Boxes*, dated 1964, with great pride and sentimentality. I treasured the world-renowned piece as a direct connection with my secretive and amazing mother.

Collage for Mum by Me

Chapter 27

The Shaw Festival Again and Howard

Contracted again by the Shaw Festival, I'd no idea what a landmark in time this venture would be in my life. Halfway through the 1965 season, while on a walk around the grounds of old Fort George in Niagara-on-the-Lake, I accepted a proposal of marriage from a new young actor from England, eight years my junior.

There was no gazing with wonder into my adoring eyes, no passionate assault on my body, only a polite statement. "I feel very comfortable with you, Mary," Howard Lever said, looking past me toward the lake. "Would you be my wife?"

"Yes," I answered, with no hesitation. "I'd like that."

My strong Catholic faith at that time contrasted with my new fiancé's unofficial creed, which pointed toward some eastern philosophies. But what did I care? Allurement too often masters us! I was almost thirty and should have known better. But he'd entranced me since the first rehearsal of *Pygmalion*—the only production we both would ever appear in together.

Howard and I became an item in theatre gossip. Popular with both the company and audiences, he carried his tall, thin body with an energetic lightness; his high forehead with its premature receding hairline gave him a majestic appeal. When he addressed me, looking down to my five-foot-two, I hardly dared glance at his full lips for fear of a Victorian swoon. The mellow young man seemed unruffled by stress. How first appearances deceive! I later found he disguised his inner agony too well for his health.

Mary, Howard Lever & Joyce Campion in Shaw's *Pygmalion*

Mary as Patricia Smith in Shaw's *The Millionairess*
in tailored suit by brother Peter

If I'd been more knowledgeable, more intelligent and street smart, I would have recognized a wrong choice. But who's to know what Fate has designed, or what primary importance in life might another person be? The engagement ring he bought should have been a sure-fire warning: a single black pearl. My friends gazed at it in silence, but I decided it was very hip.

Mary, John Horton, Rosamund Burns in
The Importance of Being Earnest

My lover and I rarely spoke of private inner matters. Yet one day, together in my rented room, he told me he suffered from emotional stress that took the form of pre-mature ejaculation.

"That's why I have difficulty making love," he confided. "We shouldn't marry until I can get help for this."

Wanting to help, I enquired "for a friend" among the people I knew in the Catholic community, and heard of Mrs. Lea Hindley-Smith, a hypnotherapist who'd recently arrived from England and was helping not only students from the University of Toronto but also many of the school's faculty. Howard applied and was immediately accepted. After his private sessions, he frequently landed in my rented room on Selby Street to smoke, ponder, lounge, and chat. He had the enviable habit of making himself comfortable in any location, reminding me of Bertie Wooster, the character by P.G. Wodehouse, as he lay back, splayed, drone-like across my bed while I viewed him from a chair at my window, inhaling both my own brand of nicotine and what I regarded as his genius.

Howard's talent not only lay in acting and directing but also in teaching. He coached me as I learned lines for my next big tour, this time with Canadian Players as Cecily in *The Importance of Being Earnest,* both of us thoroughly enjoying the wit of Oscar Wilde.

* * *

While I toured Ontario yet again, Howard became a regular client of Nessa Hendrickson, one of Mrs. Smith's growing number of trainees from St. Michael's College. He followed me to Montreal during our week-long run there and spoke almost nonstop about "this fascinating therapy business." We made love, but I was aghast at how he threw the resident cat off the bed in order to fulfill the action. The pet was owned by the couple who'd allowed me to use their apartment while they were vacationing, and I worried the animal was hurt. Howard seemed not to care.

Arriving back in Toronto after six weeks away, I developed a strange terror of going outside my room on Selby Street. Then, after experiencing a terrible emotional block on the set of a television drama, I was convinced I'd never be hired anywhere again.

Howard insisted, "Your fear is dragging you down, Mary. I've moved to a male therapist now, so tomorrow you go see Nessa."

My first three visits with Miss Henderson were spent drying my tears, not able to understand how this intelligent American ex-nun could spend time listening to me. After the lady invited me to join her in her rented kitchen, I sat on a high stool, drank her tea, and watched as she prepared a salad lunch. There, with great relief, we laughed as I was able to answer a few simple questions and to hear my voice aloud. For a very little fee—$30.00 for fifty minutes—I received careful empathy and guidance never before imagined on my horizon. I continued with Nessa, slowly learning how one's mind can deceive and how dreams can be multi-illuminating.

Kenneth Wickes and Mary in *The Private Ear & the Public Eye*

The following September, I began to worry more about my physical development than my mental. While running in another play at the Colonnade Theatre on Bloor Street—a delightful run with co-actors Kenny Wickes and Roy Wordsworth—I noticed my breasts were fattening and my waist too, even though I'd sworn off French fries for life. Afraid of those things people called "tumours," I visited a doctor's office. I went alone. One would. After the doctor's brief examination, as I dressed, he said, "Young lady, you're four months pregnant."

Impossible! I couldn't remember Howard ever fully entering my vagina! Getting in the family way had never occurred to either of us.

"I can't be," I insisted.

"I've met virgin births before in my time. I don't believe any of them," he quipped as he showed me to the door.

Just back from flying high at the Shaw Festival in Niagara-on-the-Lake again, Howard was nonplussed at the news.

"Pregnant?"

That was the only word he spoke to me during the pregnancy. While paying a therapist to cure his sexual problems, at twenty-three years of age his sperm had been smarter than his mind.

I realized very quickly that I'd more than one problem. Most imminent was my next contract. I was to play the romantic lead in *Charley's Aunt,* out-of-town, in the recently rebuilt Garden Centre Theatre in Vineland. How could I appear in a popular nineteenth-century farce looking already banged up? I phoned the producer, who was also director and lead in the play, that elfish Emperor of Comedy, Tom Kneebone.

Tom proved to be the most compassionate person alive and a friend for many years afterwards.

"Are you showing, darling?"

"A bit, I must confess."

"Well, get to Sammy immediately. She'll adjust your dress so it will give as you go. It's not a very long run. Thank God the period's Queen Vicky, love! Remember, you'll wear a corset—oh Lord—breathe in, and don't tell a soul. It's our secret!"

I didn't have to tell. Everyone knew via dressing room gossip. Why couldn't I have laughed it off? Why couldn't I have been bold and bravado, making light of misfortune as others did who made great stories out of trauma? Nessa's wrong—I'm not angry. I'm a first-rate clown.

Back in the city, I went to work as a clerk again, dressed in tent-like disguises. In those days, pregnant women were rarely seen out of doors. One morning, I remember leaving my desk for the washroom. On my knees in one of the cubicles, I made a pact with God: keep my child safe and healthy, and I'll do all in my power to do the same, no matter what it costs me. This was a new sense of commitment for me. The passion that I felt was almost overwhelming.

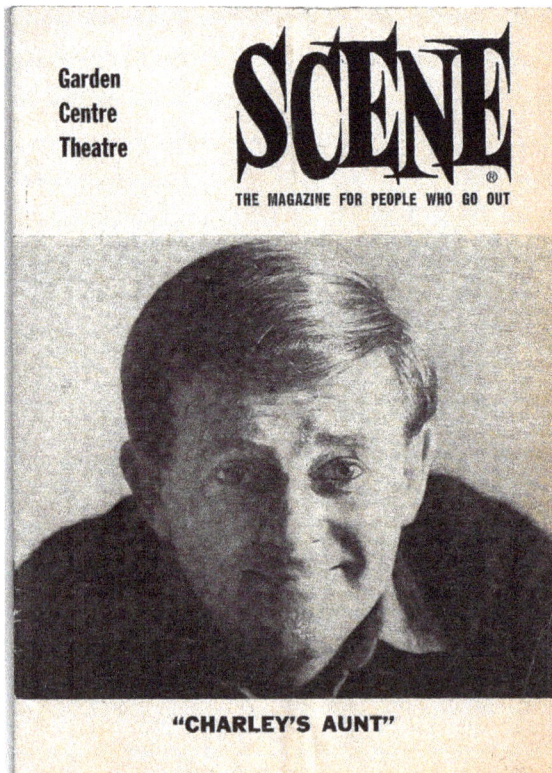

Tom Kneebone

Howard, however, was not answering my phone calls. Where was he? Nobody seemed to know. A week passed after I'd shared the news with him. Not a word. Then I heard via Nessa that my baby's father had admitted himself into 999 Queen Street, Toronto's Hospital for the Insane.

"Why?"

Nessa could give no answer. The bastard! I pictured him in comfort with doctors to look after him, nurses to feed and cheer him. Hate, resentment, rage—all mixed together with missing him, his attention, his caring, his phony actor's façade. My prince had turned into a frog.

"I'm afraid there's no sign of him discharging himself quite yet," Nessa said. "But your anger at Howard is misplaced."

Right! She was the one I should slice to pieces. She never once warned me. I had a right to be pissed off—he was giving me zilch support.

"You are in touch with your inner self. You're feeling lonely. Mary, that's a good sign."

Lonely! God, she had no idea. But I didn't dare let her know how bereft I really felt because, like my father, she'd probably tell me I'd made my own bed.

"Do you think you can rear a child alone?" Nessa asked.

"I don't know, but I want to try."

"Your work and income are very … inconsistent. Do you think that wise?"

"I don't know what's wise, do I?" I stared her in the eyes as I made my first facetious remark to my therapist—and knew at once an unusual sense of power.

My ire was up and aiding me. So with the help of Mary Carpenter and other Grail women, I made plans for keeping the baby, despite forces inside and out warning against the choice. I was one of hundreds of women lost and pregnant in a paternalistic society that was retaliating against uneducated youth who threatened the establishment in the late 1960s with ideas of following their bliss. With the help of social workers, I would have liked to prove that I could be a good, protective single mother. I searched out natural child birth classes and attended avidly, being especially enthralled with the breathing exercises, which I saw as extremely helpful for vocal work on stage. I found I didn't care who saw me large around the middle, and I walked through the streets with a smile on my face as though floating like a tall ship into harbour. Believing myself capable of any required task, my new prospects looked very exciting as I ate French fries and gallons of ice cream to help onward my new inner friend.

Chapter 28

Laurence Baines

Nessa was practical if not always sympathetic. She arranged for me to spend the last months of my internment in one of Mrs. Smith's House Groups: #477–479 Brunswick Avenue, overseen by Richard Taylor, another of the famous lady's learning therapists.

Richard welcomed me and treated me in the same unruffled manner he dealt with all fourteen other occupants of his rooming-house. A tall, attractive man from Jamaica, his interests also lay in alternative forms of physical health that would later help me.

Through my experiences with convents and the Grail, I was familiar with some forms of community living. This was different. Although everyone shared cooking, cleaning, the usual household chores, and ate together in a renovated basement dining room to accommodate more shared bedroom space upstairs, people didn't necessarily share any cause, opinion, belief, nationality, age, or anything else that I could see. Yet there was a consideration and order about the place. People argued in public as well as in private. The occasional plate was thrown across the kitchen, but there seemed to be no ongoing distress. People spent evenings enjoying each other's company: talking, singing.

The root of such ease might have been the weekly meetings to discuss emotional and practical issues brought forward by the occupants. I could not fathom. To my great pleasure, there was a large, loveable German Shepherd bitch roaming freely around the house, keeping a keen eye on Richard's whereabouts. I fell in with all the routines but had little energy for much outside my own concerns. I was assigned the ground-floor front room to re-design as a nursery cum bed-sitter.

At #479 I was settling in well and felt more secure than I had in many years, when one night I saw the vision that sealed the fate of my child. I dreamed that in a fit of frustration, I threw my infant out of a window—like a cross child might throw a doll.

"Your dream tells us clearly that you have no real desire to bring up a child," Nessa informed me during a session with her. She urged me to make immediate arrangements for adoption. With all self-confidence gone, I became convinced I wanted to destroy my baby. With the growing weight of my co-created wonder of the natural world, I set about the bleak proceedings of adoption.

* * *

The news I was most afraid of arrived late one evening, several months after I'd moved into the Brunswick house. With the baby late in the third trimester, I'd joined half a dozen residents in the basement to watch *The Johnny Carson Show* on TV.

Richard, our leader, turned up the lights as he entered the basement lounge. "Sorry to interrupt. I've just heard. Howard is at 76 Admiral, asking for Mary."

"He's out?" one of the men asked with wide eyes.

I gasped, holding close my belly.

In a steady voice, Richard said, "He discharged himself today. Apparently he seems unaware that we are protecting Mary in her condition. We have to take precautions. We don't know his state of mind."

Louise grasped my elbow to help me stand. "The good news is, you feel scared, Mary," the dear woman declared, attempting to be helpful.

The terror that Howard should reappear at any second with outrageous demands had spread throughout my nervous system. I couldn't hurry. Even walking was difficult. An underground blaze had been lying smoldering in my system since Howard had admitted himself five months earlier into Toronto's infamous insane asylum.

"Mary can't stay sleeping on the main floor," Richard continued.

Immediately, a young student at U. of T. offered to exchange with me, and everyone pitched in to move us. The next day, a padlock secured on the door of my second-floor room imprinted on my mind that I must make this a temporary arrangement. Best to keep moving. Afterwards? Who knew, perhaps home to England? No, that was unthinkable. At least in Canada I could hold my head up, could keep some semblance of self-respect without family pity and pathetic help. Here I could stay sane, like I'm told: moment by moment. I could still this nightmare once the baby was here.

Having to keep my new door locked at all times prevented Lady from continuing her daytime vigils with me. The gentle German Shepherd used to wander in as I lay on the bed there, reading or listening to the radio. The protective house mascot would come as though to assess my condition, with her long jaw resting on the edge of the blankets, her eyes blinking a while as she stared ahead, then she would wander out again, leaving behind mounds of calm energy. I missed her attentive poise in the new room as I waited behind the barred door. Instead, I remembered my first "baby," a round, white bundle of puppy rescued from a car accident when I was eight years old. I saw how much I'd fussed over him in his recovery bed that I'd made up in a corner of the kitchen floor. Bobbie, I'd called him. He grew into a lovely, cuddly adult dog—until killed on the main road outside our house, like all our other "Heinz 57" mongrel dogs. Nobody we knew then owned a leash.

The following day Richard told us that Howard had been persuaded to take a temporary home at the newly purchased Therafields Farm, an hour's drive north of Toronto, in Mono Mills.

"His therapist is taking him up there in his car," Richard explained. "That's better than letting him hang around the city."

I understood that Mrs. Lea Hindley-Smith and her assistants in the Therafields organization would keep safe the problematic father of my child. My part was to rest and wait for what would appear.

One cold February evening, my membranes finally ruptured and water poured onto the floor of Richard's kitchen. He helped me to his car and drove like a crazed cab driver to St. Michael's hospital on Queen Street while I experienced the first agonizing contractions of labour.

Midwifery was illegal in Ontario, but I'd prepared myself and my doctors for as "natural" a birth as possible. I'd taken classes for three months in how to sit, eat, breathe, and even fill the needs of baby. I was determined to be present and alert when my baby reached out. Then, on being wheeled into the surgery, a mirror conveniently positioned above the delivery table gave me a sense of both safety and excitement, like watching a grand new opening of a grand new show.

I remember a guy in a mask, wearing gloves and a white gown, holding up a syringe. I felt a hand on my shoulder from another person seated at my head as I lay with a mask over my face. I remember wanting to ask them all "What are you ...?" I woke to a strong smell of antiseptic and a form bending over me, pointing another needle.

"You be a good girl now. One more ouch."

"My baby?"

"He's fine and doing well. But we have to get *you* right," humoured the figure. "Your bladder is too full, dear. The muscle won't release. We don't want you to burst."

I figured she was a nurse with not the best news. Instructing me to raise my knees, she separated them, guided each leg—with shaking hands, I swear—into metal contraptions. Then holding down with her elbow my still-swollen stomach, with her fingers she held my vaginal lips apart; then, with her other hand hoping to find the right hole, she forced a long fine device up my urethra and pierced through the point of my peeing, thus opening floodgates. Labour pains had been a laugh!

Apparently, I learned, the surgeon had to make a last-minute decision. The baby was in breech. The operating team needed to reverse the fetus to the cephalic position and so preferred to put me under anesthetic.

During the week in hospital, I continued as though under anesthesia. A familiar blankness of mind enveloped me, although today the sensation would probably pass as postpartum depression. As I sat recovering in an open ward bed, the baby was occasionally brought for me to hold. The soft seven pounds, rounded in a blanket, was placed, sleeping, on my lap. I didn't appreciate those visits. Like an inexperienced actor, I didn't know what to do with my arms and hands, afraid to move in case I caused an earthquake or other terrible calamity. I would only stare at the pale, wrinkled face of the creature and feel an uncomfortable arm and developing stiffness in my jaw. The special scent of newborn sweetness, that mixture of vaginal discharge and baby powder, was more abhorrent to me than endearing. I would not, could not want the thing. But when the nurses took him from me, I remember noticing the coolness left in my lap, the hollowness, the loss. I determined to turn strongly against feeling that again.

Later, a stiff-capped nurse in blue came by to tell me, in loud tones, how my "perfect little red-head" had been voted the "most popular baby in the nursery." Energy leapt slightly inside my chest! Red-head? "Auburn," my mum liked to describe her hair and my brother John's, too. Strange I hadn't noticed the colour on the baby. Yet how could I? All one could see was a pale bundle in a blanket. The Irish and Scottish must be coming through. I almost laughed. Peculiar to be called English yet with few known ancestors from England. A momentary connection to the creature passed through me, a need, a kind of claiming of my family blood present here while the rest were thousands of miles away across the Atlantic.

Chapter 29

Goodbye, Laurence

I left Saint Michael's Hospital with no goodbyes to the baby. "For the best," the nurses advised. Now I was free to make the most of the rest of my life. You never know what's around the corner, my mum always said. Setting off by bus for Brunswick Avenue, I felt relieved to be my normal shape again, and never so glad of the greetings of welcoming faces at the group house. How lucky was I! Grins from Richard, a hug from Rosa, an empathic Latin American resident, and a cup of tea from Joan Goddard—an English singer presently studying at Toronto's Royal Conservatory of Music—and a lick from Lady made my return bearable. Later, after dinner and sharing stories with my amazing new friends, we listened to the singing of a long dark-haired student from New York. Carole accompanied herself on her guitar. Her singing Joan Baez songs warmed and relaxed me, although I remember thinking I still preferred Joni Mitchell.

"Did you scream?" Carole said with a giggle between songs. "In America the Italian women scream and shriek and yell their babies out, cursing blue murder, and the huge families swarm the wards afterwards, ooing and ahing, while everyone else is mortified and deaf."

We all laughed at the visions, and, still smiling, I retired early from the warm atmosphere. Just in case, I locked my door. I worried how long I'd be able to stay now that my crisis was over.

Looming largely ahead was the task of notifying the Catholic Children's Aid of my choice on our child's future. As an unmarried mother, I was the sole decision-maker. The organization had no interest in Howard Baines Lever apart from his age and race. There were no forms for him to complete. No long-term preparations. No commitments. An Ontario law at that time gave me a few months to consider my decision before I officially gave the infant as a Ward of the Courts.

On my discharge, a Catholic Children's Aid worker had taken the baby from the hospital "to a warm, temporary mother." People I knew assured me I was doing the right thing. In those freedom-loving days of the late 1960s, adoption was encouraged: believed beneficial to everyone involved. Birth mothers were deemed generous to give their offspring to parents who couldn't create families of their own. Natural mothers were "sharing with generosity their gifts with childless couples," one social worker said. Nobody in officialdom seemed to consider the best interests of the infants, least of all the infants and children of the indigenous peoples who were given no choice at all.

On Mrs. Smith's advice, a few weeks after the birth, Howard met with me at the CCAS offices in order for us both to meet Laurence. We stood in the hallway, silently waiting. Before I'd left hospital, while I was still in bed, a man from the main office had come with another form. He'd asked my child's name. Despite not having given the notion a single thought, I answered with sudden pride, "Oh, wow! Laurence! Yes, after Laurence Olivier. The world's greatest actor." Then I quickly added, "Laurence Baines. He should have a name from his father. Laurence Baines Barton."

Then, before I could share this memory with Howard, a woman in a blue uniform and a crisp, bleached apron brought out our sleeping son for a ten-minute viewing. We each took turns holding the warm, eight-pound bundle wrapped in a soft white blanket while the attending nurse politely stood aside. I worried about a reddish rash on the baby's right cheek. The nurse assured me this was a fairly routine condition.

"Nothing to worry about. He is well looked after in his present home."

Howard seemed quite cheerful after we left the building. In the street, as he moved quickly across the road, he called, "I'm off, back to the farm."

"Any other plans?" I shouted, hoping to hear words of bygone praise.

He moved off. "No," he shouted, with a skip. "And I'm not giving up my son."

But how can you or I not? Tell me. Talk to me. Share with me, you double bastard! This baby is ours, you mother-fucker. My lips trembled as I saw my ex-fiancé laughing at the expense of other people, or so I thought. So throttled by my own sense of abandonment and guilt, I couldn't see the truth or even a glimpse of Howard's mental state.

* * *

The CCAS had informed me of the procedure. Although I'd pestered them—repeatedly calling on the phone, begging for my child to be adopted by a couple who understood the creative personality—nothing, they said, could be guaranteed.

"It's out of our hands," Gemma Nicholson, my case worker, explained. "We're overloaded with unwanted children."

"You'll be lucky to get a foster home," another co-worker informed me.

The Juvenile and Family Court called me to attend. Standing in a witness box, I was required to swear to the presiding judge that I freely and unconditionally gave my child to the protection of the Welfare Department of Metropolitan Toronto, where, it seemed to me, the officials were even less concerned about the child than I. Wouldn't we all be better off if all this effort and personnel and money went into helping the mother keep the baby?

"Do you swear? Yes, or no?"

A barrage of fingers poked me in my back, digging in their accusations, pushing through their moral message of a just punishment for dirty animal behaviour. God help me, I chose to believe my accusers. Facing the judge, I made the oath.

As though crazed, I haunted the offices of CCAS in the weeks following, harassing them, they claimed, insisting they find my child a perfect home.

Chapter 30

Montreal Expo '67

Children's theatre was definitely not on my wish list when I left St. Michael's Hospital, so Ernie Schwarz's phone offer was no thrill. A year earlier I'd performed and helped create two of his popular children's shows, and I shouldn't have been surprised to hear from him that spring. Needing work, I accepted, although dreading the jolly high-spirits of cheery little ones that would remind me of what I'd lost. On the super plus side, I knew we'd be playing at Canada's Expo '67 in Montreal—the greatest show in Canada's history.

The Children's Studio Theatre's *Pinocchio*:
Bruce Armstrong, Guy Sanvido, audience participators,
Mary [waiting]

The Children's Studio Theatre Company: Guy Sanvido, Barbara
Armitage, unknown, Mary Barton, Bruce Armstrong

I wandered the sights of the festival, surveying the greatest
of extraordinary international exhibitions yet seeing very little.
Around the grounds, I may have passed my future soul-mate
among the millions attending that world-famous show. Three
years later, I learned he was there. This memory reminds me
of a cartoon strip I once cut from a newspaper: a princess sits
in tears with her pretty head bent. A handsome prince, in black
tights, appears. He stops, greets her, smiling. With head still
bent, the girl shouts, "Go away!" The bemused prince obeys. All
in its time, as the saying goes.

* * *

After two weeks at Expo '67, from few offers, I chose a ten-month
tour contract to bring English culture to high schools across
Ontario, again. (In case I sound as though I only worked in

children's theatre, I must add that I'd previously performed in two adult productions at the Crest Theatre in Toronto, then situated in an old movie house on Mount Pleasant Road). I said goodbye to my friends at the Brunswick House Group and hoped they wouldn't forget me. I would never forget them.

Gin and Diet Sprite knocked me out each night in dull, cheap motels. Each 9:00 a.m. show by The Crest Theatre Hour Company was followed by long, dozy drives in our washroom-less bus to the next appointed town. I spent that time leaning my forehead against the cold bus window, welcoming the deadening of my senses. Then into the rigid atmosphere of the next school, where the crew set up and the actors prepared for the p.m. show. The performances became an appreciated routine, but the question periods in the high-school auditoriums afterwards could be wearisome. Are any of you married? To each other? I wonder what a group discussion of birth out of wedlock would have initiated. What a perfect opportunity was there to really get down to questioning—are you all knowledgeable about birth control? D'you know where your sexual urges come from?

I didn't do a lot of thinking during that time, and perhaps that was my best therapy, although at night I would pray Howard and Laurence would one day forgive me if I ever enjoyed my life again. I remember telling the cast in the bus, one day, that my brother was a tailor and sat on a table. Of course they didn't believe me. Yet, after the Christmas break, I returned to the tour with a magical letter from Mum with a photo of Peter. I didn't care whether they believed me or not. I had a picture of my beloved brother, working on his table in the Isle of Wight.

Peter, the tailor, with one of his dogs

Despite my depression, I was involved in the life I loved and yearned for. I taught myself to play the ukulele on the bus until the company requested me to stop. Life wasn't easy for any of us. Nor, we found, for the students of our next school.

The show in Red Lake, a town 850 miles from the province's capital, the most northern town on our tour, was the most painful. Beyond the town there were no paved roads. The last time the children had seen "outsiders" had been five years earlier when a group of travelling musicians had played in their gymnasium.

On arrival at the school, we were met by. "The Grade Twelves will not be seeing your performance," the man said smugly. "That is their penance. Unhappily, they have not been on their best behaviour."

We tried to dissuade the bully. Did the punishment fit the crime? Unsuccessful in defending the Twelves, this thickhead, we saw, believed more in penance than help.

One day, Ed Stephenson, one of the four actors on the tour, took me on an aborted visit to a "relative who lives just outside Toronto," he said. I enjoyed Ed. We had played together before the Hour Company and had a kind of empathy for each other.

"We've been asked for tea," my friend claimed as he bounced beside me, puffing clouds of breath in the winter air as we trudged through the greenless countryside. "I thought we'd come for a ramble first. You see, I have to get my spirits up for this."

He laughed. We often laughed. I remembered my past gay friends and how comfortably I'd enjoyed fun with them, not worrying about sexual feelings. As Ed and I trudged through the fields, I thought how very well we were working together, reading and singing Canadian poetry and presenting great dramatic scenes. I admired him for his depth of expression and of making such a grand King Henry V with his slim figure, good looks, and barrels of exuberant talent.

As he moved ahead, he called back to me, "The trouble is, I'm afraid I'm on the black-sheep side of the family."

No understanding, we trekked on, through brown hedges and across earth-frozen pastures, until, breathless, I stopped beside him and stared. Below, in the distance, at the head of a long stony driveway, He pointed toward an elegant mansion with turrets and many windows.

"Your family lives there?"

"Yes. The Eaton family. This is only one of their homes."

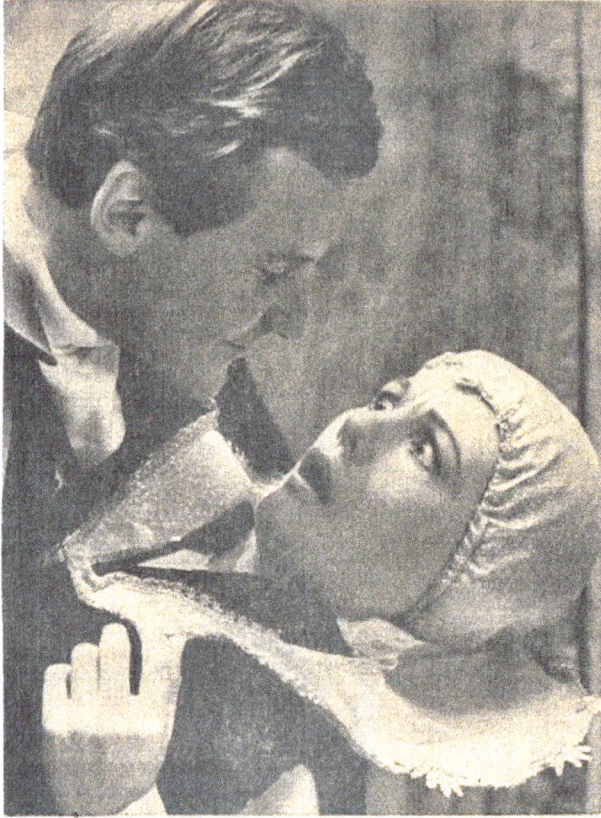

SAYING IT WITH HORROR IN SCENE FROM SHAKESPEARE
Mary Barton reacts to lines by Ed Stephenson

Ed Stephenson and Mary in *Henry V*

His words echoed in my ears: *"their homes."* I waited while he continued to stare. Then he turned and began walking back the way we'd come. Ed explained nothing as we trudged back across the fields. I understood. The protection I'd given my emotional state around my unwed motherhood allowed me the space to accept the circumstances of the bastard "black sheep." He was in total empathy with my situation. Ed and I continued a friendship for many years afterward. With much comfort, I figured that in future years, my son could grow to be a fine a friend as Ed Stephenson.

On returning to Toronto, I received news—Laurence had at last been adopted, by "a very fine couple, the mother once a dancer." He'd been taken not only out of Toronto but out of Canada. My life was full of endings. I needed to get used to it. I decided that I'd passed with flying colours the one-year anniversary of separation anxiety. I could only wonder how my child had experienced the time. I left Howard to his own wondering.

Work saved me having to live with the loss of everything I loved, or could have loved. But remaining connected with Nessa was a lifeline: an essential semi-guru constant. She was an authority figure willing to let me come and go, succeed and fail. After my ten-month touring contract, I was admitted into a weekly psychotherapy group session back in Toronto, led by Nessa and a colleague. Advancement in self-discovery seemed promising.

Then one day, not long after the end of the Crest tour, Nessa called me to come a few days earlier than planned. I found her sitting with another of her colleagues. Her expression unusually serious.

"Markus has agreed to join us today to help me in telling you some very difficult news." After I was seated, she continued. "It's Howard. I don't know whether you have heard or not." She listened a moment while I emitted a quizzical silence. "I'm sorry, Mary. Howard has killed himself."

I felt a sudden steel stab in my chest that made breathing hard. Then I felt nothing.

"He admitted himself into the Clarke Institute on College Street two days ago. It happened there. He threw himself from a window."

I stared at blackness.

"I think he felt it important to be away from Therafields when he … did it."

The vision of my dream came back to me, of throwing my doll out the window—my doll, my baby, my lover.

"Thank you," I said, as politely as I could.

A haze began forming in my head. Before wrapping myself up completely, I was conscious of an odd feeling of thankfulness—gratitude that my son was free of both his natural parents. He could only benefit now.

Part Three

1969–1983

"Understanding is the essence of love."
—**Thich Nhat Hanh**

Chapter 31

Will

My first impression of him was of an intensely annoying young man. Clearly, he was too much: audacious, irreverent, loud, and totally insensitive to my uneasy psyche—too handsome and neurotic to be anything but trouble. Will Kennedy entered my shielded world like a Barnum and Bailey Circus into a funeral parlour. The most vexing thing was that he was so damned attractive. I'd known the worst and the best in romance and was not in the mood for anything close to the like again. I was now working toward becoming a mature human being.

His voice reached me first. I stood, comforting myself with a mug of cocoa held close to my chest, doing my best to appear at ease in a roomful of chatting participants: an island unto myself in the largest renovated barn of Therafields Farm. Trying hard to find grounding during the fifteen-minute break, I was focusing on my socked feet on the wooden planks of the flooring, taking in the lingering, strangely comforting infusion of hay and dung.

"Hi!" The call cut clear through the heightening babble.

Turning toward the sound in the dim light of the barn, I saw a young stranger, one certainly not in my group, sitting on a bench near the wall.

"Wow! Are you ever pretty!" he called, beaming a wide smile.

Cheeky young devil! And during a marathon! Feeling a gentle flutter in my stomach, I turned away, concentrated on cocoa and my reason in the first place for being there: to find some peace of mind.

Our group had trudged in from a nearby barn where we were holding the first of a weekend of group psychotherapy sessions. Of course we were. This was 1969. There were many groups, many people from Toronto and the surrounding areas, who even came from the US, to take extra time out to explore how we might rid ourselves and the world of phobias and neurotic hang-ups. The farm, purchased a year or two earlier, became the host for hundreds involved in Therafields' "Great Experiment."

Will Kennedy, 1969

Cutting through my efforts at mature contemplation, the young guy persisted. "D'you wanna come with us to town tomorrow?"

Astonished, I turned to him. Tilting up my chin, afraid he might be seeing me as amusing, I answered with a straight face. "What?"

Without a response, he turned away, then stood. I watched this tall, agile guy move swiftly to merge with stragglers buckling up their boots at the main entranceway. He was heading back to another barn.

Impertinent pup! Ignore him!

But the young man was shouting at me, holding open one of the magnificent, masterly-made, heavy wooden doors. Waving at me, for God's sake.

"Tomorrow night!" he yelled and closed the door.

"Who were those others I saw during the break?" I asked one of my group members as we tracked through the springtime mud back to our own designated and almost-heated cowshed.

"I think they're from one of the House Groups back in Toronto," the woman offered.

He lives in one of those? They have therapy 24/7.

My attitude toward the stranger softened, remembering how grateful I'd been at the warmth shown me by the Brunswick House Group. Still, this Will Kennedy was clearly not sensitive to unwritten rules. He seemed a bit over-crazed, not needed in my world right now. Resettling into our circle of sixteen stoic souls in Nessa Hendrickson's Standard Group, I relished the stillness that calmed the air as we listened for the most urgent feelings to surface. I liked when people revealed "from the depths of their unconscious," as one member put it. Not quite knowing what an unconscious was, I felt safe knowing that we were listening and offering help with someone's dark, self-destroying secrets. Life in group was intense and felt emotionally dangerous.

As we all left the meeting room, I felt a hand on my arm. Nessa smiled and took my elbow. "I want to share something with you, Mary."

Guiding me outside to the back of the barn, we walked up a straw-covered slope leading to the loft. Inside, the temperature dropped as the chilly wind gusted through the broken sides of the old building. I glimpsed low bales of last year's clover and alfalfa illuminated by strips of daylight shining through the broken barn walls. Standing, breathing in the thick country-rich aroma, we were silent. I'd only known this woman as that knowledge-able lady in Admiral Road who sat in the chair opposite as my psychotherapist. This seemed more than a tad eerie.

After a lengthy moment, Nessa spoke, still staring into the rafters. "He talks to me, Mary."

"Who?" I dared to ask, feeling slightly queasy, although I guessed she might be referring to my deceased fiancé.

She whispered in an undertone, "Sometimes I come here and I meet Howard. He comes to me. I can feel and hear him if I listen." She stared up again, and her weak smile reminded me of pictures of a madwoman with the wide, unblinking eyes. Then, turning again to me, she excitedly said, as though to reassure me, "He's quite happy now."

Feelings of anger welled in me. I turned away. I didn't care if Howard was happy. I wished I could call out to him, to say, "I'm so sorry you felt so bad but you didn't talk to me." Yet like in a recurring nightmare, my voice had no sound.

Nessa then spoke in a more realistic tone. "There's going to be a memorial. Did you know that?"

"For him?" I asked, picturing a prayer ceremony.

"Yes, in Howard's memory. A smaller barn in one of the outlying fields is being renovated for intensive emergency cases—such as we would have loved for him. We're thinking of calling the new house *The Phoenix*. What do you think?"

A large lump grew in my throat. I wanted, oh so much, to be held by her. I so wanted to say, "Please, talk to me about ME. While we're here, close, alone." With a huge deep breath, instead of letting out a loud howl, I was able to utter, "Sounds good!"

Nessa and I returned to the dining room, her arm on my shoulder before, with smiles, we separated. Wandering off to find my ride home, I wondered why I wasn't obsessed with my ex the way Nessa seemed to be.

During the following weeks, I heard no more of any "memorial." If there was any kind of ceremony, I wasn't invited, and the lack of any news where Howard was concerned convinced me of my insignificance in the world of love.

* * *

By the following day, the mood around Therafields farm had generally lightened. Saturday afternoon help with the farm work stimulated muscles and got the blood moving for the later sit-down meeting. That evening was, however, ours to do with how we liked: play ping pong, mingle, read, play music, cards. After dishes were done, on heading back to the group room for solitude with an Ayn Rand novel I'd brought with me, just in case,

I changed my plans. Crossing the parking lot, who should I spy but this pushy guy.

"Come with us. Come on," he cried, indicating a blue, two-door car. "We're going for a sing-along at the local."

He took me by the elbow and guided me to the front of a Volkswagen Beetle. Who wanted to read, anyway? Already secured in the back were three laughing, welcoming women. I soon discovered why they preferred squashed bums in the rear. It was some wild ride. We took off down Airport Road at the speed of a racing car being flagged at the finishing line. In the darkness, as the car, following flickering centre-lane lights, rounded countless winding turns at a terrifying pace. I saw forest trees on either side whizzing past, creating one long, black tunnel. I prayed.

"You don't have to worry," the driver shouted at me above the noise of the engine. "I know these roads like the back of my hand. Born and raised not far from here. In Schomberg. We're heading into Orangeville now. Ever been there?"

I couldn't speak. I needed what breath I could catch to stay alive. He turned on his car radio and sang, beating time on the dashboard, rocking with a number from The Doors.

"*Come on, baby, light my fire,*" he screamed, sounding exactly like he'd cannons going off inside him.

As the song was finishing, he called, "I'm Will Kennedy. My mother calls me Bill. Why Bill when my name's William?"

"I'm Mary," I managed to helpfully shout back.

"I know," he responded.

Inside the tavern, rather than talk and drink, I liked to be active, so after my legs had stopped shaking, I moved to the shuffle board, away from the juke box corner where he and his passengers had plunked themselves. I found myself hoping he'd join me. Listening to him jabbering on was better than playing a pub game by oneself while Tammy Wynette wailed *"When the Grass Grows over my Grave ..."* But the man sat with a beer throughout the long hour we all spent in the place. I remembered this occasion many years later and wondered if, on that evening, I'd been ignoring a clear foreboding of perhaps another side to the gregarious guy—his reason for participation in the Therafields' weekend.

For the ride back, I was first to grab a spot in the safety of the rear of the car, with no objection from Will. In my ignorance I thought that would be the last I would see of this wild young man. Well, it was the last at the farm.

Chapter 32

Toronto Meeting

Many tears had passed since I'd first cried in Nessa's office. She'd instructed me in numerous ways of the world—whether I asked for the tutoring or not. She had become my main semi-trusted friend. Returning homeward from my first therapy session after the weekend at the farm, I ruminated around my problems—like whether or not attempts at waitressing showed strong masochism. That evening, as I pondered on my gypsy way of life, I sensed an unusually hopeful lift in the air. Suddenly, through the sharp chirruping of robins on rooftops, I heard a voice from the other side of the street.

"Mary! Mary!"

Turning, I saw him leap the steps of a three-storey apartment building. Tall, lanky Will Kennedy, he from the farm meeting, strode toward me, his shoulder-length dark hair and sideburns wilding flaying, a fringe ruffled over a high forehead, and that wicked smile. He who had invited and then, I believed, neglected me at a pub was now appearing super-friendly. Dressed in jeans and T-shirt, he walked alongside me with one foot on the sidewalk and one in the curb. Skipping around the trees, he chatted in a long soliloquy. Then, at the quiet crossroads of Admiral Road and Lowther, he turned and was gone. These weekly encounters became a habit I rather enjoyed, although I forgot about him the minute I turned the corner, as one might forget an affable street cat.

Each time he appeared I enjoyed Will's outlandish enthusiasm; his insistent charm wore well on my melancholy. Probably mid-twenties, I figured. Feeling flattered and attracted, my facial expressions must have uncovered inner pleasure. I have one of those faces that instantly reveals the truth of my state. One's face, however, can be easily misread. I remembered an incident as a schoolgirl, a bus conductor in London saying to me, "Cheer up, ducks, it might never happen." At the time, I was a little hurt to be seen as a "sad face," as my father used to say, when all I was doing was thinking. Yet here today was a guy who didn't seem bothered by how I was feeling or thinking. I was sure he believed me ten years younger. Most people did. That was how I was able to work on stage playing teens or the young comic friend of the ingénue lead.

Recently, I recalled, I'd returned from out west after playing—I must say, most triumphantly—my first invigorating thirties-something at Edmonton's Citadel Theatre. But I wasn't going to discuss my stage work—and especially the lack of it—with this young man. Definitely not my leaving Alberta after refusing a prime offer to play a romantic lead. Sean Mulcahy, the Irish-born artistic director, had called me into his office during the run of Neil Simon's *The Odd Couple*. "We will up your salary for the next role but not by much," he said. "Even though you're sexier now than when I first knew you at Shaw." He had grinned through slitted eyes.

I guessed Mulcahy's first choice of actress had thought better of his contract. I surmised he was desperate. "Sorry," I had lied, assuming a perfect forlorn look. "I have other commitments in Toronto."

Never before had I been offered a lead romantic role, but I knew my nerves would collapse under the pressure of his sadistic tongue. I could see it: me breaking in front of the whole cast, letting down everyone. Besides, my growth in psychotherapy was suffering with all the upping and going in and out of a home base.

"Perhaps you were afraid of *succeeding*?" Nessa suggested when I was able to tell her.

Will Kennedy, the guy hopping beside me, broke through my thoughts. "You ever think of living in *our* place? In the apartments?" he asked.

We had reached the crossroads.

"Never did," I answered, turning from him. But he was already gone.

* * *

At our following session, Nessa astonished me beyond belief. "How about moving into a House Group? This time for your own reasons?"

My pulse quickened.

"I'd like that," I said, remembering the friendliness of #477–9 Brunswick.

She smiled. "You're beginning to grasp your poverty deficiency. I think you're ready for twenty-four-hour therapy," she stated. "A vacancy has just come up in the building across the street."

An odd little laugh gurgled inside me. Of all the thirty or so houses owned by Therafields in the Annex area, Nessa had to choose that one. Well, it was her idea, and she was unmistakably right about everything.

"I think that would be the best place for you, for your restart, as it were," she continued. "You have enough Freudian ego now to benefit from group living." My therapist rose from her chair, retrieved a pad from her desk, and scribbled a note to Mrs. Smith.

"Lea began these experiments in her own home, just further up Admiral," she continued. "She believes in help made available any time of the day or night."

With curiosity, I asked, "Will I change from you?"

"Oh, no. We'll continue with weekly sessions, but two very honourable male therapists oversee the building and meet with you all regularly. Both Martin and Gus live elsewhere. Remember, we're an experiment, Mary. Anything can change."

"Yes," I said, too amazed at her invitation to have any further questions. I thanked her, paid my thirty dollars, and let myself out through her front door. My face beamed with excitement as I marched back down Admiral, impatient to prepare for another giant leap toward health and maturity. I believed in Therafields' power of transformation as naively as a young religious novice. Will didn't appear that day.

Chapter 33

#32 Admiral Rd.

"You know someone here named Will?" I asked of a chap the morning after I'd settled my things into what felt like a clothes closet. In the third-floor kitchen of the elegant Victorian apartment building on Admiral Road, I sipped my second coffee and ventured a question of the other lingering person. I'd loads of time before studying the want ads in the *Globe and Mail*.

"You mean Kennedy of Will and Cathy?" the chap said.

"Cathy?" I groped around my mind.

"In the second floor? Weren't you at the last Friday group?"

I shook my head. He rambled on.

"I knew Cathy had wanted out. Finally handed back the engagement ring, right at the meeting, then as much as said "fuck off" to us all. Well, I used to live in their floor, and anyone could see that couple wasn't working."

In? Couple? This is most discombobulating. The news sent a kaleidoscope of colours colliding inside my head.

"Tell me, how come residents here live *in* floors, not *on* floors like normal people?" I didn't want to appear too interested in his gossip, for surely that's what he was talking.

"No idea," he muttered as he picked up a briefcase and headed for the door. "Must go or I'll be late for the library."

As I washed my coffee mug, stirred to embarrassment by my fantasies of a welcome to the place—the open arms and shouts of glee—I knew I should put attractive guys out of my mushy mind. Unconsciously, I think I'd imagined entering a kind of semi-permanent repertory company, what might later be known as a "hippy kingdom," where we all toiled together for a common magical goal. Instead, I'd received a blow to my sense of reality. My purpose in moving here, I told myself, was to live reality. Nessa had told me, "Therafields living is expendable, disposable, to be utilized for a time but not to be seen as a lifetime's career." Extraordinary how complicated words can be, because I was sure she also told me that when one truly enters therapy, one is "committed to a way of life."

Within months of moving, I received fabulous news from the office of a new theatre company in town. Fairly bursting with excitement as I returned along the second-floor hallway from answering a call on our common telephone, I met him.

"I have an audition," I blurted.

"Great!" Will answered, echoing my excitement, immediately calling after me as I hurried off. "D'you want to come see my studio sometime?"

I stopped and called back a hearty, "Sure thing," and hurried on my way up to the third floor to sort out my repertoire of audition pieces.

While I was high on theatrical employment that month, I did indeed visit Will's art studio. The keen painter had recently moved his art supplies from a smaller space into a brightly lit room near the railway tracks, above a warehouse that was used for storing grand pianos. He told me he'd live accompaniment coming through the floor while Glenn Gould was in town. The Canadian icon would practice for hours.

Will in his studio: photo by Dougal Bichan

"Right below me," Will whispered, his eyes wide, his finger pointing to the floor.

Fascinated and impressed, this meant we both loved music, yet I was more interested in this guy's paints, brushes, and canvases. I could smell the aroma of turpentine and oil, reminiscent of

231

my own thrilling memories of dressing room Leischner stage makeup. We both had our homes from home. There was no seducing, no "come up and see my etchings" type of atmosphere. Usually more interested than flirtatious, he became nicely sober in his own surroundings. This creative young man's intense interest in me certainly had turned my head, but his preoccupation with making art had the most immense attraction. I loved his work. Joyous and raucous as well as soft and playful. Always colourful. I now knew why he was so seldom seen around the apartment building.

The artist swayed around his space as I watched him cleaning brushes, tidying his busy wooden worktables. "Is your family OK with you being an actress?" he asked.

I answered happily, glad he was including me. "Much encouragement. Both my brothers are gifted artistically. As kids, they spent hours painting, drawing, carving. Peter, my eldest, taught himself gardening too. He's a gentleman's tailor now. Trained in Saville Row. That's the best in London."

"How about you? Did you paint?"

"I once won a National Award when I was at Grammar School for something I painted in class. Some watercolour I did. Don't know which one." I settled myself on one of the work tables he offered me. "It may have been when I was imitating Renoir. He was my favourite. I tried to show life like he did, with his sort of vagueness of look. So I just washed out the edges of all my figures, like I thought he did."

Will didn't laugh. He didn't mock me.

"Did they give you a prize?" he said.

"A little book on Botticelli." I felt touched he would ask. "I still have it. I never did find out which painting won. But it didn't bother me. My big passion was entertaining."

He stopped washing out a bucket in the open toilet, looked at me, and said, "Someday, I'd like to design theatre sets."

And he did. But that was way into the future. As we chatted that day, like a couple of teens on very high energy, I became less self-conscious and more comfortable around the handsome Canadian artist.

Chapter 34

Accused/Guilty

For many of my neighbours at #32 Admiral, I presented as a distant non-participant. Interaction was a key element to success in any of Therafields' many communal living setups. Martin, the handsome ex-priest who shared with Gus the task of leading our weekly Friday night sessions, to my surprise, had defended me when one of my neighbours accused me of being a stranger to the place. He'd told the whole group, "It is the *quality* of presence that matters, not the amount of time given." That I'd liked. All actors are travelling gypsies, created for the entertainment and edification of audiences wherever they're found. Martin understood I could only survive on the periphery by straddling the worlds of both psychotherapy and my unreliable profession. But I wished he'd said he *admired* my quality of presence.

I did my best to participate but almost never spoke at these groups and rarely attended—other than on the one occasion when I was spotlighted for the full two hours. Usually I rarely spoke, partly through shyness around my opinions, but mainly because my career was in full swing and seemed to take off through 1970.

Participating as I could in the day-to-day of this community, I didn't expect such wild and extreme life-changing eye-openers as met me. How could one help not be influenced by the small, informal round-table get-togethers, listening with hypo-objective ears to agonizingly long arguments, the parties, sharing cooking, cleaning, the parties, pondering excuses, shopping together, the parties, nightly ponderings on one's own "unconscious motivations," the sobering weekly groups with Martin and Gus—and the parties?

Saturday nights I would join the folk from all floors mingling in the largest room of the basement. The carpet would be rolled up, the TV off and replaced by someone's record player or ghetto blaster, armchairs and sofa pushed back to form a spacious wood-paneled dance floor, cushions around, and the entire room gently lit by candles and shaded lamps. People in depression were welcome but not encouraged to completely take over the mood. Incense might be attempted but often dismissed as not to everyone's taste or smell. The imperative ingredient of these gatherings was beer. Piles of twelve-pack bottles of Molson's or Labatt's best were held in the two basement fridges—the larger labeled BEER ONLY—waiting to be consumed along with, or not, homemade munchies offered by the women.

Not patient enough for large weekend revelries, each floor might hold their own private celebrations, or a few select friends might gather of a weeknight over a drink in someone else's shared room. Never any drugs. No to that trend. We all knew, many from painful experiences, what disastrous effects LSD and the likes had on psyches. All, that is, except me. I look back and wonder if I could have been that innocent.

Early in my life at #32, at one intense Friday evening House Group official meeting, I was accused of drug dealing.

"Yes, I suppose you're right," I answered when confronted. Then I added in my defense, "But I didn't think of it that way."

"She's trafficking in drugs!" declared a guy who stood up and pointed at me.

At the time of this affair, I was rehearsing *The Dog and the Stone* for Young People's Theatre.

Guido, my young partner-in-crime, because of his age and temporary time in the building, was not invited to attend Friday night groups. I was grilled for both of us. Remaining seated in my chair, I tried to quiet my racing body heat and sick stomach. I explained that it had all started off as a good deed. The theatre administration department at YPT had advertised for help. They needed a gofer between the business office and the Colonnade Theatre—a job that computers would replace a few decades later. I suggested Guido apply. It was brilliant. This would help the company and at the same time settle the problem of the boy's financial needs.

Guildo, an Italian-American runaway, had been temporarily bunked at #32 while decisions were being made about his future. He had recently left his home in the United States to be with Uncle Ted, who lived in an overflowing Therafields' house further north on Admiral Road. Grapevine report was: this kid has a bad reputation. After meeting him, I thought the opinion nonsense. I saw the sixteen-year-old as a pleasant and talented youngster. He could entertain like a pro on the guitar, and his music enchanted us. But he did need an honest occupation. I figured him a perfect match for Young People's Theatre.

Not surprisingly to me, Guildo quickly proved himself not to be wild and unruly around the theatre but reliable and cheerful. However, Guido was somewhat wilier than I'd guessed. Despite being new to Canada and now busily occupied with work, how and where in the world he acquired the illegal weed, no one knew.

"Now she's blaming the boy," a woman's voice interrupted me.

"Continue, Mary," Gus said after a moment of quiet.

A few evenings ago, I'd walked in on a small party in Stephen, Claud, and Kevin's room and was offered a few puffs of Guido's grass. Yes, the boy was there. He had a bed in the linen cupboard along the hall. I was happy to see everyone and glad to be invited to share, although I'd a nonchalant attitude toward the drug, having tried it on several occasions years earlier with little obvious effect. I always thought hash would be hard on serious stage work and on your concentration, sort of thing.

"That stuff fucks with your brain," one heated elderly man interrupted.

A woman sitting near him disagreed. "Usually, this foreign weed is pretty harmless. A good relaxant. I've tried the harder stuff, and marijuana's dull."

Taking a gulp, I tried explaining again. "Then I thought, what the hell. Someone suggested we make brownies with it, and I thought this would be fine. I love brownies. Guido offered to sell me a stash for cooking. I bought it. Gave him a fiver. I think it was a fiver. Then the folks there also wanted some, and when Guido had none left, I sold him half my stash."

A young woman stood with tears already glistening on her face. "I must say," she said, "I'm speaking not only for me—but there are many that I know of who came here in order to get *away* from all that, who are seriously in trouble because of these hallucinatory drugs, people who are struggling every day to get

238

over habits that have made us sick in the head. I can't believe she sold it under our very eyes."

Gus spoke. "There are indications here of psychopathic behaviour, Mary. What do you say to that?"

No longer able to open my mouth, I sat stunned and horrified. I'd caused someone to publicly weep. My utter stupidity was showing up again. I sure was out of it, thinking blasé thoughts about therapy and me getting on with life so well. When my therapist hears, she'll go on about it for years.

Strangely, the next day, many in the building greeted me warmly, even grinned. People who generally grumbled—like the man who said I woke him every night coming in late, or the woman who complained I sulked through the last party she gave—made a point of greeting me. I think these people must have seen a kind of "hutzpah" in me, as my Jewish friends, like the Segal brothers and Jessica from drama school, would say. My sense of wonder about Therafields also began to build again. Perhaps I wasn't so bad after all.

Looking back on the event, now in 2024, when thousands of people in Canada (mostly through no fault of their own) are dying in terrible destitution, caught in the opioid crisis, while cannabis retailers are legally springing up more frequently than dollar stores, I wish I could have fought more openly for marijuana. Times change, but people do not seem to.

A few days later, Uncle Ted sent Guido packing back to his parents in the US, and I returned to my world of theatre, only to find there, shortly thereafter, a reality shock that would affect me more deeply than the Therafields "hot seat."

Chapter 35

Young People's Theatre

The announcement on Equity's noticeboard—that I'd recently seen since moving into #32—had requested auditioners "include a two-minute mime." That had made my heart race. *The usual two-minute speech, plus Mime?* Never since leaving drama school had I heard the word *mime* even spoken let alone requested. Guildhall school had taught no intricate mime techniques such as the amazing Marcel Marceau would later demonstrate on his world tours. The silent influences of Jacques Tati and Jean Louis Barrault—whose riveting performances I'd seen in England on film—had long been stored away in my heart, believing them to be fantasies I would have to leave behind as I crossed the Atlantic. With this Actors' Equity opportunity, dreams could come alive.

Finding a subject to base a mime on nagged me through a sleepless night and after until right before the appointed hour. Just as I sat waiting to be called in from the corridors of the Equity offices, I had my topic.

A slim, rather shy gentleman greeted me as I entered the audition room. We shook hands. After answering a few questions about my background, I stepped back six feet from his table and delivered a well-rehearsed speech, followed by my silent improvisation, entitled: *The Audition*.

That day, I won the sole female role in the next two plays at Young People's Theatre, a promising new company for children.

Still looking very teeny in years, at thirty-four I possessed an instinctive sense of physical play and a goodly flexible body.

However, YPT was full of surprises, including the end of my contract. Firstly, 10:30 a.m. on Monday of the second week of rehearsals for the first show, the cast members were still waiting in the foyer of the Equity building, wondering at the delay. Loitering also yet separating himself from us, was a stranger. Eventually, a woman from the office appeared. She brought forward the thick-set young man. "Heath will be joining you, replacing your male lead." Heath Lamberts was an actor I would admire and respect enormously in the coming years. But that morning the insecurity was tangible.

We continued rehearsing *The Dog and the Stone,* written by the innovative British playwright and producer Brian Way, whose workshops in drama for children had inspired me and many actors, therapists, and teachers in Britain. Although my female role was small, I was proud to be knowledgeable about this playwright's work and thrilled at the benefit his creative ideas would have for Toronto. The performances at the Colonnade, and the following inner city school tour, resulted in a great review from the only Toronto critic at that time who would willingly suffer the ignobility of reporting on a children's play. Herbert Whittaker, however, didn't think it beneath him to take along a young relative and then give us all high professional praise in the city's *Globe and Mail.*

Through various media, Mrs. Susan Douglas Rubes, founder of YPT, expressed that she was offering "the very best" for her young audiences: David Kemp, the director, had been brought over from England, and Adrian Pecknold, a professional Canadian mime who'd recently returned from studying with Le Coq in Paris, was contracted to cast both plays plus perform in *The Circus*, the second.

What happened around recasting *The Circus* should not have surprised anyone. With no "excuse me" on the morning of day two under my second contract, Susan Rubes marched into the rehearsal hall. Bob Adams, director, this time from New York, was beckoned to join her in the hall. Several minutes later, Adams returned, alone.

"I had no idea, Mary. Susan has a substitute. I'm so very sorry. My dear, I feel very badly about this. She says you'll get the full rehearsal salary. You are asked to leave, now."

The mandate for the new Young People's Theatre was described in the media as "long awaited … revolutionary … outrageously modern thinking." Toronto had always welcomed semi-professional entertainment for kids, but, for actors, these shows were considered stop-gaps between better gigs. The enterprise of Rubes and Company had stupefying plans to own and run a theatre building devoted, year-round, solely to children's theatre. A grand and courageous affair I was honoured to be part of it.

I tottered out of the building with ice, not rain, falling on my parade. Wandering the street, I shook with terror, as though in a nightmare, extricated like a foreign intruder. Why? What had I done wrong? Usually slow to learn, maybe, but eventually I always gave the goods—stacks of glowing reviews would prove that. Hadn't I mounds of experience with children's shows?

That evening, with a sick stomach, I left my room at #32 to answer two unexpected phone calls: one from Adrian Pecknold in anguished sympathy, pleading total ignorance. Then I heard from the director.

"I want you to know this is causing me considerable upset, Mary." Mr. Adams sounded sincere.

"But why, Mr. Adams? Why did they fire me?"

"She believes someone younger should play the role. They are a young people's theatre! My dear, listen, if you're ever in New York, please look me up. I will recommend you to anybody I know there. If I'd any say in this, believe me, I'd never let this happen."

Appealing to the Equity Association never occurred to me. Actors' Equity would surely have simply shrugged its shoulders had I complained. I'd taken my pay envelope from the YPT office and swallowed my humiliation with a hamburger and double order of hot poutine at a soda joint, far from Bassel's.

In Nessa's office the next day, my pent-up rage had freedom to vent. Trying to make sense of my situation, tears flooded my face as I blurted, "What does age matter when you're making art?"

The wisdom in my therapist let me weep for a while. Then, "Don't you think, in some ways, she's right? How old are you now?"

Were my ears blocked?

Nessa calmly continued. "Aren't you getting a bit too old for juvenile parts? Princess roles?"

Suddenly shaken out of self-pity, I asserted, "We were making theatre." I tried to explain. "Theatre art is about illusion!" *How can this squat, dull figure in front of me be so ignorant?* "On stage, one gives the *impression* of being young or not young." I felt a moment of sheer clarity, stating, "Performers stimulate the imagination. It's called *acting*!"

244

I sat silent again. Fuming. My mind raged on. *Everyone knows no girl of fourteen can play Juliet and show the fullness of Shakespeare's tragedy. That range of immense insight and passion needs a mature, experienced actress.* My mind reminded me, *a grown man originally played Juliet, for God's sake. Sarah Bernhardt played Hamlet when she was sixty and had a wooden leg! Children absorb the stories they are told. Kids don't say, "Oh, the storyteller's not the age for this part." Children's theatre should stimulate inventiveness, help kids to think creatively.*

Roused from my thoughts, I heard Nessa say, "As you were growing up, my dear, you didn't see adult life as anything to look forward to. Unfortunately, you had no good mature models, so you stayed safely in childhood."

Theories, theories! I hate your book theories! I wanted her to say, "You can play any age you choose. Don't let others make choices for you."

"Aging is a hard reality to accept," she continued. "But … *I never promised you a rose garden*," reminding me again of the recently published book title to make her point. "Psychotherapy doesn't intend to make life pretty. It gives us a second chance to change destructive patterns of thinking." (Later I was to learn the teachings of ancient Buddhism was far more effective, but that is for another time and book.)

I submitted. Here was I, again repeating self-persecution. I could see that I habitually crouched when shat on. I took abuse in a cowardly fashion, even adding to it, throwing dirt on my coffin.

Nessa asked, "Why can't you laugh at misfortune? Write a poem about it?"

A poem? You mean squash it onto paper? Her timing in telling me to turn the other cheek was not helpful. I was seeing even Nessa had failings. No. What happened to me was not right. I wanted very much to continue feeling wronged. There is nothing more soothing than caressing the secret weapon that empowers one to vindictively punish. But fostering the fire inside me was also dangerous and scary.

Telling myself to be patient, I ate meals in huge bites, as though shaken from an earthquake, followed by cigarettes burned to their nasty, bitter stubs.

My effort to get comfort and understanding from Nessa left me feeling worse. Yet days later, I found positive energy flowing as I took courage and walked again to the Equity Notice board, and checked out new auditions. Performing was my only real life! I would show new auditioners what others were missing. Thank God I had an art.

* * *

One afternoon, some weeks after the firing, after returning from yet another day of office work, I was called again to our third-floor telephone. My dreary mood was only slightly raised at receiving yet another call from Adrian Pecknold. Surprisingly, the pleasant voice of my ex-casting director and fellow performer, who had last called with such touching sympathy, now sounded decidedly chipper.

"Harro and I are going to take a children's show on a two-week tour around Winnipeg starting in a few weeks." He was laughing. "Can you guess which show we're taking?"

"Not *The Circus?*"

"Yes! And we're interested in you playing Miss Julie—again."

To be fired and then rehired for the same part—could heaven be so cruel to be so kind?

"However, after the tour in February," he continued, "and this is the thing, we're planning on creating a mime company … for adults, and all ages. We're very excited. Manitoba Theatre Centre has also invited Harro and me to present an evening of our own mime pieces on their main stage. I expect you know that we have been wanting to start up in Canada, preferably in Ontario."

"I didn't know."

"Well," he went on, "Winnipeg seems to be our gateway, our leap into it, if you like. But I need to know, most importantly, Mary—would you be willing to join us as a company member, become our female mime?"

"Would I? Oh yes," I said. "Yes, I will. Yes! Yes!" I shouted, ecstatically echoing the triumphant words of James Joyce's Molly Bloom.

That phone call began a very rich time of theatrical creativity for me, only thwarted by occasional frustration with having no avenue then for vocal expression. With mime, was I sidestepping my career? I didn't care. I only wanted to celebrate the opportunity to move, pretend, fascinate folk, make people laugh. A sense of pride surged through me at the thought of learning new skills and sharing with people of such calibre.

Adrian Pecknold and Mary in *The Circus*

Hailed as "triumphant" in and around Winnipeg, *The Circus* for me was pure joy. A review by critic Peter Crossley, after claiming Adrian and Harro as highly successful, also added: "… Miss Barton as Miss Julie, the romantic element in the pantomime, is beautiful, gracious, and graceful. On her first entrance, the audience of 1,000 young school children 'Oooohed' appreciatively. She is the perfect counterpart of Gillou" (*Winnipeg Free Press*, April 1, 1970).

Vindication, you taste delicious

Chapter 36

Canadian Mime Theatre

Mime was a refreshing novelty for Canada in the 1970s. After the Winnipeg tour, the Canadian Mime Theatre (CMT) supported by Brian Doherty, co-founder of Ontario's Shaw Festival, became a registered company. It settled in Niagara-on-the-Lake, Ontario, under the artistic directorship of Adrian Pecknold in a wee old fire station on Queen Street. The place was renovated into a one-hundred-seat venue: Fire Hall Theatre. The little town was bustling with Shaw theatre buffs and visitors from across Canada, the US, and around the world. Gift and specialty shops were popping up and new hotels surfacing. Around the area, the grape industry was flourishing. I was amazed to see a world of change had happened in both the town and my life since I'd last performed at Shaw five years earlier.

Our company, for a while, consisted only of Adrian, Harro Mascow (Adrian's assistant artistic director), our devoted stage manager, David Satterthwaite, and me. Through the spring, as we created shows together, I offered ideas for new sketches, but mainly I followed direction, not having the expertise of the experienced guys. My frequent supporting roles of wife, lover, victim, patient, or odd body became less frustrating when I found my niche by creating and adding the character of Card Holder: a figure who displayed, with a card, the title of the following sketch. For each, I designed a posture, with a simple gesture or two, to illustrate what might unfold. I got a great charge out of listening to the whispers and giggles in the audience as they connected what I did with what was to come. An example: for *The Tightrope Walker* (wearing the traditional black leotard and tights) I stood tall and held the sign high with my arms above my head, then, with one foot raised, I slowly swayed to one side, my expression showing growing terror until I almost lost balance. Blackout. At first there were reservations from the guys, thinking I should stand static with the sign, that I might be giving away too much.

Canadian Mime Theatre Company

"So put the titles back on a music stand," I declared, fury burning in me.

I think I would have left them then and there had they not reminded me again that I was "a natural" at mime and to work out the details. I refined the techniques until they laughingly agreed to the idea. Soon, having learned a great deal from Adrian's teaching, I agreed to stand in for him, relieving him of instruction time for beginner classes. With mime, I discovered I much enjoyed teaching, learning as I taught, and was paid more.

With audiences rapidly growing, our company expanded, with Raymond Wickens added as company manager and George Uri Stanislav as a fourth Equity performer. Uri was younger than we three, a recent newcomer to Canada, spirited and keen to make a success of his energetic abilities. Although shorter in stature than the other two men, his brash athletic style supported Harro's subtle comedy and complemented Adrian's slow pathos. Uri was also welcomed by me as a relief from mounting sexual tension from the other two. On different occasions, Adrian and Harro had each offered me their bed, but only once. Harro made the invitation while very drunk in a small tent in a park, surrounded by partying witnesses, so I didn't take him too seriously. I couldn't spoil the joy and camaraderie of our working days by smutting up the mornings after the nights before. Besides, my therapist would call such actions incestuous.

Working together, my heroes soon fell several notches from the high pinnacles I'd first seen, becoming normal needy, stage-struck guys. Still with respect and awe, I kept them at a safe emotional distance and concentrated on work.

Uri and I, however, became typical siblings, and from him I learned more than mime skills. His lack of awe toward our two veterans was refreshing. During rehearsals, he butted opinions against Pecknold and Maskow, his effrontery emboldening my rebelliousness, and I began to question more. After evening shows, on tour, Uri and I often walked the streets of a city, improvising loud scat tunes as we skipped along the sidewalks, popping the stoppers from out our vocal cords.

To my delight, that guy Will Kennedy occasionally drove down to Niagara and surprised me. Several afternoons that summer, he added to my mixture of men. But I found the lanky young man's company easy and relaxing. He'd grown a wide, dark moustache, which I thought quite dashing. After strolling around the sunny golf course, we'd sit at the edge of Lake Ontario, he chattering nonstop like a mime off-stage. He revealed himself as a shy person beneath his flamboyance. I enjoyed his innate joy of life and passion for creativity, and I slowly discovered a blossoming within me that I thought I'd never feel again.

* * *

I knew my future in mime was dim. I'd no commitment to it as my sole medium. I had to talk. Surely there was work in regular theatre waiting for me somewhere.

However, that August, Ray Wickens had landed CMT a major coup, and one I couldn't resist. Although Adrian knew my conflicted mind, he asked if I would accept as my final contract a three-week tour of the Northwest Territories. The company had been chosen to be part of the two-hundredth anniversary celebrations of its (so-called) founding. For a newly designed two-hour show, Ray Wickens had promised expansive publicity, good touring salary, and a once-in-a-life-time chance to step into a vast, mythical area of Canada.

We were all at liberty for a few weeks before the Northern tour began. While biding my time at #32 Admiral, I bought two new books. The Maya Angelou I packed, and I started to read Rachel Carson's *Silent Spring*, but found her claims too terrifying to believe, so I turned to less-scary magazines, wrote to my mother, took long showers, listened to the radio, attended House Group sessions, and partied.

The night before I left for the tour, the residents of one of the larger rooms in the second floor gave a Friday night splash. Somewhat anxious about travelling so far away just as I was settling in, and attracted by the loud playing of a Cat Stevens record ringing down the halls, I went along. Electric lights had already been dimmed by the four occupants, and the room lit by candles in various holders donated by other roomers. The air was already smoky and smelling of yeast from cracked bottles of beer. The carpet was rolled back and a table was laden with chips, dips, and vegetable snacks. Partner or no partner, we danced our feet sore to music like the Guess Who's "American Woman" and Simon and Garfunkel's "Cecelia."

After drinking much wine from a paper cup, and hoping for at least an hour to be invited by Will to dance, he finally asked and timed it for a very slow ballad. Will held me tightly and we both swayed to the sound of Bob Dylan's "Lay, lady, lay / lay across my big brass bed ..." How could I resist? Taking me back to my room, on my single spring mattress we culminated the magnetic force between us. He didn't stay the whole night. He knew a taxi would pick me up at 5:00 a.m. Would he be at my door to see me off? Not a sign as the taxi took me away. *Serves you right, you little flirt. When will you learn?* Stop this! I'm off on another adventure.

Chapter 37

Tour of the Northwest Territories

My image of the North before visiting was no different from that of most southerners—a desolate place of endless ice and snow. I believed the North to be inhabited by people wrapped in parkas and appearing from igloos whenever a plane passed over. We found the reality far different.

Company on tour NWT

On the first step of the Arctic tour, our six-member company—Adrian, Harro, Uri, Ray, David, and I—flew directly on a commercial flight from Toronto to Frobisher Bay (now named Iqaluit). Looking down from the plane through the window beside me, I could see thousands of miles of undulating, bare grey rock. The businessman sitting beside me leaned his shoulder against mine.

"There's nothing down there," he muttered. "It's a wasteland."

How wrong he was. However, there were no roads. The plane grounded on asphalt. The first implanted local we met drove us and our baggage in a truck from the airport a short distance along a bumpy pathway. He pointed out the low rocky hills dotted with scatterings of pale clapboard cabins.

"Eskimo families live in those," he, a local government representative, informed us. "The buildings have to be on concrete blocks because of the permafrost. Don't die here, folks, because you'll get buried under a pile of rocks," he added, with a loud laugh.

We were more curious than amused.

In a loud Ottawa Valley accent, our guide told us we would be billeted in an ex-U.S. air base on the outskirts of the settlement. "Still there and always occupied from the days of WWII," he said. "Cheaper than the hotel in town. But you'll be in the old officer's quarters, seeing as how you're special. The Americans knew what they were doing. This place has a future. It's the location, you see. Lots of traffic going back and forth across the Atlantic from this area."

"Where is the snow? There's none that I see," Jiri asked.

"You'll be gone from here before we see any. The natives are tired of the summer, even though it's very short," our representative said. "They can't wait for the fall. When the snow comes they can get about with dogs and snowmobiles."

The Chinese cook at the base prepared a late lunch of cod and chips, "in our honour," and we were shown our quarters. Then, well-fed and finding I'd been given a clean bed for two nights, I felt compelled to get about and explore, find my feet. So, I set out in my warm coat, gloves, and toque. The air was a balmy 40 degrees Fahrenheit, slightly above freezing, with a brilliant sun still warming the day.

As I wandered along meandering stony pathways, I saw children dressed in bright-colours playing on the higher rocks. I passed a few of the crude pastel-painted cabins and was greeted by barking husky dogs tied up in fenced-in yards, one with a greenhouse at the back, with small plants, and clothes drying on a line alongside hanging fish. No roadways. Fascinated by the otherness, I moved onto the undulating landscape that was edged in the distance by ugly large pipelines. Yet, wonder of wonders, under the wide-open sky, I found the rocky tundra to be green and bracken-covered, speckled with sorrel and wild flowers of many colours. Later, I discovered from reading that many varieties of berries grew here: partridge, blue, crow, and cranberry. Many birds, too. Apart from the seabirds that I watched flying overhead, that day, I learned of migrating loons, plovers, falcons, and even larks that flew high above arctic fox and hare. I was walking in a story-book wonderland.

The following day, our rep. drove us a short distance into the formal "town" where I caught sight of a few larger cabins.

Our first performance was given, that evening, in the local "Eskimo Community Centre." The large clapboard building surprised us with a decent-sized, warmly-heated hall, an area for a stage to be erected with wooden rostrums and curtaining either side, and a generous auditorium area not yet set up with chairs. Our audience, we soon learned, would happily sit on their leather and fur outerwear, right on the wooden floor.

While David, our stage-manager, set up lighting and arranged for some semblance of a stage, we four performers were able to rehearse, discuss, or variously prepare with some attempt at privacy. Usually, if I had no prior set up, I used the women's washroom. On this occasion I was given a private area plus a female dresser in the form of Mrs. Brian Pierson, wife of the mayor and town councillor who ran the one and only general store. Mrs. Pierson was a woman only too glad to volunteer help and information for "the artists," as she called us, which, of course, endeared her to me.

When I told her of my wandering about town, Mrs. Pierson said, "Some call the scenery "volcano vomit," others call this place "the dump." Brian doesn't like that."

She chatted on as I got into my basic blacks, glad of the local company.

"We've been here fourteen years, me and Brian," she said as she folded my discarded jeans and sweater. "Quite a card he is. An Aussie, really. Very proud of being mayor. He says the Queen's tour planners have sent you to the wrong settlement. You know, to give an example of the North. This place doesn't do it justice, Brian says." Then she added, still holding my clothes, "Did you know, Eskimo women have never seen a half-naked woman. You couldn't have one of them helping you out."

Thinking the time was not now to discuss native knowledge, I asked, "Are there other events going on for the Centennial?"

"The people are holding something, somewhere. They're always up to something. We never really know. The natives can't do much, though, without the government coppers to fund anything. But the Cathedral might get a boost. Did you know? The Church is building an Anglican Cathedral! Here! Can you imagine? I'm not a believer myself but the Eskimos are, and they're all for it. Very proud, they are. Next, the minister says, they're going to have a high school. Well, that'll be the day! They've had a Junior one for years, a day school, you know, for little ones. Very popular that, they say. For the whites, anyway."

Little did we imagine, then, that before the turn of the twenty-first century the settlement of Frobisher Bay would grow in population from a village to an official town to be known, as it is today, as the most northern city in Canada, although with only a population of less than eight thousand. Now the Capital of Nunavut—the Territory having broken from the Northwest Territories—Frobisher Bay has been reverted to its original Inuktitut title, Iqaluit, and much in the news for its criticism of the present and past's Federal Governments' lack of support for the indigenous peoples.

In the main hall of the town we presented a few evenings of *Visual Delights,* a two-hour collection of mimes we had devised for the occasion. Our entertainment almost everywhere we travelled brought either breathless wonder or hearty laughter, and always vigorous applause. However, after arriving up north, it occurred to us that some of our planned sketches must be beyond the comprehension of these Inuit, Dene, and Metis peoples in the small settlements who made up the major part of our audiences. A four-minute piece by Adrian was based on the symbolism of a tree. These people lived way above the tree line and most likely had never seen a real one. Another, titled *Traffic Cop*, was an obvious problem. But Harro, who wrote and performed the comic piece, insisted on including it. Rightly so. Laughter resounded through the halls as the audiences recognized themselves, watching Harro's character desperately trying to organize the uncontrollable.

As we continued on, it occurred to me that there was a problem with the placards I held up as cardholder before each sketch.

"It seems rude to show them information in English," I said to Adrian. "Is there anyone who could translate? These people must have their own language."

Adrian agreed. "I'll check it out with Ray."

Our manager found a local authority figure who phoned ahead. It took some time, but finally they came up with Aliaka, a teaching assistant in Baker Lake, our next stopover almost nine hundred miles west.

After arriving in Baker Lake by the next commercial flight, I enjoyed an enormously liberating afternoon with Aliaka in a small, well-heated cement schoolroom. This petite, perky young woman, who surprised me with excellent English, wrote out her translations of all the twenty-one titles in our repertoire, plus the signs *Intermission* and *The End*, listing all in pencil on sheets of paper. Then I carefully copied her fascinating Rune-like script onto the reverse side of each of my signs.

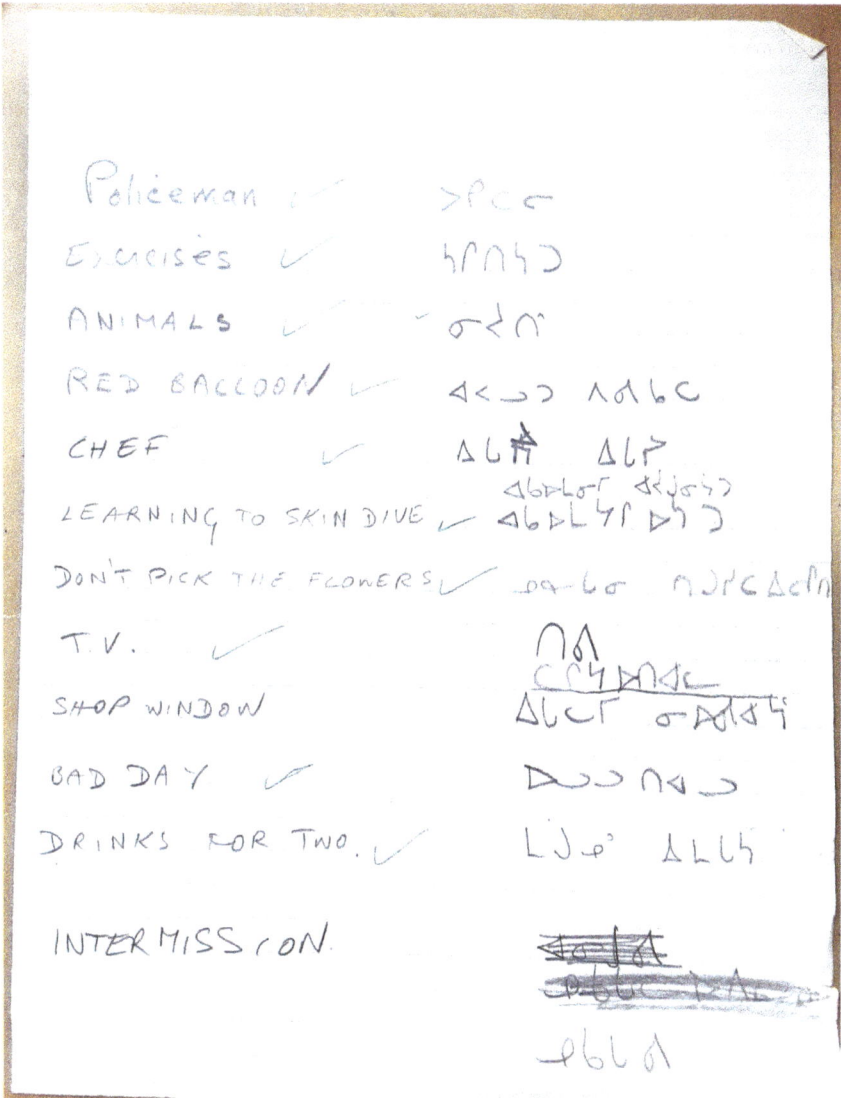

A page of my notes for Inuit signs

The cards showing the local script were greeted with prolonged applause at each showing that evening. However, my pride took a plunge when we moved to the next community several hours' flight away. How little we understood. There, in Copper

Mine, the sight of my title cards brought guffaws of laughter completely out of keeping with the information. The sign *Doctor's Waiting Room* brought raucous hilarity. *Animals* and *Don't Pick the Flowers*, likewise, had the halls rocking, and on throughout the night. Knowing my miming could not have been the complete reason, I eventually discovered the cause. After the final curtain in Copper Mine, a sympathetic English tradesman explained.

"Believe me, they loved the idea," he laughed, "but, you see, the script is written in Baker Lake. It was the dialect they all thought was hysterical."

People definitely are the same the whole world over. Sadly, my scheme was canned.

Then, the tour took another turn. We were given our own single Otter seaplane that came with our own handsome, accomplished pilot: Norm joined our troupe for the next four weeks. This dark-haired, middle-aged Albertan pointed out spots of interest as we flew over vast areas of rock and moss. One time, he took the plane very low.

"Down there!" he called. "See the musk ox?"

As the small plane dipped down, we flew very close, and from the windows behind him we stared out.

"See them all collecting in a ring? They do that around their young," Norm shouted over the noise of the plane. "No idea what the danger is."

Up we sailed again. Would our cameras capture the wonder of it all?

As we travelled from area to area, Norm cruised and allowed us, one by one, to sit in the pilot seat of the cockpit to "fly the plane." This sure beat most stage tours.

Our pilot was the strong and silent type—a widower, we guessed. Gradually, Norm became more than an air-born chauffeur as, over and above his call of duty, he helped erect and take down sets as though taking on a new trade as a teenage apprentice, although a rather mathematically and analytically inclined one. He became indispensable to our troupe. Toward the end of the tour, about 2:00 a.m. one morning, he knocked on the door of my single, monk-barren bedroom in one of the sleepovers we had. There were never any locks. That night I broke my rule of no sexual ties at work and let him into my warm bed out of the northern cold. He left around five—the only time I had Norm to myself.

I decided there were two types of non-indigenous people to be found in the Northwest Territories: the heroic or the scum. Norm was a hero. So was an English minister's wife I met who excitedly showed me brown potatoes she'd succeeded in growing in her back yard. Visitors from away either saw their time there as full of possibilities or as a sentence in icy confinement.

In Fort McPherson we met serious scumbags. Our show floundered when we played our only school children's matinee to almost complete silence. That is, apart from our yells during the blackouts between sketches when we were attacked with stinging pellets.

"They won't bloody use those pea shooters again," a voice announced in an English-public-school accent. The comment came from the school principal after the curtain call (our time to bow for applause) revealed an empty stage. We'd had enough.

In the changing room, when one of the teachers stormed on about the shocking behaviour of the students, I laughed. "I've been in North America fourteen years and never been shot at 'til now." He was not amused. I remembered all the sombre white faces at the long dining table as we'd arrived late at the town that previous morning. We had trudged a mile journey from the water where the seaplane had landed and we'd squelched our way along the deepest, muddiest pathway imaginable, with not a sign of snow, to arrive at the school, covered above the knees in brown guck, with as much of the theatre equipment and our personal bags as we could carry on our backs. We were told, "dinner is in process." We dropped our gear at the building's entrance and proceeded down the hallway. Not a word was spoken to us or an eye looked up as we clumped into the dining hall. We seated our disheveled selves at the end of a long table set with cutlery. In silence, dishes were passed to us: beef liver, baked beans, and a kind of suet pudding. My share stayed down in my aching stomach for an inordinate length of time. Finally, a large man seated at the head spoke, but to one of his neighbours. A strained, muttered conversation began between all the diners, who we presumed were school faculty. We left, having received not one word of greeting. In the middle of a continent, perfect strangers, and not a word. They definitely went on my scum list. I cheered on the rebellious students of that afternoon.

In general, I found the Inuit people extremely polite and peace-loving toward each other and foreigners, to the extent of accepting the foreign Christian religion. At least, they outwardly accepted. The native people were patient beyond comprehension of the opposition to their own cultural beliefs and traditions. Was ancient wisdom wise in this? The government buildings were strongly built while the indigenous peoples were forced to live in cracking, leaking substandard homes. Yet, what alternative was there for these people?

Eventually, we arrived in the town of Inuvik to join the celebrations of the Northwest Territories' Centennial Anniversary of being gifted by the British Government to the Dominion of Canada. We were then the honoured guests and treated with dignity in a large room bearing banners and paper streamers reminiscent of a Christmas festival. "Eskimo" men and women sat against rock walls, well-clothed in leathers and furs, some men bare-headed or with simple cloth berets or Western-style hats, the glistening black hair of the women decorated with feathers and beads.

Song, print by G. Ianuguk

Welcomed officially by the head of the newly elected council, we were given medals in memory of the occasion. Then they offered entertainment. We sat spellbound at a rare display of drum dancing. Strong, rhythmical booming emanated from large, skin-covered hoops, held by wooden handles and beaten on alternate sides with short sticks by wrinkle-faced men in heavy parkas. The dancers were also elderly but wearing gaily coloured, patterned, calf-length dresses with belted waists down around their hips, reminiscent of European 1920s fashion but with arms fully covered. Sealskin boots in a variety of styles and colours shielded their lower legs and feet, and identical-looking grey knitted mittens warmed their hands.

The dance filled the room with mesmerizing solemnity as the handful of women moved in a slow motion, telling of the hunt, the catch, the celebration, the passing of milestone times together.

Following this, we witnessed an astonishing performance of the unique throat singing of the Inuvialuit People (Real People). Oh, how did they do that? We were told privately that only the very aged knew these traditions now, the ancient arts disappearing as the people died, although some elders were making an effort to pass on stories, songs, and dances to anyone interested. But few of the young were. Hearing this, I was saddened and valued even more my purchases from the Baker Lake artist's community: the stone carving and silk screen print. These I would always cherish.

After the entertainment, gifts to fill our bellies were offered: morsels of ptarmigan, seal liver, and whale meat. It was an evening I wish I could have taken home with me and kept in a box somewhere to be opened when I felt lost in my own world.

* * *

Moving on to Yellowknife, the capital, we learned about city life in the North: how the cost of living was extraordinarily, unmanageably high, how there were only two Eskimo/Inuit students in Teacher's College down south— "And they are girls." This I took to intimate educating females was wasteful. Also, I was told how, only two years previously, a project was begun to allow Inuit people to choose a family name rather than keep the numbers they'd been allotted by the government.

"Many people here are beginning to question the helpfulness of the residential school system for the native children," I heard. "Maybe the government is too paternalistic in their policies."

And I thought I had identity problems!

When the tour ended in Yellowknife, farewells were hard all round. Norm left a message for me at the hotel. His note read, "Thanks and good luck. I'm going to look for my wife." When he told the company he had "lost" his wife, we all presumed she was dead. I tried to sooth my loneliness with the thought that perhaps I'd helped him in some way. We'd never know.

In the final days, I accepted a surprise gift of a yellow beaded necklace from a young Dogrib woman—that I still wear on occasions, and it was in Yellowknife that I received two anonymous audience messages: "Thank you for tonight," one read. "You have made my year." The other enclosed a ten-dollar bill with the note, "In thanks for your inspiration. You will probably need this more than I."

With gratitude and regret, I broke the bill a month later.

Chapter 38

#316 St. George St.

To calm my mixture of high emotions I opened my first pack of cigarettes in three weeks. I was on the bus back from the airport, leaving behind the Northwest Territories, and my mime. Filled with the wonders of my life, I was returning like from a distant planet.

As I carried my bags up the stairs of Admiral Road's apartment building, a neighbour immediately jolted me into home reality.

"We're all moving October tenth. Thirty-two's been sold!"

A Therafields custom was developing: every fall, residents of all House Groups were moved, shuffled like cards, and relocated with fresh sets of therapeutic family life.

Nessa delivered the official news on my next session with her. "If you wish to, you can move to a double-house setup on St. George Street. A few blocks away. A large portion of #32 will move there. It's still in its final stages of renovation, but you'd need to share a room, if you don't mind. A young teacher who'll join you all a little later."

Eager to stay wherever assigned, I agreed, even though I found the place still a construction site. Our small room under the eaves was a grim dip. Totally black! Everything painted matte: walls, door, doorknob, windows (and I mean the glass too), even an abandoned bed frame, left behind on the ebony wood floor. A blackened ceiling completed the hell-hole, although that was relieved by splats of twisted silver paper hanging by stale chewing gum, probably spat up from the floor during daily contests.

Quickly, gangs of volunteers scraped, scrubbed, and painted to make livable not only ours but all the rooms—mostly rendered off-white, although one new occupant strangely produced his own shit-brown.

As we all settled into #316–318 St. George Street, I grew more miserable. This time, adrenaline deficient, I spent many Indian summer evenings sitting on the front steps, eating quarts of ice cream from the Becker's Milk store opposite while staring blankly ahead at passing traffic. Fortunately, William Kennedy was rarely seen, even though his new art studio was now situated even closer to home. Yes, he'd moved in too, apparently.

Cleaning gang at #316 St. George St.

Many gloomy morning hours I loitered at the kitchen table, looking through newspapers for the perfect temp job. Perhaps I was feeling despair knowing that even acting doesn't bring everlasting satisfaction. Maybe by attempting professional mime I'd believed I'd messed up acting possibilities. One bleary-eyed Saturday morning, Stan Bachinski confronted me in our communal kitchen at 316. The usually gentle high-school art teacher suddenly woke me from my musings inside the newspaper.

"Mary! I'm sick of your self pity!" he shouted from the sink for the street to hear.

I plunked down the paper. Stan was a fellow art lover, usually receptive to problems. He and I had even written some funny poems for a magazine we were going to print up.

"Unemployed doesn't mean un-alive!" he declared as he left the kitchen.

My God, I thought, *just sitting here minding my own business really affects some people.* But I'd been well shaken.

Yet my moods of despair were reason for my choosing to live in a Therafields House Group, for the penny to fall on what I needed to do to pick myself up from the ashes of life. Mind you, I was better off than Bruce, who had the single in the #318 section. As neighbours moved him out of #32, they found his room smelling of putrid urine, coffee mugs filled with green mold, and Bruce lying in bed. Still, even he was better off than Mary, who suffocated and died from an asthma attack in our new living room. For weeks we all spoke in whispers, then, and nobody was confronting anyone for quite a while. The sudden emptiness where she used to be—that was real life, that death.

In order to survive, waitressing was the shoo-in for earning cash. My charming qualities, fully up front when hired, were impossible to keep up. I failed Steak 'N Burger almost immediately, quit Dairy Queen, leaving a line of gob-stopped customers, and had no humour for the nightclub bunny work that I think should have been the most fun. Unfortunately, my good English diction secured me market researching gigs where I'd put poems to pen while waiting for the calls to be answered. Mostly, however, I worked office jobs for agencies like Office Overload and Manpower. Never having learned long multiplication, I discovered a solace in simple accounting gigs, reminiscent of my early days at Consumers' Gas. Abstract numbers brought my imagination alive. Sitting at my desks, my number symbols developed characteristics. The letter eight with its double roundness would giggle its bubbles at me. The sevens I'd tease for having been cut off from the letter T, and threes I'd bully for empty-headedness. However, game playing fast lost its attraction as slow time ticked by.

The October Crisis in Canada came and went by the end of the year, causing not too much high anxiety in our community. The parties that had been so regular and popular at #32 were exchanged for smaller group creativity sessions. That Christmas, in 1970, handmade gifts were given around, and a few teenagers even visited their parents. I still have on my wall to this day a framed painting by Stan Bachinski, and many people received gifts from Will. I remember his wooden PEANUT BUTTER SANDWICHES, each with string attached to hang around the neck. He'd given me one previously, but when I saw him spreading them around, I suspected him of testing his art on me rather than showing me special attention. He joined one gathering that Christmas, dragging by rope a small cart on wheels that carried an indecipherable sculpture made from an old purple sweater. To admirers he explained, "It's a *WARM AND FUZZY*. See? *You can take it with you anywhere you like.*" He had many offers and finally sold it to the highest bidder.

Mary by Gary Balabanian

The New Year saw me unemployed from any job, although a few radio gigs helped my sanity. However, Jerome Nicholl, an artist friend of Will's, had been encouraging him to ask me out for dinner. Three Small Rooms, a very classy downtown restaurant, was Will's choice. We supped on splendid steak dishes, with burgundy wine adding to the relaxed atmosphere. But we never did make it back to bed that night. Before heading home, Will invited me to take a walk down to the lake to look at the moon. All I remember next was Will falling and badly cutting his head on a rock. I spent the rest of the evening playing nurse. We didn't try again for weeks.

When she discovered that Will and I were more than friendly, Nessa tried to wizen me to the hormones and tensions of young men.

"You mustn't believe everything a young man tells you. What men promise is only their own dreams."

She then encouraged me to think about one of the therapists, a close friend of Nessa's, who, apparently, was "enamoured" of me. Horrified, I asked Will if I could visit his studio again. I helped him move some of his work to a new studio that Ben Woolfitt and other artist friends in the community were organizing at 390 Dupont Street: a mini-village of studios out of a large Creeds fur storage building that would eventually add spaces for dance classes, and even a live theatre, and where Ben began his art school and art supply store that would eventually move into his own building. On that Dupont site I began children's creative drama classes to help finance my therapy, and to have the luxury of talks, walks, and general hanging around with the people and friends I admired the most: the artists. And, of course, my favourite, Will Kennedy.

Chapter 39

The Stratford Festival, Ontario

My time as a stage teenager was past, that was clear. Convinced I'd never play the role of a mature woman, at age thirty-seven I received a call from the office of the Mecca of Canadian theatre.

"Mr. William Hutt would like to audition you here, at the theatre. Is that possible?"

Hutt, the most renowned actor in Canada, wants to see me in Stratford! I think one's nerves get worse as one ages, or perhaps our worrying more quickly replaces that glorious exhilaration. Experience is no help. I was a big bundle of all emotions as dear Will patiently drove me westward in his tiny Volkswagen two days later.

On arrival at the Festival, I was immediately ushered into the auditorium of the magnificent octagonal-shaped theatre. In the stark houselights, I made my way down a long aisle toward the front to shake hands with a gentleman rising from a seat, the only other person in the house.

"Find a spot, Mary, and give me what you've brought. Take your time," Mr. Hutt said in a well-resonated, reassuring voice as he reseated himself. There was no preamble. He wanted the goods, and on Tanya Moiseiwitsch's award-winning thrust stage, the jewel of the Stratford Festival Theatre, I couldn't wait to thrust it to him.

Breathing deeply, I mounted the wide steps and chose a position near one of the two permanent stage pillars. Looking around, I saw before me the vast horseshoe of expectant seats. *This may be my one chance to ever see this view*, I thought. With a sense of victory, there on my mountain top, I sent forth the words of furious and confounded Katharina in *The Taming of the Shrew:* "The more my wrong, the more his spite appears ..." A speech I always thrilled to give.

Hutt thanked me with elegance and gentleness. He may or may not have been impressed, but I knew I'd given him the required style: big, bold, and beautifully articulated.

Will drove me back to the city, chatting all the way, while I sat like a tight spring bud, silently berating myself for what I should, and should not, have done.

The next day, a secretary offered me a contract.

"You're needed ASAP because you're replacing another actress, and rehearsals are already in progress."

Lucky or what? An actress must have died, or was fired? No matter, I was in ecstasy with six months of acting work. This job would raise high the level of my resume—even though I was contracted to play only two minor roles and to understudy two leads.

Hesperia in *As You Like It*, which I was to rehearse immediately, is never seen or heard, only referred to in all published editions (and clearly a "lady of the world"). It was William Hutt's first go at directing. He had interjected the character and created his own lines for the woman. What superb gall!

I wrote home to Mum, "An actor here thinks he's improving on our Bard. I'm speaking in a Shakespearian comedy with lines written by Bill Hutt."

"The new speech helps clarify the plot," Hutt later claimed. Apparently, there was a lot to catch up with.

That afternoon, after visiting the Festival office to sign my contract, I went to a large hall behind the main stage and joined the cast of *As You Like It*. I walked into a roomful of people in street attire, people of varying ages who were moving, standing, or sitting around an open central acting area marked out on the floor with chalk. Having a role to play in any company, professional or social, always relieves a terrible vulnerability, so I should have had more aplomb. I should have seen the triumphant nature of my place there.

Nora, our stage manager, handed me a script.

"The official copy," she said, then added with a wink, "Don't let the gnats irritate."

There was no time to question her comment, as she blew a whistle to signal silence for our director.

"Now that we're fully here, we'll begin Scene Two."

Beginning actual work, one could centre one's purpose. Excitement rose in me as I was placed in position among a courtly crowd to watch a wrestling match. Representing Hesperia, the forceful mistress of Duke Frederick, I stood beside a tall, serene-looking gentleman whom I recognized as Bill Needles, a long-time veteran of Stratford. He nodded down to me.

"I'm your wicked Duke," he said. Then, with a grin, "We have to stand here—very regally."

I smiled back and breathed more easily. That is, until Hesperia's speech. But with well-assumed assurance, I sounded Hutt's lines. Receiving what I considered an admiring look from my Duke, I felt I'd finally arrived. My new-found poise, however, was disrupted by giggling. Turning, I saw two young "courtiers" nearby whispering behind their hands, eyeing me. My cheeks burned. I glared at the boys. What was wrong with me? The tedious, unprofessional razzing made concentration impossible. My apparent scare set off the two morons with more guffaws. I was losing cool.

"Can we go from Hesperia's speech again?" Hutt called, either ignoring or unaware of the unconscionable disrespect for artistic proceedings.

My stomach wrenched. Too filled with anticipation, I hadn't slept five minutes the previous night. The room and the company all seemed to sway. I was supposed to be understudying Rosalind too, the female lead in this play.

"Hecklers belong in Vaudeville!" Hutt suddenly boomed, glowering directly at the boys. The giggling stopped. So did my shaking body. The room and the people in it came into balance again. Slowly I continued, quickly realizing these young guys were riding not me but Hutt.

As we left the hall, among the chatter I heard an actor say, "Bill should've cut the play, not added lines."

"Don't worry," Needles whispered to me. "Some hope for more time at the bar before it closes."

Each time I spoke Hutt's lines on stage, I thrilled at my triumph, and his. The critics were very kind.

"Hutt thinks he's Tyrone Guthrie," I heard one of the boys say that first evening, sitting among half a dozen of the cast in the watering hole of the theatre's Green Room. "Guthrie poured hundreds of actors on stage and made dynamite drama."

"The critics love Hutt. Everyone does," another muttered into his rum and Coke.

"Who's on next?" cried another, waving his beer in his hand. "You think Bawtree's gonna be any better?"

"I've had a dose of Bawtree. He's a lambchop," another quipped.

If Michael Bawtree was a docile director, he wasn't without hazards. During a dress rehearsal of *She Stoops to Conquer* on the main stage, I would witness a disgruntled actor lose patience and punch him in the face. A scuffling fist fight followed, broken up only by another actor. I was to feel the impact of the scene through my whole body—and the thrill. In the theatre bar after the opening of this Goldsmith classic, the two combatants laughed together like old war buddies. Audiences can't pay to see some of the best histrionics.

* * *

Displayed on the great Stratford, Ontario stage, the wondrous spectacles were produced through miracles when one considered the ghastly conditions most of the company put up with. Backstage, we all were cramped together, the aroma putrid with sweaty bodies and damp clothing. Financing the whole building with air-conditioning was impossible. Only the audience and office areas enjoyed cool comfort.

The hallways leading to and from the stage were necessarily dim, but entering the narrow dressing room I shared with four other actresses—spacious compared with the guys' quarters—the lights were dazzling. The smell of the greasepaint made my blood race. Well-laced by a dresser into my handmade, artistically-designed costume, I would sit in my allotted chair before a wall-length table. This bench was sectioned to accommodate each actress' personal belongings where we prepared for the makeup ritual. We talked with one another in the broad wall of mirror as we painted our faces. Then, in preparation for our crowning glories, we would brush our hairlines with sweet-smelling glue and wait for Clayton Shields, the wig-master, to press down his masterworks, covering the skullcaps that tightly hid our natural hair.

"You'll do, ladies," he'd say, checking his work in the long mirror and giving our shoulders a pat.

I have watched and chatted with Clayton in his studio as he worked, nimbly and deftly, hair by hair. The workshops, in general, fascinated me. Fantastic wonders were created behind those theatre walls.

One day as I sat in the dressing-room, lounging before the half hour call, I lit up the routine ciggy and set it to smolder in my newly purchased ashtray from the local flea market. I gazed afresh at myself through the smoke. *I have everything here I ever wanted*, I thought. *Here is the answer to all my prayers. So why am I puffing at cigarettes that ruin my throat?* I stubbed out the cigarette and never smoked again.

* * *

By the time I joined the Stratford Company, much of the pecking order had been established. Groupings were still in flux, but most were already formed from previous seasons. I needed to find my niche and settle into the hierarchy of life in the "Factory," as the company was familiarly called. I found my favourite grouping from the voice, movement, and fencing classes held every afternoon. Voice training, for me, became a blissful fascination.

I absorbed the Warren-Linklater approach to voice like a bear takes honey. Taught by two North American women who had learned the method through study in England, I remember wondering why more of the mature actors didn't attend classes. Very few did. I supposed because, originally, the instruction was planned only for the apprentices, with government grants. The elders, keeping up with current vocal trends, had their own private classes.

* * *

Late in the season, informed backstage of the presence of visitors for me, I entered the auditorium to see Lea Hindley-Smith standing in front of the thrust stage in conversation with an entourage from Therafields. Visvaldis, her ex-client lover, I spied with horror. The beefy-looking guy, dressed in boots and a Western-style leather waistcoat with fringes flying, was standing on our Holy Green as though he were crew. There is an ancient law that no person should walk across a stage when the holy green is not open. Theatre people never walk on a "dark" stage. But Visvaldis, who usually greeted me with "Hi, Mary. How's your love-life?" was sitting on King Lear's throne! Seeing me approach, he hailed, "Friends, Romans, countrymen, lend me your ears."

I wanted to obliterate him. With no reverence for the art, Visvaldis was violating our sacred mysteries—and quoting from the wrong play! How could intelligent Lea admire this middle-aged architect schoolboy, this cock? After I accepted friendly comments from Lea, they all departed, reminding me of how much I did not miss their company. Although this amazing woman had taught me, helped me through her work in so many amazing ways, I'd never felt comfortable in her company.

Finally, life was contenting me. Yet one can outgrow content-ment. Pleasure can stagnate. My roles as understudy kept me far from a holiday mood. Like a bad Boy Scout, I was never prepared. I figured that because I'd arrived late to the company, I'd missed understudy rehearsals. Perhaps directors thought I would pick up from observing in my own time. If nobody pressured me, I was not in the mood to study other actress' lines.

The day I was told Elizabeth Shepherd had lost her voice I experienced a kind of no-woman's land. The incredible dread of everyone knowing I'd no idea what or when she did anything as the lead female in *Lorenzaccio*, let alone the dialogue, filled me the whole day. I was simply told to "stand by." Then, at the twelfth hour, with influenza and a croak, she appeared. The actress made her entrance and whispered her way through the rest of the play. I should have known Miss Shepherd would have made the stage her deathbed, if need be. I have to admit, I was never so glad to see anyone. Not a single understudy went on that year.

There were days off when I felt really constricted in Stratford with the ever-growing number of picnicking tourists along the

Avon River, or shopping crowds in the town's high streets. I'd take off into the silence and natural beauty of the countryside. It was then I began to write again. Short passages of prose or poetry. Back in Toronto, I showed a story or two to a friend, who suggested I write in my own media.

"Why don't you write plays?" he suggested. I liked that idea and decided I'd try that one day.

* * *

By the time October arrived, I landed another major goal. I won two bonanzas: a Tyrone Guthrie Award plus a Canada Council Grant, both moneys for me to train as a teacher in the new Warren-Linklater approach to voice production. As an instructor, I could be undeniably useful. I might even make a living with my newfound absorption.

As the season ended, everyone's mind wondered: Who would be chosen for the coup of the century? The European Tour, with William Hutt starring again in *King Lear*, to begin in January the following year, playing Quebec, Holland, Denmark, Poland, and Russia—the land that not only produced the geniuses of modern theatre arts but the nation opposed to Canada in the hockey Summit Series! On the afternoon of the finals, Bill Hutt, re-entered the main stage still dressed as the king, and interrupted a school presentation of *King Lear*. He walked toward the audience and in a loud clear voice announced the final score: "It's Russia five. Canada (pause) *six!*"

The news brought the duteous crowd into a cheering mob and made their day.

Although I could celebrate a booming year with the Festival Theatre, my frustration at getting stuck in the vicinity with no easy means of escape was starting to worsen. I'd wandered, one afternoon, into a local Toyota dealer in town. A neat two-door white Corolla was for sale, and I was praying I'd soon be able to afford payments on it but I needed to prove guaranteed income for the following year. I made an appointment to see the Stratford Company manager.

From behind his desk, without raising his eyes, Mr. Max Helpmann said, "The listing for the European tour is not yet posted."

"You see," I begged, "the dealership needs to settle the sale. I need to know from you, sir, whether I *can* buy my car." My desperation around an objective other than a role in a play must have been a novelty to Mr. Helpmann.

Without raising his eyes, he said, "I don't respond well to hustling. But"—he looked up— "if I have your word, Mary, that it *goes no further in the Company*—"

"Yes, oh, yes, sir, my word!"

"You *are* listed. Now, remove yourself … and close the door *quietly!*"

Thank you, God! Now I can drive myself to heavenly bliss! And see Russia! Oh my, and Poland too.

My bright and shining white Toyota Corolla, with its old gear shifts, put me in immediate ecstasy. I drove out of the dealer's lot into the countryside, round and around. I'd received my license the year before but hadn't seen a standard for years. A handbrake! I vaguely remembered there might be one. On I went, confidently showing myself how to shift gears, but while doing this, the car suddenly lurched and dove, nose downward into a roadside ditch. I tried reversing the thing. Found the gear and stepped on the gas. The car slowly dragged itself upward. As though resisting all my efforts, it gradually agreed to reach the top of the ditch and out to the middle of the road. Then I realized my mistake. The handbrake had been on—ever since I'd left the car lot.

What a long-suffering, brilliant guardian angel I had.

Chapter 40

Canada's Stratford Festival Tour of Europe and USSR

Forty members of the Stratford National Theatre of Canada—so termed for the great tour—in early 1973 performed on some of the finest stages of Europe and the Union of Soviet Socialist Republics. We presented Shakespeare's greatest tragedy, *King Lear*, as requested by the USSR Embassy, plus the popular comedy *The Taming of the Shrew*, chosen by Jean Gascon, then Stratford's artistic director.

For psychological comfort on tour, I placed in my suitcase *Man's Search for Himself* by Rollo May. I needed a stable grounding of humane truth if I was going off to foreign countries. Before we left, first for Montreal's Place Des Arts, the tour's first stop, foreboding January weather set in. Will and I spent two days and nights under blankets on a double mattress on the floor of my single Therafields room. Separation was imminent. Between cigarettes and sex, we took turns searching out beer and refrigerated leftovers to bring back to our confine. We bonded then to such an extent that we both could part happily.

* * *

Danish poster *Taming of the Shrew*

Danish poster *King Lear*

In Copenhagen, our first stop in Europe, I suffered seventy-two hours without sleep before eventually succumbing. I toured my legs to trembling. Then in the evening, after the Stratford tour's official opening, many of us from the company went out again. We window-shopped the official red-light district near the docks, ogling at the "wares" lying in recumbent positions in window after window, some still, some doing the slow undulation bit, some moving only their eyes, all in attempts to tempt desperate wayfarers. Each day, there was much to stimulate us on the streets, from the sale of silverware to superb Danish pastries.

Ontario's Festival Theatre's cramped and stuffy backstage accommodations compared sadly with the picturesque dressing room of the Copenhagen's Royal Theatre—built like a castle with six frontal arches. It took me further into storyland. In the room I shared with Trudy Cameron, the high chandelier threw a bright glow on the original nineteenth-century furniture, which included an ornate chez lounge. Against a floral-patterned wall stood two independent dressing tables, each with its own gild-framed mirror reflecting a linen-covered surface. Each table held a personalized greeting card embossed with the golden crown. The view from the towering windows showed clusters of closed-for-traffic streets among slanting red rooftops. A cloak laid at my feet couldn't have amazed me more.

The Taming of the Shrew—in which I played Widow with several lines—on the first evening was a proper royal affair. We were instructed to follow imperial tradition at the final curtain: before turning to acknowledge the audience, we were instructed to bow firstly to the Royal Box. Of course, in the excitement, as we all lined up at the finale, on cue I bent my body to the audience and collided with an actor going toward the box. But everyone was good-natured about the error, and I discovered others had made the same faux pas. I smiled on hearing that Her Royal Highness, Queen Margrethe II, had so enjoyed her evening that she planned to bring her sister the second night.

During the opening celebrations, with the press from both sides of the Atlantic flashing and demanding interviews with whomever they could, a woman approached me backstage.

"You may not remember me. I was Jackie Foster—at Guildhall?"

My eyes took in this face from drama-school days, fifteen years past. Jackie! A spunky, petite girl with smart intelligence, as I remembered her, who was now married to a Dane and living a half hour's drive from Copenhagen. Driven to her house the next morning, I enjoyed tea in a most grandiose house, met her children, and conversed all afternoon. As I left, she handed me two matinee tickets for the Danish Ballet, and I invited jolly Jack Wetherall to join me. With eyes only for the flying, floating figures and the glorious music of Tchaikovsky, I felt a deep satisfaction that I'd chosen my own path and not sought marriage.

* * *

Holland was soft and peaceful in comparison with the Danish city. We played The Hague after beautiful Utrecht, where the moment I remember mostly was a luxurious breakfast the following morning in a grand Dutch seventeenth-century hotel that was interrupted by a loud New York accent.

"George!" a sharp female voice called from a neighbouring table.

Looking around, I saw a middle-aged couple. The woman was fingering their centrepiece. "Look, George, they're *real flahrrs!*"

When I told Powys Thomas, who became my buddy on the trip, the phrase became a fun gag between us.

Powys Thomas

Before heading behind the Iron Curtain, we were to have a day's respite in Amsterdam while waiting for our flight to Poland. I heard whisperings among the company that this could be a perfect opportunity to take a quick flight, there and back, across the English Channel.

"Max would never notice we're gone," Powys whispered.

Powys Thomas, one of the original actors of the Stratford Festival, was respected by all who saw and worked with him, temperate in nature but with an extraordinary range of extravagant characterizations. He was also overly fond of alcoholic consolation for unknown reasons, but on the tour he and I became fast friends, sharing afterhours philosophizing in his hotel room or getting out sight-seeing in cities to be discussed for hours afterwards—he tippling, me sipping.

"Meet me!" the Welsh actor whispered with a wink.

At 6:00 a.m. Sunday morning, we were in a taxi to the Amsterdam Airport for a half hour flight to Heathrow, London. I could never have dared make the trip without him. He even stayed in the London airport with me while I phoned John. I later wondered what would have happened if I hadn't reached my brother.

"Well, I s'pose I'll come and get you," John drawled.

On that short spree, I heard tell the latest news of John, Margaret (his wife), and their three children: Belinda, John Jr., and Austin. I met briefly my Guildhall friends Jessica and Stanley and their three children: Danya, Magda, and Gaia, and with them all was Tom, my ex-boyfriend—long now married to Sally, a descendent of the author Charles Dickens. He would soon be opening an English Language School for foreigners in London.

My mother saw little of me those whirlwind hours, but Dad's few words spoke tomes: "I received the earmuffs you sent me. Much appreciated." Those words were worth the trip.

In all the excitement of bringing my theatre news to England, I took a later-than-intended flight back to Amsterdam Monday afternoon, and by a shade made it to the aircraft. Dear Powys was settled at the front of the small, crowded Polish Airlines plane when I collapsed beside him in my seat. We both grinned at each other as a stewardess handed us each a small orange. Powys leaned in to me.

"Look, George, real fruit … We must be flying Polish first class!"

I laughed irresistibly at his racist joke.

* * *

With this tour Stratford Festival had taken on a worldwide, newsworthy undertaking with many surprises. My only lengthy letdown was not to witness, on their own soil, the great Polish Mime Theatre I'd fallen in love with during their run at Toronto's Royal Alexandra Theatre. Such clever, mischievous artistry I'd never before witnessed. I remembered thinking up a scheme to smuggle myself inside one of their storage bins so that I could forever learn from them, or at least shine their shoes. To my great disappointment, all the while we performed in Poland, this outrageous company was touring in the US. Yet, during the two weeks we visited their homeland, I learned a great deal more how and why their brilliance shined so much.

In both Cracow (the Polish Mime Company's centre) and Warsaw, we found lasting impressions of endurance, courage, and artistry that Canada might quickly learn from. While in that poor but galvanizing country, I observed amazing performances; to spectacular effect, many and various companies used live entertainment—on the streets or any largish venues—as creative sounding boards for political opinion, defiance, education, national pride, preservation and cultivation of their language, and celebration of life. Performances had a passion, a purpose, and clever humour. True clowning only a resilient people can master bubbled around grand pathos and heavy messaging.

Poland was again overpowered by one of its foreign neighbours, as it has been for most of its history. Mother Russia dominated the country. The oppression was evident in the social sufferance discovered by us through their own Polish jokes and innuendoes, and even in the architecture. Standing like oversized implanted white elephants, the enormous white "wedding cake" structures rose high among the beautiful historic buildings of both cities. These monstrosities were erected by the Russian oppressors in an attempt to house local cultural activities.

"They're left empty," one Polish actor told me. "Apart from the brothels in the basements."

Poland was at the height of its national spirit, its cultural "Golden Age." I remember the energy of the people, the artistry in the marketplaces, after-hours jazz clubs, beer parlours where I learned that ordering two beers brought three when one held up two fingers to the busy waiter. In Poland, one begins to count using one's thumb as number one. I remember the day we explored the salt mines: caverns larger than five playing fields with carvings of magnificent statuary in tunnels leading to an actual underground cathedral with an extremely high ceiling and—imagine it—a music gallery in salt air, smelling as pure as Virgin Mary. I remember walking for hours around Cracow with Powys while most of the company sat in the hotel bar all afternoon before they took a sleep ahead of the evening show and then, the bar again. There was so much to see, especially how the city had rebuilt and flourished from the flattened ashes of World War II. We never dreamed all this productivity would come to an end the autumn of that year when the socialist government changed leadership and the country's massive debt was eventually addressed.

One morning during breakfast at the Bristol Hotel in Warsaw, I heard news it was possible that evening to see the final performance of a play presented by the Polish National Theatre School. Our curiosity was overpowering at a chance to see fourth-year drama students prove themselves. But a conflict arose when our company manager, Max Helpmann, made an announcement.

"Today is a free day, yes, but listen up, everyone. This evening, we're all, I repeat all, honoured guests—it is listed in your itineraries—at a reception given especially for us at the Warsaw Canadian Embassy. Buses will transport everyone at six o'clock. The occasion is to celebrate Canadian culture, so all members of the Stratford National Theatre of Canada, be bloody well on your *best behaviour*."

Max had given me no flack about my tardiness on leaving Amsterdam, or to any of us leaving the tour for thirty-six hours. He was really a muffin. I figured he thought, *No complaints, no stress*. We dutifully attended our reception and ate supper of the grand assortment of hors d'euvres. After twenty minutes of routine geniality, fifteen of the forty company members quietly passed the nod and slipped away, boarded a waiting bus, and were transported to the entrance of a large theatre. We found the curtain held and the audience waiting in the dark while we squeezed to our seats. I sat spellbound between the Canadian actors Bill Needles and Butch Blake as we witnessed Sophocles' *Antigone* performed by graduating students, with members of the school faculty also cast. Bill stared throughout as though frozen to see such creative brilliance. Butch and I both wept, we were so moved.

"How did they learn to do that?" Butch said at the intermission, wiping his eyes with a handkerchief—and he a senior actor admired in Canada for several decades already! I sat stunned, wondering at young talent primed to perfection, every moment attuned and attended to in minute detail. Not understanding the language in which it was performed but knowing well the play, my attention was free to observe the actors' ability to resonate, to listen, to react, to move, to express with classic precision, and to sense the audience in awe of it all. Here, to be an actor was, in itself, honourable. I wondered again if there wasn't a way of staying around. But isn't the grass always greener over the fence? Hadn't I ogled at every performance given by Pat Galloway, the actress I understudied as King Lear's eldest daughter and the lead in *The Taming of the Shrew*? In the wings, I would hang on every word of hers, not only that I might know the lines better, but that I might learn more about her endless variety of approach, her genuine extravagance of sound.

* * *

The Embassy of the USSR in Canada had recommended we carry small Canadian items with us to be given freely as gifts: objects such as ballpoint pens, postcards, little maple leaf flags, pins of any kind. The Polish people we met were wild for anything Western, the more modern the better. One actor, having given away all his little goodies, took off the Levis from his legs for a group of girls who waylaid him after one of the shows.

"They ripped my jeans to shreds. Desperate for just a piece," he said.

Simply by being North American, our shows were a hit with audiences behind the Iron Curtain, but not all critics were supportive. We, the general company members, were denied an opportunity to read reviews either in translation or in the original. But we found ways of detecting. One evening off, most of us accepted an invitation to dine as guests of a local Warsaw theatre company. The members put on a splendid spread for us. Fifty or so sat on benches or old chairs at planks pushed together to form a long, winding table that stretched at one point between open double-doors. The snakelike line of tabletops was covered with white sheets set with mounds of luscious and sweet-smelling home-cooked food and bottles of homemade wine, all served by smiling women bustling back and forth from the hot theatre kitchen. That evening, half my Canadian trinkets were hungrily grasped from me.

William Hutt as King Lear in Moscow

Well-nourished with wine and noticing some lead Stratford actors were absent, including Mr. Hutt, I took courage. In a voice loud enough to be heard above the resounding din, I addressed one of the newspaper critics who sat nearby.

"Tell us, sir, what was your impression of our *King Lear?*"

I had him chained. All around us went quiet. His response brought a roar of laughter from both the Polish and the Canadian guests. In perfect English, he replied, "Let me answer you this way—they are going to love you in Russia."

And, of course, the audiences went feral over us in Russia. After two weeks in the land that I believed I'd inhabited in a past life, we left Poland and moved on by train to cross the Great Plains to Moscow and then to Leningrad, playing throughout our stay to packed houses. Despite laughing at *The Taming of the Shrew* in all the wrong places—the Russian audiences listened through individual earphones to a tentative translator who sat on stage left—dozens of rose blooms were thrown onto the stage at each curtain call in classic style. *King Lear*, their "favourite" Shakespeare play, had been especially requested and moved them to tears. Our company was officially allowed to see one Russian review—a translation of the writing by A. Bartoshevich in the magazine *Sovetskaya Kultura*. This declared the Canadians' version had "de-romanticized" *King Lear*, saying the production had "the language of heavy prose" rather than poetry.

Arguments erupted. How could the land that spawned Chekhov and Stanislavski—the fathers of the Method—denounce us for "naturalism"? Were they not the creators of the style? If not romantic, we prided ourselves on Shakespearian speech reflective of today's North American audiences. But most agreed with the Polish.

* * *

In the USSR, we were labelled as "workers" rather than "tourists," and regarded as high on the social ladder. This afforded us much hospitality and some of the best lodgings. But in our large hotel rooms behind the Iron Curtain, all was very bleak. All seemed big and barren. Everyone seemed misplaced. In Moscow, the dining hall reached the size of a city block. Furnished with rows of folding tables, each accommodating twelve, they reminded me more of wartime boarding schools than a home for tourists. Unbeknownst to us, we ingested tapeworms from what the proprietors called veal cutlets. I was fortunate in that my critters were successfully murdered then eliminated after I returned to Canada, but some people in the company would never be rid of them.

"The Russians have infiltrated well," commented one Canadian doctor.

During our off days in Moscow, we were herded around on organized tours to "pertinent places of interest." As workers, we were led ahead of waiting crowds: a privilege we were commanded by our Embassy to accept with smiles. Coaches drove us en masse to the Red Square, where we were allowed inside the sacred walls of the Kremlin. Apart from the red thick walls surrounding it, the building is memorable to me now only for the many large flags on rooftops and the beautiful jewelled Fabergé eggs on display. Then, of course, one can't forget filing back onto our buses, all "baaing" like sheep despite Max's protests and the smiles of Natasha, the delightful young Russian translator-guide who had a hankering to follow us back to Canada.

"I long to be one of you," she would whisper with impish exaggerated misery.

"Jack," she called back to us one day on the tour bus, "Tell again about room carpet, the naughty screwing."

Our guide's choice of words made us laugh. We knew to what she was referring, and we needed some group fun. The story was going around that Jack had caused a minor disaster.

Kneeling up on his seat, Jack Weatherall repeated the story. "I tripped on this bump in the middle of my hotel room. When I lifted the bit of carpet on the floor, I found a large metal bolt. I unscrewed it, more and more, until I heard this huge crash. Looking through the hole, I saw on the floor below a shattered chandelier."

One afternoon in Moscow, I deftly avoided being seen by authorities. Escaping Max, Natasha, and the flock, I needed to explore alone to discover Moscow for myself. I managed to board a crowded local bus, where I stood crushed along with other passengers. But in the squeeze, I'd passed the female driver without paying.

"Sorry, sorry!" I called as more people surged on. I'd no idea the cost of the fare.

Halfway down the vehicle, I held up some coins to let her know I wasn't intending to deceive her. The man beside me took them. He passed the roubles to another, and so they went down the line to the front. Well, that was lovely … but then change was passed back, all the while people chatting or sitting, watching as though this were a daily occurrence. What was so fearful about these courteous Russians?

A store displaying books on the street attracted me, so, when the bus stopped, I squeezed out. With two volumes written and published by Russians but printed in English under my arm, I found my way back to the hotel just before the coach took off to the theatre for our evening show. I'd conquered Russia.

Another day, greatly encouraged by the bus event, I secretly took off to see a matinee show. Here in Moscow stood a professional theatre whose mandate for many years was to present only works for children. This type of theatre continued to fascinate me, and I was curious to discover how their plays compared with Canada's new beginnings in this field. I wasn't ready for an audience of soldiers. Apart from my own, every seat was filled with a Red Army uniform. We watched the dramatization—in a language foreign to me—of a boy befriended by a soldier in a forest setting during the time of war. Were the child audiences as attentive? There seemed no indication of humour. The play seemed to be indoctrinating something. Care for the innocent? What a mystery! But theatre for children, about children was undeniably valued.

Leningrad was calmer. We were taken, still "baaing" on buses, to the extraordinarily vast Hermitage Museum and allowed to wander through the miles of gallery rooms. I stood mesmerized before sections filled to overflowing with Impressionists and Van Goghs rarely viewed by Westerners yet so badly protected from the devouring daylight.

At the tour end, I gave my finished copy of *Man's Search for Himself* to the delighted Natasha, receiving tears and hugs and more hugs in gratitude. I saw nothing of Powys afterwards. He continued at Stratford but died in Wales not many years later, from a failed liver no doubt. I also later discovered he'd been a renowned teacher and one of the founders of the National Theatre School of Canada. A more loving and talented man I could not have wished to share precious time with.

Chapter 41

Early Teaching

"Why did you leave Stratford?" I dreaded that inevitable question.

How could I explain to young, progressive directors that I'd left a company because I'd fallen in love with a new approach to vocal instruction? How could I explain, "There's no more lasting satisfaction than seeing your enlightened student progress," and still expect to be hired.

On leaving the Stratford Theatre Company, I possessed more of a sense of social purpose than when I'd entered eighteen months earlier. I'd trained in the Warren-Linklater approach to speech with Lloy Coutts, one of Canada's leading coaches and directors, after the season's end and even before the European tour. Now, however more from self-discovery that from altruism, I was aching to try out this exciting and inspiring new method. I'd learned that actors and public speakers previously often worked under great muscle tension. I'd known this from my experiences with the work with the Alexander technique during my drama school days. Now I knew that one need not unnecessarily stress the vocal cords, or any other part of the body. Unfortunately, at the Stratford Theatre I found this approach useful only in theory, as I'd had few opportunities to speak on Stratford's stage. Although when I did, the result had exhilarated me.

By my mid-thirties, my passion for theatre hadn't abated, but discoveries of new universes of self-expression were bringing fresh hope of that elusive happy life of creativity. Work diversification worried me. Others might teach, direct, write, along with acting, but I always took to distractions so whole-heartily that I find fascinating satisfaction with no stage in view.

George Bernard Shaw's famous quote, "Those who can, do. Those who can't, teach," had me wondering. *Yes, but for an aging actress, satisfying roles are rare.*

People flocked to my classes. Not only actors but real people, giving me both thrills and challenges! I began with several occupants of the 123–5 Walmer Road House Group where I returned after the big tour. Community living has a large number of advantages. A very generous woman who worked during the day loaned me the use of her ground-floor bed-sit. It conveniently contained a piano, an instrument of sound and pitch necessary for the new method. Admittedly, most of my early students with many varying occupations and interests came through Therafieldians' word of mouth: two with vocal disabilities looking for help, lawyers or teachers with public speaking difficulties, therapists, secretaries, clerks, even the unemployed. I exuded calmness, patience, and steady amazement at the wonders of human potential. I charged $2.00 per individual class.

* * *

After finding my feet teaching at home, I was able to convince the University of Toronto to bring me in for students of University College Playhouse. This opportunity gave me some group experience as a voice instructor. Intriguing! When twenty-five young people divided almost equally into two camps of opinion as to whether their bellies moved forward or backward as they breathed out, this was an eye-opener to the students. I didn't expect a heated argument as to the correct direction, but one ensued. After settling into the whys and wherefores of our disagreement, one student said, "I didn't know I changed my breath like that. Why isn't this taught in school?"

I could see an exciting future in this work for me: an honourable and possibly a lucrative profession.

I was already spending Saturday mornings as a mime instructor at Niagara University in New York State. Travelling long distances in my little Toyota Corolla became routine. I became familiar with college and university classrooms, also with little theatre groups. My car took me all around the eastern half of the province. I facilitated evening and weekend workshops in acting, voice, and mime through Theatre Ontario's Community Theatre Training Programs, driving to towns as far west as Kincardine, easterly to beyond Ottawa. I had nervous energy to spare in those days. Gas was cheap, and possessing my own car was a godsend. For distant cities: Sudbury, Espanola, North Bay and Thunder Bay I was flown.

* * *

I continued creative drama with children, also, around this time, giving workshops in junior schools through Canada Council for the Arts and the Ontario Boards of Education—I enjoyed the experience despite overhearing one faculty member refer to me as "the weirdo." Brian Way's book, *Development through Drama*, was my teaching Bible. The British theatre director's vision and techniques, blending with those of Peter Slade and Viola Spolin, were useful in the adult classes too. Most of all, I enjoyed my private students in my Bedford Avenue rented studio, with its upright piano left for me by my golden-haired singer friend Joan Goddard when she quit teaching.

I might have built a career as a drama therapist had I not been so very unsure of what career I really could make a go of. If I'd been male, I could have done well in acting as a TV cop, earned a steady income, and retired early. During my fifteen years living in the Therafields community, I practised not only as an instructor and actor but began to write and even took gigs as a stand-up comic. I studied sound poetry after being inspired by the popular Four Horsemen, a band of Canadian respected poets.

My friend Francie declared me a "dilettante." That bothered me.

"Why can't I stay with one thing and work at that?" I complained to Adam Crabtree, one of our original community members and a valued therapist and teacher. "It worries me that I'm all over the map."

He explained something that resonated profoundly. "Look at your hand," the wise man said. "You have four fingers, a thumb, and a palm. But they all make up your hand."

My many facial parts came together then and formed a grateful grin.

Chapter 42

Noah's Flood

Frustrated by Equity restrictions demanding permits to appear in amateur productions, I moved into the area of directing. I gathered together a few friends who had no previous experience in acting but who enthusiastically responded to my idea of presenting a Medieval mystery play in the big barn at Therafields Farm. *Noah's Flood* would not only entertain but also be a perfect metaphor for Therafields as the "Ark" of courageous experimentation in a world at sea in ignorance and confusion, guided by wisdom handed down from above. As you can tell, at the time I was sold on the saviour flavour of the organization. I was also beginning to understand metaphoric symbolism. How could we lose with a classic script—copied from the library—a universal story, and a captured audience?

Rehearsals were fun, the cast was fun, but the script proved beyond us with its sermonizing and obtuse, flowery, middle-aged way with words. When we moved from initial warmup games and exercises and turned to the script, all eagerness and inspiration faded. We believed the play was significant but fast becoming a humourless stumbling block to creativity.

Wil Ellis, cast as God, while stroking an imaginary long, grey beard, seemed to be the only one relishing the script. He'd learned his lines since first reading and suggested we find a way to hang God by a rope from the rafters and for Him to enter, royally, by descending from above. Yay, we really liked that. The more fun we had designing and improvising, the more foreign the script sounded.

In desperation one day, I let out my frustration to Nessa, still my therapist. "The play is utterly embarrassing. I don't like what we're doing with it, and we're scheduled to go on in two weeks."

Nessa came through with her objective eye. "Who said the show must go on?" she clipped.

She had a way of stunning one. *Did she mean give up?*

Noah's Flood

"Aren't you being theatrically superstitious?" she queried. "Why present something you don't like?"

"I like … the rehearsing … that's great!"

"Well, then, show us rehearsing."

I sensed a settling happening in my stomach, and like I was opening a gift-wrapped box, I muttered, "When they improvise—you know, put the lines into their own words—it's really fun. We break each other up laughing."

"Well, if that's settled, I'd like to finish early if you don't mind."

I floated out of her house as though I'd won a lottery.

At the emergency cast meeting that evening, I redesigned my whole direction. Rather than trying to recreate a classic English drama, performed as it might have been originally, we brought our modern images, language, and insights to the play. I asked the cast to speak the lines in their own words, which was "enormously liberating," they said (although Wil Ellis insisted that he keep God's original lines, and we all agreed that God could effectively sound superior).

We created imaginative props from modern day objects and made use of the audience's imagination in many different ways, a la "story theatre" or creative drama as encouraged by Brian Way and seen recently by me at the Tarragon theatre with James Reaney's groundbreaking Canadian play, *Sticks and Stones*.

The show came together very swiftly, and *Noah's Flood* was so well received at Therafields Farm that six weeks later, another performance was requested and presented in Toronto. My directing debut had been an enormous learning curve.

Chapter 43

Break with Will

If only my health, my acting, and my love-life could have been as successful as *Noah's Flood*. The pain I was experiencing in my right groin was worsening. Although I'd tried numerous doctors, I'd received no clear picture as to what was crippling and sometimes keeping me prostrate much of the time. An orthopedic surgeon had explained, "It's your corroding right hip. You're too young for surgery. Change your work habits. Find work where you're seated. Always walk on level ground, and you should be ready for a hip replacement in ten years."

Richard Taylor, master of many healings and who was helping out at 74 Admiral Road (my latest Therafields abode), gave me a set of physical exercises to try. So successful were they that I took up an offer that I'd previously refused. Vivienne Muhling, a feminist to be reconned with, was producing the first Festival of Women in the Arts, to be held at the St. Lawrence Centre.

Women in all aspects of work, art, and entertainment were then campaigning for more power and recognition. We had all read Germaine Greer's *The Female Eunuch*. I created and performed two solo mime pieces.

FESTIVAL of WOMEN and the ARTS

join in six great days of celebration
women in the arts in concert
a unique festival of creativity

June 5, 6, 7, 12, 13, 14
evenings at 8 p.m.
tickets $5.00, on sale May 1st 366-7723

St. Lawrence Center, 27 Front Street East

Thursday/June 5

CATHERINE MCKINNON
well-known, well-loved Maritime star
CAROL ROBINSON
comedienne, now starring with Dave Broadfoot in "Take a Beaver to Lunch"

ANN COOPER, soprano;
KATHLEEN RUDDELL, mezzo
courtesy Canadian Opera Co.
LYNNE GORMAN
noted actress; dramatic presentation of Canadian writer.

RITA MACNEILL
Composer and singer of songs about women
DANCEMAKERS
premier a new dance
Choreography by
ANNA BLEWCHAMP

Friday/June 6

SALOME BEY
powerful singer. Obie-award winning stage, T.V. and recording artist.
ERICA GOODMAN
harpist with the T.S.O., major concert soloist

ALANIS ABOMSAWIN
will share songs and stories of her native Indian tradition.
SELYANI
Macedonian Folklore Group

"THE KISS" choreography by
ANN DITCHBURN
performed by artists of the National Ballet of Canada
JUDY JARVIS
and her modern dance company

Saturday/June 7

SANDRA O'NEILL
AND
BARBARA HAMILTON
in an excerpt from their new Revue

DARLENE HIRST
singer-actress, Ann of Green Gables medley
MARY BARTON
mime. Winner of Tyrone Guthrie Award.

MONICA GAYLORD, piano,
PETER SCHENKMAN, cello
pay homage to Eckhardt-Gramatte
PAULINE CAREY &
PHILIP SHEPPARD
dramatize the life and work of Pauline Johnson

Thursday/June 12

SYLVIA TYSON
Capitol recording star
MARS AND MAYA
Doug Henning graduates, performers of magic and illusion

KATE REID, Ph.D., O.C.
distinguished actress
GISELA DEPKAT
cellist

DEBORAH JEANS
lyric soprano;
Dvorak's Gypsy Songs.

KATHRYN MOSES
JAZZ QUARTETTE

Friday/June 13

DINAH CHRISTIE
popular revue star
SHEILA HENIG
pianist. International, concert and television artiste

JANE MALLETT
unique performer; champion of causes
BEVERLIE ROBERTSON
folklorist sings songs from our heritage about Canadian women

BEVERLY GLENN-COPELAND
celebrated singer and composer
PATRICIA BEATTY
Co-founder, Co-artistic Director Toronto Dance Theatre

Saturday/June 14

DENISE PELLETIER
renowned French-Canadian actress presents Sarah Bernhardt
MARGARET CHRISTL
singer of ancient folk songs dulcimer accompaniment

LIONA BOYD
classical guitarist, recent Carnegie Hall triumph
MARIA ENRIQUEZ
Chilean actress

AURA
jazz singer with spectacular range
MIRIAM ADAMS
in a Dance Poem.

block ticket bookings - Susan Shapiro
967-6768 evngs.   programs subject to change

narration—Pamela Fernie
continuity—Dodi Robb, Pat Patterson

direction, production—Vivienne Muhling.

poster Festival of Women and the Arts 1976

314

During that two-day concert, I joined such up-and-coming talents as Rita MacNeill, Ann Ditchburn, Peggy Baker, Catherine McKinnon, Judy Jarvis, Salome Bey, Barbara Hamilton, Sylvia Tyson, Liona Boyd, and many more. The festival of all festivals for me proved that I could present my own ideas, say my own say loudly and clearly, albeit in silence, and take pride in my efforts. Rather courageous of me, and of Vivienne, because mime as an art form was then receding in popularity. Having goals such as this gave me energy to exercise on. I even used the opportunity to further develop my mind. I practised staying aware of my actions from moment to moment. I didn't allow those pessimistic thoughts to take over. I didn't "schist out," as the saying went. I moved house again, despite my disability, and happily delayed the inevitable for many years.

While not walking I'd continued writing. I bought a typist's *HOW-TO* book and a Remington typewriter. Suffering much guilt about the purchase of such an expensive object, it stood for months unused. Meanwhile, I scribbled "funny stuff" and moments of "intense impressions" in a notebook that are still lost in the Annex. Eventually, slowly, encouraged by the people at 74 Admiral, I learned typing letters on my imposing new machine and on it even produced a children's musical *Evolution Cheer*, which eventually was produced and published, despite the Toronto Board of Education blacklisting it because "clowns did not exist with dinosaurs."

* * *

Will Kennedy and I boogied better and more often after he signed a contract with the Royal Ontario Museum. His coup of permanent employment as an exhibit designer at the museum ensured acceptance of his imaginative construction skills and was rewarded with a very decent monthly income. Proud of his achievements, we ate out more often at sophisticated restaurants.

One novel idea of Will's we sold on the streets. Hundreds of little pin-on buttons. A popular trend in those days. Into each circle of clear plastic—bought from a wholesaler—we inserted a black and white print of my naval. We called our products "Belly Buttons." We imagined the whole world would welcome and laugh. Described by some in the community as "disgusting," others thrust dollars into our palms and went away laughing. The novelties sold very well for a day or two until we tired of passers-by ignoring us on Yonge Street. I lugged around a carton of hundreds of assembled and unassembled plastic Belly Buttons until lost altogether.

Being around Will and his artist friends, with the talks we all had about art and ideas, was extremely stimulating, but the guy was here and not here, someone whose warmth I melded with in the dark but who could change the next moment into some spikey alien. A thousand and one times others had talked to us, or about us, trying to fix our problematic affair. The lack of satisfaction between us as a couple I found infuriating. The problem to me, clearly, was Will behaving like in Woody Allen's movie *Zelig*. He even recognized the enigmatic non-descript resemblance after we'd seen the film.

"Leonid Zelig is me," Will had cried with delight.

316

The undulations, no doubt, kept me chained, but eventually I wanted to stand my own ground. I didn't want to always anticipate one mood and he arrive only to be off again in ten different directions—probably because I would be going in ten opposing directions. I didn't want marriage. I never had wanted the ties, the attachment, the children—but I wanted a lover with whom I could see building a trust beyond our last date. In one of my learning groups, I'd heard of a sexual problem called "coitus interruptus." I figured that fit Will. That was our problem.

Each year before the annual relocation, people begged not to be housed with us.

"Why don't they just have a good fuck and move in together. Save us all a lot of counselling," one resident suggested.

One year, Will moved where I was not invited. As I helped carry his bags, his manner toward me seemed abrupt and harsh. Probably nervous about his move, but that I didn't consider. Too habitually I'd face fears with aggression. Will settled into a large mansion of a residence at 9 Elgin Avenue, a block within the most eastern edge of the Annex. The place was handsomely built with expansive, well-lit rooms. There, a new assemblage of Therafields residents was establishing itself, which included therapists, learning therapists, artists, academics, and a number of oddball types. One resident described the place as "a home for those who walk to a different drummer." My boyfriend—who definitely walked differently—rented a minute "servant's" bedroom near the attic, plus space for an art studio in the basement laundry room. In the house, comfortable common-room areas were set up for "dialogue."

As I was only a visitor, I saw the scheme as elitist. I figured this arrangement had been made for the resourceful and ingenious, the really interesting ones among us, in order that they might have fun 24/7. Will developed habits, infuriating to me, like spending great lengths of time socializing with other house members, something I'd never seen him take part in before.

I was a doer-type person. I didn't know this new Will. He didn't need me. I didn't need all this discussion stuff. He never discussed art alone with me; we only dreamed together. We imagined life, told stories, and after fights we occasionally fucked. With all this stimulation and interest at 9 Elgin, Will wasn't spending any time in his studio, less with me. He loafed around, drinking and bull-shitting, was my opinion.

Ian Dowel, one of Will's friends, one day said, "I know how Will feels about you, Mary, but for the life of me I've no idea how you really feel about him."

This comment jolted me, twisted me around. I respected Ian. He was intelligent and cared for Will, I knew. Yet I determined to find Will at fault.

Back in my room, Will's gifts kept niggling at me. On my bookcase sat his carved fingers in the Victory sign, which could be reversed depending on one's mood—with its two fingers down in the fuck-you signal. He had asked me then if he could make multiples, but I'd refused, feeling nastily powerful.

My finale to our relationship occurred before my return to Niagara to teach basic acting at the new Mime School. Will had plenty of admiring people around him who thought him fabulous, so perhaps that was my out. I'm not sure; it was all so mixed up. I took my leave of our love, not in a delicate, sensitive way, but as my last piece of ammunition.

Will with Rail Fence at Bau-Xi Gallery

"That's it, Will. I can't take us anymore. I don't want to even see you."

I didn't care to think how my "Dear John" message would affect Will; I was too involved with my own mental survival. The abandonment of his "muse," as he called me, affected Will in his usual flip-flopped manner: instead of going into deep depression, he began work on his art again. Several pieces from his Rail Fence series were shown in a group show at a major gallery in Toronto, the Bau-Xi Gallery on Dundas Street.

I didn't go to the opening—I made sure I was especially busy that day. I was surprised to find my senses became not less but more strained as I distanced myself, so I turned again to stage acting, which had always been my best cure.

319

Chapter 44

Magnus Theatre

An offer came for stage work at a time when I was being referred to more and more as a "teacher." The term bothered me. I'd never wanted full time teaching, nor, it seemed, any other full-time profession. So at this opportunity, I gave up my voice studio. Excitedly I signed a two-month contract with a theatre company in Thunder Bay. I think, in retrospect, I needed a holiday.

The name Magnus Theatre (previously Magnus Theatre Northwest) had a great ring to it. Less prestigious than the Shaw and Stratford Shakespeare Festival Theatres, but Northern Ontario was now the land of the future—no longer a place where people came *from* to "make good" further south. Thunder Bay had a thriving cultural life, or so I understood from my audition with the Cockney-accented artistic director, Burton Lancaster. Previously unknown to me—looking quite unlike his famous namesake of movie fame—the chubby man sounded genuine in describing provincial cultural life.

"We have a thriving audience. Membership numbers grow every year," he said. "I'm looking for professionals who know theatre."

Learning that he had stage managed the first production of *Look Back in Anger* at the Royal Court Theatre in London, my interest grew. I'd been awestruck by that production as a drama student. (The play astounded the theatre world in the 1950s with its realism of emotion and working-class theme.) Also, Lancaster, since emigrating, had begun several regional theatres in Canada. So I trusted the guy. Besides, if I accepted his offer of two months' work, I could travel further across Canada. Already I'd worked my way into New York State, Inuktitut, and Moscow. One day I might proudly say I'd played Canada coast to coast to coast.

Lancaster impressively flew half a dozen "stage troupers" from Toronto to begin his 1976 fall season in Thunder Bay. But our enthusiasm was soon dimmed. An elderly Mrs. Latt, chairman of the board of directors and box office manager, met us at the airport, squeezed our six bodies and luggage into her family station wagon and drove into town. She too disappeared, leaving us on the street with our baggage outside a wooden shanty shack. We stared up at a setting right out of Steinbeck's *The Grapes of Wrath.*

Under the neon sign reading "St. Louis Hotel," through double doors, a mountainous rickety staircase faced us. Its sheer front needed to be scaled before reaching a distant landing. Dragging my luggage behind me in an independent manner I huffed and puffed my way up to find a wall of chin-high desk at the top, and no assistant in sight. Eventually, a glum-faced youth, no more than fifteen, showed me to my patch of the plywood building. As we passed down the narrow, mildew-smelling hall, through an open doorway I glimpsed several half-dressed male bodies and heard the clinking of bottles. Through another doorway, I stared at a huge TV with a large hole in the screen.

"On the dole," my young helper moaned. "They party all night after they get their welfare cheques—so you're best to stay out those nights."

I figured my bank account was somewhat similar, but not as regular. Then, roaring down the hallway toward us, came Vern Chapman, the high-nosed, high-voiced thespian I'd squashed up against, bum to bum, in Mrs. Latt's station wagon, politely reminiscing about the Red Barn Theatre days. Now Vern was dragging his bags back toward the exit.

"There has to be a better place in town!" he called. "Can you imagine me offering martini cocktails in this cesspool?"

Another actor joined Vern. My allocated room, further down the hall, was what I'd now come to expect. Lit by a swinging light bulb from the ceiling, I saw bare walls and an iron bed frame covered with a striped mattress and matching pillow. Fortunately, white folded sheets and grey blankets were laid on top. Above the linoleum floor, between the bed and a rickety chest of drawers, a small window looked onto what seemed like another shack. The room provided no TV, not even broken. Its adjoining bathroom had no bath. All this amounted to $125.00 a month—one quarter of my salary. Another quarter paid Toronto room rent. This meant I could save something over two months—enough to pay a month's rent until my next job.

Three weeks after I arrived, Steve, the serious young man who had first assisted me, came with a TV from a vacated room. He lingered after plugging the thing in.

"Are you going to be an actor?"

"I've been one, on and off, for twenty years. I love it. But it's hard to find work."

"I can't understand you like work," the long-faced boy said. "I hate it."

I wanted to tell him how one didn't always have to work at miserable jobs; one could dream and see them come true, but the boy was off.

While Vern set up his martini oasis in a slightly more high-class room up the street, the St. Louis became our temporary home for most of the cast. In my cubicle, I even came to admire my interior decoration—a $3.00 poster of Van Gogh's chair bought in Magnus Theatre's variety shop. On my bed I'd lie listening to Andre Gagnon or Mozart sonatas on my radio-recorder to drown out noises from the bar below. While studying lines for Alan Ayckbourn's comedy, *Absurd Person Singular,* my eyes hurt under the dim ceiling light in the St. Louis. Marilyn Gilbert, my great friend in Toronto, relieved my pain. By Greyhound bus she forwarded my own bedside lamp plus its sixty-watt bulb.

The morning after settling in, I walked the long main street to the address of the theatre and there found a small brick building with a sign indicating "Polish Legion Hall." Above it another sign read "MAGNUS."

The company of players for the new season 1978–79 was already assembling in the small hall. Soon we learned the good fortune of sharing a building with a Polish Legion. Our organization was quite compatible with the other. We thrived on lunch-time perogy dishes, cooked on the premises, that filled the rooms with stomach-warming odours, while we brought stimulation and much gossip to the local audiences, who were very curious about our antics on "their" stage.

Our artistic director was a theatre rarity for me—a teetotaler who drank no coffee, who ate healthily, and was a family man. Burton's round, short physique reflected reliability. Beneath his dark eyes, a neatly trimmed set of grey beard and moustache gave his balding head distinction. Wearing always freshly-laundered shirts, his middle-aged body moved slowly yet with determination as he trod softly around the stage, giving firm notes in his London Bow Bells accent. During one of the rehearsal breaks, I made an attempt to get to know the man. I joined him while he sat, thinking, in the dim auditorium.

"What are the audiences like here?" I asked, trying to sound casual.

"They talk back to you," Burton answered without glancing at me.

Magnus Theatre ink drawing by Desmond Ellis

"Good!" I nodded sagely. Feedback is always appreciated.

"No." He turned to me. "Not good. They *answer* you when you talk on stage!"

We laughed.

"Truly?" I had to know.

"It's been known to stop the show. These people can really get into it. We did *Inherit the Wind* one year. About the evolution trial, and that was too much for them."

"Which side won?"

"Neither. We didn't finish the play. We did better the next night. It sold out and we had to announce at the beginning that the audience could discuss this matter at the end of the play."

"So it worked?"

"Sort of. We lost a lot. But the audience is growing, slowly. Not just the Legionnaires, but the locals too and the university. We get many through the colleges and schools."

Burton was easy to talk with. So began many laughs, many discussions, personal and professional, and more associations over the following years as we both moved around the country.

At Magnus, like any other gathering or herding of humans, we found our own kind. One likes to find a buddy or two. Groupings magnetically configure and relationships establish, as in any family or organization. On our first day off, Nolan Jennings, a very entertaining and attractive actor who hosted a TV show back in Toronto; Aaron Schwartz and Marcia Bennett, a recent immigrant couple from the United States; and I rented a car and went up Mount McKay. We stood, ogling at the view from Indian Lookout, then drove on to Kakabeka Falls, then Amethyst Mines, where we found people snapping photographs, all spellbound with awe at the view of water and countryside.

At Ouimet Canyon we had the scare of our tourist lives. First, we parked the car, then wandered along a lightly travelled grassy trail. Working our way through trees, we arrived at the open space of the gorge and stopped to admire the distant cliff view. Thank God! If one of us had walked another foot onward, the sheer drop from our level would have been 350 feet. No warning signs, not any indication of any changing terrain.

"It's more impressive than the Grand Canyon," Aaron said, staring in wonder. "Here, it's so immediate."

"Come back," shouted Marcia. We all took off, back across firm ground to the car. To overcome our fright at being so close to nothingness, we drove back to Vernon's hotel to refresh with several cocktails.

After *Absurd Person Singular* opened—to unanimous acclaim and much back-slapping—the company of actors increased fourfold for rehearsals for the following show, with many of the character roles in Shakespeare's *Taming of the Shrew* to be played by both imported pros and local amateurs. Also included were a couple of faculty members from Lakehead University who "greatly valued the expert experience."

But not all Thunder Bay supported professionalism. A promo for Magnus Theatre was scheduled to be shown on local TV one evening. A large number of the cast and crew gathered around in Aaron and Marcia's room to see nothing but fog on their set—or on any other TV they tried.

"I called the station," Aaron told Burton the next day. "They said the tape broke."

Dean Hawes as Petruchio, by kind permission of Mr. Hawes

Burton roared a hiccupping laugh. "Sure," he said. "Last time we approached the alderman for financial support he said actors should starve. He said all they do is leave and go to Hollywood and become stars. So there you have our local leadership."

It wasn't hard to see the obstacles in the way of regional theatre in Northern Ontario. But one of the pluses for some actors, part of the appeal of working out of town, was that we were semi-celebrities and treated as such by the local theatre lovers. Some competed to have us for dinners on our Sunday evenings off and were very generous with their kitchens, liquor cabinets, and Swedish saunas set beside the icy waters of Lake Superior, into which we leapt screaming like ten-year-olds.

I'd joined a local Y.W.C.A. and was able to swim and sauna regularly. I read novel after novel, and Marilyn was sending me mail and the current news. I heard from Maureen Jennings, inviting me to join a murder mystery dinner theatre drama (later to become the TV series *Murdoch Mysteries*), and then a letter from the Ontario Arts Council telling me I'd been accepted for an "Artists in Schools" project. Offers of work were coming fast! Now was a time of holiday, of health and rejuvenation.

Because my roles in *The Taming of the Shrew* were small and already known, time lay plentiful on my hands. So during rehearsals, I sat in the auditorium, took out some crimson wool from my huge carry-all bag, and carried on knitting my new winter hat. That is, until Burton sent a request I leave.

The stage manager officiously reported, "You're reminding him of Madame Defarge at the guillotine."

I acquiesced, even though, as elected Equity Deputy, I knew one's rights if one kept the noise to a minimum. Recently as Deputy, I'd complained of the dreadful state of the unclean basement, where twenty people congregated not only for dressing but for practising, exercising, resting, meals, or exploding our feelings. Burton responded by sending his family and friends down with buckets and brooms to clean the place. I'd been heard. After all, we were high-minded actors.

After the *Shrew* opening, Burton took me aside, saying as he shook his bearded head, "I wish I could use you again this season, Mary."

I wished so too. Yet Burton and I became very good future friends as we joined forces to start another summer theatre the year I married.

Chapter 45

Artists' Marathons

I'm not sure from where or how the idea of the summer arts festivals at the Therafields farm in Mono Mills, Ontario, came into being, but I think the artists' marathons held there were surely an influence.

Photos: ELIZABETH BARNES • DOUGAL BICHAN • CATHERINE FROST
Photo Preparation: D. BICHAN

● CO-ORDINATOR / COMMUNICATIONS   JOHN ST. JAMES   ●   THERAFIELDS, 510 DUPONT STREET   ●   964-7910
● ADVISORS   V UPENIEKS, R. HINDLEY-SMITH, bp NICHOL   ● CO-ORDINATOR   Profiles / People   JOAN KUNTZ
● PRODUCTION   AXIS PRODUCTIONS   ●   WITH THE GENEROUS HELP OF VOLUNTEER TYPISTS
                AND LAYOUT ARTISTS
● OPINIONS IN THIS PUBLICATION, OTHER THAN THOSE SO DESIGNATED, DO NOT NECESSARILY
   REPRESENT THE OFFICIAL POINT-OF-VIEW OF THERAFIELDS.

Therafields Arts Festival

331

Mary as Amazing Gracski (the first of many original characters)

Many Therafields folk in the late 1970s were wrestling with creative unease and difficulty in effectively expressing themselves. Several artists were openly questioning the effectiveness of psychotherapy in art or life.

"I can't sit and talk about problems," I heard one painter complain. "I don't have problems when I'm sitting talking. They're there when I'm fucking well trying to paint. I don't paint the painting; I paint the fucking problem. That's if I dare pick up the brush."

Lea shocked us one time by saying, "If you're an artist, do art. Don't get involved too much in this psychotherapy business."

In answer to a formal plea for help, Grant Goodbrand, art historian, and bpNichol, member of *The Four Horsemen*, concrete poet extraordinaire and winner of Canada's Governor General's Award for poetry, organized a series of annual Artists' Marathons. Designed only for active artists, amateur or professional, involved in Therafields' psychotherapy, they offered, according to a flyer, "an opportunity for artists in all fields to explore emotional blocks and/or disturbances that stand between them and the furtherance of their art."

Sitting in an interview with Grant and Barrie (also known as bp) before the ten-day course was to take place around the farm's grounds, I fought back tears.

"I don't know if I'm qualified to join. I can't call myself an 'artist.' I like to dabble around with comedy monologue stuff, but that's so I can perform it. I'm more of a part-time actress. I write the odd poem and plays, but mostly sketches."

I took a breath. I hadn't talked much about the quandary of artistry, even to Grant, my current psychotherapist. Both Grant and Barrie stayed silent.

"To me an artist creates art … that's making order out of our chaos. I don't do much of that. But, all the same, I want to be … art*ful*, skill*ful*." I gained courage as thoughts came to me while I spoke. "I'd like to be artful in everything I do," I said, with a bit of sparrow's cheek. "I want to go on the Marathon because I want people to think I'm creative, yes," I finally added. "Actually, I want to *be* artistic, but I'm not sure *how*. Perhaps I can practise audition pieces at the artists' marathon … wow the others to tears. Or perhaps I could develop my writing skills and make them laugh."

Barrie said, "Mary, what do you *want* to do?"

"Write," I said immediately. Then I added with a final surge of courage, "So I can make people laugh. That's what I've longed to do ever since I can remember. A good clown's an artist!"

There, it was out. How embarrassing! How presumptuous! Of course I didn't only want to make people laugh. I wanted to make them cry too, to see, to feel. But I said no more.

Grant smiled. "You're describing one of the reasons we're offering this time together—time to work and talk through conflicting thoughts."

"You're in, girl," quipped Barrie. I departed, elated.

During those times of Artists Marathons, Therafields farm in Mono Mills took on an exhilarating, provocative atmosphere. For ten intensive days, one could work, talk, relax, share, develop artistic ideas, and dream. All my agoraphobia vanished. My two almost favourite guys in the world were leading eighteen nervous, shy, but passionate warriors toward creative productivity fighting inner obstacles.

In loft corners, behind barns, under trees, or in makeshift tents, we planted our stakes, our solitary spaces. Several wanted total privacy; others thrived on company. Dancers and musicians moved around the whole campus. I remember two painters laying out their oils, watercolours or acrylics, stretching out canvases on folding tables or on the grass, but not twenty yards from each other, each with a ghetto-blaster, each machine happily blaring out different music. A table with a typewriter sat between the two while the writer wandered the fields making notes and then returned to type another sheet, not bothered in the least by the dissonance. Nobody cared. My choice was to wander the woodlands around the barn where I stored my papers on a make-shift desk.

The sculptors worked in stone, clay, wool, silk, even weeds; the ceramic makers created machetes of fun, and fantastical pieces. The intensity of struggle was infectious.

Many of the experimenters were very familiar to me. Apprehension filled me when I realized Will Kennedy would, of course, be present. Would we be a distraction for each other, being ex-lovers (we had separated twice now)?

I needn't have worried for Will. He dove right into the action with humour and intensity with work his clear focus. His attitude helped me enormously, of course, as the activities became so absorbing I forgot my erotic concerns and began to write.

The air smelled fresh; birds sang in the green woods and farmland. Early morning walks as the sun was rising prepared many for work—others worked all night and simply slept until group time. Art bliss! If they wished, individuals could present their work-in-progress to the group while talking about difficulties. Criticism was not in the picture. Here we were, a bunch of artsy folk intent on helping but not criticizing—this was radically new. We weren't about art therapy. The point wasn't to assess or analyze the work in order to reveal personal problems. The point was to listen to what was trying to emerge in the work and to hear what was preventing the work from its free realization. We grew in knowledge and understanding of each other—even if we didn't always like or approve.

Several left me dumb with admiration, but I remember one young woman I resented and belittled. Leisa wanted to join a modern dance company but had no confidence in public. The lithe young woman requested that she might dance for us all. We were curious as she set up a large battery-run tape recorder, then, as we sat in an open field, the sweet sounds of a violin filled the morning air. As she moved, the swimsuit-clad girl sweated and waved her arms around, gyrating back and forward, around and around, moving to and fro. The music ended and the dancer stood, arms raised to the skies.

"You did it, Leisa!" Barrie called. "How was it for you?"

Breathing heavily, she mumbled something, wiped her face, and grinned.

Barrie and Grant praised Leisa's success in "going public." They seemed to delight in her performance. But I'd found it agonizing, her body embarrassing. I hated her—hated her "foolishness," as I saw it, her wanting to dance professionally when she obviously was a turkey. But I couldn't voice such a negative reaction. Leisa had triumphed with enormous courage and I was thoroughly jealous.

Later, I talked about the event in a session with Grant.

"You saw yourself in Leisa," he said.

Yes. My impulse was to squash all youngness, stamp it out, demolish out of existence anything tiny, freshly emerging, unsafe. I'd hated her for putting me there, in an openly vulnerable place. Was all this so, or was I simply too empathic to her stage fright? Either way, I'd clearly wanted to destroy her initiative.

For my own work I felt ambivalent. At times when I read aloud to the group, I was rewarded with laughter and praise. Other times, the effect was dull. When the creating flowed easily it was fun, but generally, I doubted. I believed then that one either achieved something or failed, was a good artist or not, a success or a bomb. My work was derivative of the great comic writers I'd enjoyed in my childhood. In my mind, I heard past voices of the revue artists I heard on the radio: Beatrice Lilli, Gracie Fields, Joyce Grenfell, and the uproariously silly Goons. Under the spell of Grant and Barrie's example and guidance, I explored my own voice.

Boisterous, witty Barrie and Buddha-like Grant made a well-balanced pair at these marathons. They grounded our battered, confused egos, drew out the hesitant fires.

I regarded Goodbrand as a man of great artistic integrity, of enormous intellect and courage. He might, on first meeting, have appeared like a big teddy bear with his large body and thick bearded face, but on closer encounter, one met a no-nonsense, direct, and searching man who cared more for honesty in work than pleasing anyone. Since he was my psychotherapist at the time, initially I was quite wary around him. We were all rather like goldfish in a bowl, but some, like Barrie, thrived in the light.

Barrie, the intuitive, the outspoken lover of word play, was the most socially congenial of the two therapists. With bp, one first met his hair—a frizz of fair, curly locks hanging shoulder-length, a strand or two flipped back from time to time as he listened or spoke, revealing sharp blue eyes beneath his high forehead. Whenever he entered a room, perhaps wearing a long summer smock and open sandals, he was the focus, within seconds relieving any unspoken tension. He could catch the drift of any negative mood prevalent in a group of people. Immediately, he would address it.

"You all look slightly stunned," he might say on looking around a roomful of people surprised and silenced by his entrance. "Like you've found a short and curly in your sink." Laughter would ease the room.

I admired Barrie for his personal magnetism and his vocal magic rather than his published brilliance.

"Most of my friends don't read my work," I remember he said one day.

His comment embarrassed me, realizing I'd be in the non-reading category should I ever be regarded as a friend.

He also told me, "You don't write so you can perform, Mary; you perform so you can write."

This, of course, perplexed me for years. But I felt stirred by his perspective of me. He had a way of making one feel unique. I remember feeling quite disappointed to discover many people felt themselves special to Barrie. Nobody and nothing seemed too heavy for him. He wanted everyone to enjoy full lives—he certainly seemed to enjoy everyone else's. What a profound influence he was on so many lives.

I must have attended eight of the dozen Artists' Marathons offered over the following seven years, with me, in the final run, as one of the facilitators, directing a course on creative drama.

"It's the *process* that counts," bp famously claimed. A wise man, indeed.

Little did I dream that within a few years I'd be working alongside this master on not one but two projects.

Chapter 46

In and out of Mime Again

"Could you go to my class, Mary?" the instructor pleaded, "It's … Lionel."

"Lionel?" The name was unfamiliar.

"He's … upset."

"You need *me* to help?"

"Well, he's just sitting there. I don't know what to do. He's … just like a rock."

At the time, the winter of 1977, we each were teaching at the Canadian Mime School in Niagara-on-the-Lake. I had returned to teach drama—commuting two days per week from Toronto—hired by Myra Benson, the school director, and Wayne Pritchett, the new artistic director of The Canadian Mime Theatre.

Puzzled at the teacher's distress that wintery morning, I asked a student to take over while I hurried to the small auditorium where Joe taught. The place was empty apart from one twenty-year-old, sitting on the school stage, his feet dangling over the edge, arms hanging like strands of rope. The rest of the class had taken off. I never saw Joe McKay again.

I walked up the steps of the stage and sat beside the boy, letting my legs hang beside his as he stared before him with blank, wide eyes. Lionel's pale, freckled face looked unnaturally still below wisps of long, disheveled hair tied roughly back by a rubber band. I waited for a sign of what could be done. He was an unknown student to me. I wondered if he were actually breathing.

Venturing tentative contact with him, I said, "I'm Mary, Lionel! I've come to sit too, if that's OK?"

I didn't expect a reply. There was no sign of one. After a few minutes, I took his limp hand and felt the semi-warmth of it. His muscles didn't resist or respond, so we just hung our legs and held hands. I heard sounds from the hallway of people coming and going, but nobody entered. There was nothing to be done but follow my instinct to wait. I imagined his class had probably been too intense with emotional challenges and this had activated a psychotic episode—terrifying everyone, including the teacher. This was not an exceptional case. Many instructors dive straight into the inner territories of their vulnerable students, having read only a scrap of instructions in how to train actors. Stanislavski, the great Russian modern theatrical influence, had serious concerns about his own methods.

The boy and I continued to sit for what must have been an hour until suddenly I sensed a few jerks shiver through his body. Lionel turned his head toward me. We made eye contact.

After permission from Wayne Pritchett, Lionel was allowed to go home but continued class the following day. Joe did not return. Did he and all in his class think Lionel dangerous, contagious? The incident stirred a curiosity in me to someday find more schooling in mental disorder. That afternoon, I sensed an inner assurance, a deep knowing within myself, that I was in the exact right place at the exact right moment for everything, everywhere. A most calming sensation.

I had parted company with the original Canadian Mime Theatre (CTM) years earlier. The friendly accord between the founding members, Harro Mascow and Adrian Pecknold, I remembered, had been cracking even seven years earlier. The tension must have finally exploded, because the board of directors proved helpless in solving their rancour, resulting in many of the members convincing Harro to found his own band of mimes. This he'd done—around the corner, in the same little Ontario town. Adrian had carried on, with Ray Wickens staying loyal to CMT as managing director. But bitterness and the mystery of the breakup remained. After two years, Pecknold also had quit, to do solo work. His book—requested of him for many years by teachers and students of theatre arts—was published a few years later, entitled *Mime: The Step beyond Words*. Curiously, Harro's very successful new company had used a similar title: *Theatre beyond Words*.

* * *

When the school ended, that spring, Wayne Pritchett, a world-travelled mime of the Etienne Decroux school, invited me to join his newly mobilized group that would be presenting the CTM's season of '77 in the newly renovated Royal George Theatre on Queen Street, Niagara-on-the-Lake. I hadn't dreamed of mime again, for me.

That summer, I rented a tiny house in town and began rehearsals with Wayne, Peter Townsend, and William Finlay—two actors with a mime flair—and two talented young female apprentices from the Mime School, Peggy Coffey and Paula Schappert.

Star Week

TV listings and entertainment guide

May 28 to June 4, 1977

**Canadian
Mime Theatre
opens its season at
Niagara~on~the~Lake**

Paula Schappert, Wayne Pritchett, Mary

Wayne Pritchett's direction for the newly-formed company was to create images on stage "less formalized and more life-like" than the previous company had offered. No "Marcel Marceau tricks of the trade," as Pritchett maintained. Hence his choice of actors over specialized mime artists trained in Europe and, I figured, more easily obtained.

"I have in mind long pieces rather than the little vignettes usually associated with this art form," Pritchett explained at our first meeting. "We will present important storytelling, not quaint magic show stuff. We're not into that."

Mary at mime

The season of '77 was definitely a change in style, yet historic, in that the whole company created the summer shows together. During the season, Pritchett had us performing with the Canadian Brass and the Hamilton Philharmonic Orchestra,

345

studying and presenting a story around the local Inniskillin Wineries, generously aided by the owner, Don Ziraldo. One of my unusual contributions was to incorporate a section of prose by bpNichol into the programme, read by yours truly. However, the opening night taught me a forgotten basic acting lesson: let the audience clearly understand that it is the character that is trembling, not the actor—a skill only learned with experience.

During difficult times, I wrote. In happy times, I wrote. Whatever my emotions, I wrote more each year. During a break from mime, one Monday free day, I'd taken the beginnings of a short story to Dan MacDonald, once a manager of the Catholic Book Centre in Toronto, and a good friend.

"Short stories are everywhere, Mary," Dan had tactfully commented. "Why don't you write for the stage, your own medium?"

More as a doodle than anything significant, I began writing comic monologues. *So much easier than me trying to write perfect English.*

Toward the end of the mime season, Ray Wickens, still manager and essential company glue, found me in one of the dressing rooms revising a speech.

With curiosity, he asked, "Have you ever performed your work?"

"Only for friends!"

"Would you be willing to perform some for us?"

A series of evenings were being organized in the Royal George after the close of the season; time for the local talent and the mime students to shine on stage—another of Pritchett and Wickens' ideas for CMT fundraising. Was Ray asking me to stand on a mime stage and give voice to my own words?

346

Chapter 47

Mirth Music and Mary B.

"While currently working one gains employment more easily than while at liberty," the truthful saying goes. The following winter, while playing in the run of *White Marriage*, directed by Saskia Noorkhoek Hegt, brought from the States by Toronto's Redlight Theatre (for their final production under that title), I received a call from Brother Augustine, my Saturday mornings' boss at Niagara University. He asked me to perform the lead in their play of the year, *The Prime of Miss Jean Brodie*, as guest artist. I had to decline. A role in Harold Pinter's *Old Times* at the Toronto Phoenix Theatre enticed me more. During that run, after I was awarded the *Toronto Telegram*'s Laurel Wreath of the Week for my performance as Anna, I had a call from Raymond Wickens, manager of the Canadian Mime Theatre, with an amazing proposition. Before I'd finished telling him there was no way I would sign another mime contract, Ray had me off my feet.

"Would you have enough of your writings for a whole evening, Mary?" Ray asked.

Gulp! "Ooooh, sure," I lied.

"Wonderful! We don't want your mime this time, Mary, but you and your voice. We're fundraising. If you could give us three nights in March at the Royal George Theatre we would be over the moon. What do you say? I can get you a director, an accompanist, full lighting, even a dresser."

"Good God!"

"I know we can get audiences. You have a month to prepare. Of course, we'll sort it all with Equity, and you'd get 50 per cent of the house."

Cash from writing? Unheard of! *Good God, where will I start?* In my notebooks, I kept mostly scraps of dialogue, a thousand ideas but few satisfactorily pieces. But, from that moment, feverishly I set to work. What a great chance! *Don't blow it! Use your common sense. Add a couple of comic songs, tell your favourite jokes, give them audition pieces, extend the dramas.* Ideas burst up like fireworks.

One-woman shows were rare in Canada. Lily Tomlin was yet to astound the world I knew. Revue artistes of the calibre of Joyce Grenfell, Beatrice Lillie, Hermione Gingold, with songsters like the great Eartha Kitt, had been my inspiration for the sketches, yet my resulting solo programme reflected more the style of the mostly forgotten art of Ruth Draper. This wondrous American monologist and brilliant interpreter of observations of life was unknown to me until later when I saw myself following a fine tradition. However, encouraged by all around me, I came up with some agreeable additions.

Like Draper, I presented each piece against a backdrop of basic black curtains. Yet unlike the Master-Mistress who often used elaborate costuming, I utilized simple accessories. Less was better for me. Wearing the mime uniform of black leotards and tights, I added a change of skirt, scarf, hat, or boa, choosing from an assortment of clothes and accessories that hung on a coat rack on stage. I created an intimacy with the audience, who, I hoped, followed me with fascination through each transformation.

"Mary Barton ennobled the Niagara-on-the-Lake theatre season with her performance of *Mirth, Music and Mary B.*," wrote the *Niagara Advance*.

What a sock in the eye for The Shaw Festival—the larger company down the street from us, who had informed me, with regrets, "unfortunately, unable to cast you this year." I imagined the actors reading the paper that morning heard my shouts from across the road and were muttering, "Well, get *her*!" Unfortunately, I doubted they ever read the local rag.

During the week of rehearsals for my show I had many helpers. Leading these volunteers was skilled actor and mime Larry Lefebvre, who directed. He was off-season from Theatre beyond Words, our rival company in Niagara-on-the-Lake. Larry gave me a fine objective eye both in the staging and the script. Expert pianist Harry Picken, the well-loved aging local—who had played the organ during silent movies at the Royal George Theatre—rehearsed and accompanied me during the shows, sitting in full-view, visibly enjoying every minute. What joy!

Not only was I writer and performer, but I became involved in many aspects of fundraising: publicity, front of house, and favour-begging, but I'd no hand in organizing a mass visit from Toronto. A "Dinner and Coach Excursion," Marilyn Gilbert— my friend of the brilliant light bulb, etc.—and the entrepreneurs of Therafields' Vivaxis Restaurant, brought two dozen patrons in excellent spirits one night.

"The bus was packed," Kevin, another organizer, said. "We should have rented a boat and come across Lake Ontario."

To be the centre of attention, to hear the acclaim, the congratulations, and to be cheered afterwards with raised glasses at the drinking hole, for me was a right turn on.

E. H. Lampard—familiarly known as Betty—was most flattering. She wrote in the *St. Catharines Standard*: "It's about time she struck out on her own, really, for with talent like this, she could make a new career for herself in the relatively uncrowded field of solo performance."

One becomes affected by opinions if one listens to critics. I did. One brief article concluded with: "… Miss Barton clearly has ability. What she needs is a more clearly defined philosophy. Mirth for its own sake just isn't good enough."

This hugely puzzled me. I understood stage plays had themes, central messages, but this was revue theatre, a collection of paintings in words, a variety of studies, an offering with many different emotions. Of course, people like themes—they help an audience know if they're still in the right theatre. But if there must be a cohesive lesson in my show, let it be joy of life, wherever we find it. Laughter is a gift from the gods, and whosoever feels the urge is blessed. But I also heard this critic as asking for more of what I personally chose to say for the evening. If I had a more extensive repertoire, I might change my tune toward a theme or two. Where was I going with my interests and talents? No idea. Happy to be on a beautiful plateau.

I knew I was no Noel Coward, no Bea Lillie, but I also recognized a need in me to entertain. Perhaps I wanted to continue sharing the cheeriness that had kept people going during the Great War, as we listened by radio to great comics like Arthur Askey and Tommy Hanley as they connected and relaxed all in the British Isles after the BBC's scary six o'clock news. That cheeriness I longed to hear and share in this foreign and undefined land of Canada to keep me going without my old friends, my family, my ex-lovers, my homeland. I was ever wary of becoming defeatist. Was I merely "creating for its own sake," as the common phrase goes? Great balls of fire, weren't New York productions given months, sometimes years of touring before letting in the critics? Did I expect my first attempt at a solo show to be suddenly brilliant? Yes. But I also wanted to see if I could do it.

Mirth, Music and Mary B. went on tour in and around Toronto. The show was revised again as *Mary Barton, Revued* for a Toronto festival, with Burton Lancaster directing, and another titled *More Mary* (title suggested by Paul Dutton, poet and member of *The Four Horsemen*).

When I say tour, don't imagine the large motorcoach with kitchen, dining and bedroom, plus storage space for wardrobe, props, and company. I mean my little Toyota Corona in and around the city, although often with stage management help from my psychotherapist and author friend Nicholas Power, who witnessed our visit to an out-of-town library where we found a couple already seated in the tiny auditorium. And that was our audience, until we announced the start of the show, when they immediately up and hurriedly left. My talent for publicity was zilch. Yet we smiled and took a day off, remembering the theatrical custom: Cancel only if audience less than number in cast.

Yet one of the later shows at Scorpio Lunchtime Theatre on Toronto's Yonge Street was so successful, it was held over a second week.

poster *Mirth Music and Mary B*

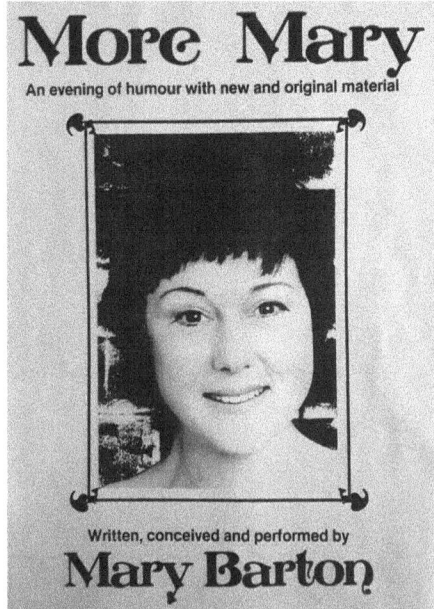

poster *More Mary*

Scorpio poster

After one of these shows, a visitor to Toronto approached me.

"What part of Aberdeen are you from because that's my birth-place," she asked with bright, eager eyes.

I'd presented one sketch with a Scottish accent but had to disappoint her when I said that I had no idea of my accent's locale, me being from England.

My producer at Scorpio, Len Gibson, ex-dancer, restauranteur, insisted I apply for a Canada Council national tour. Yet after my ten-minute audition for that opportunity, the adjudicator said, "I would recommend you for a university tour, but in my opinion, your work isn't suitable for the man on the street."

Not suitable? I was already succeeding on the central street of Canada's largest city! But I didn't get the grant.

*   *   *

While continuing to teach mime each week at Niagara University in New York State, I was invited to join a large group of artists in open-air showings and workshop presentations for Art Park 1981, held near Lewiston, N.Y. During the following two summers, I spent two weeks in residence on the university campus while I plied my comedy trade. The atmosphere over the park grounds during the days was relaxing and very agreeable. Left very much to take care of myself, I thoroughly enjoyed viewing other artists' amazing works, watching them demonstrate and talking after hours as we watched the setting sun and drank martinis before the early nights before rising with the robins the next day. I was fascinated by their creations, the potters with the kilns and ceramics, and the large wrought steel work that stayed erected in the park for years.

Often, my self-denigration was so strong that I fantasized wandering off and disappearing altogether, as I was placed, twice daily, with half-hour sets, in a remote woodland area of the park that sat on the cliffs of the Niagara escapement. Viewing the magnificent fast-running river below, I didn't imagine throwing myself off, as was rather common, I'd heard, but my pleasure at having freedom to wander was so compelling that I'd a hard time staying around my designated platform. To help me before

I went, Grant Goodbrand, my therapist, had given me input and guided me in self-hypnotic exercises. I listened. When I found a quiet spot, I lay down, and physically let go by counting down one to twenty and was present to how it was to be within myself and noticing my breathing. I felt no longer filled with stage fright—only happiness! The discovery of a peace and contentment within my nit-picking, frantically torturing self-spite, surprised me and helped carry me through many days of self-criticism.

I would have loved Will Kennedy to have joined me at Art Park. We were again living in the same house but still not speaking.

* * *

The temptation to accept extra teaching at Niagara U., get a green card, and emigrate again was intriguing, but knowing I preferred my connections and friends in Canada, I declined Brother Augustine's request that I add more days and join the drama faculty. Then, as border patrols became extra fastidious, I rarely visited. My Saturday morning replacements were always happily filled by Ray Wickens. I've applauded, many times, my choice to stay in Canada.

Chapter 48

University Teaching

My contract with McMaster University included directing lunch-hour entertainment on two days of the week, presented on campus by the second-year students who had chosen theatre arts as an elective. Few attendees had theatrical ambitions. Most had never witnessed a live performance—perhaps a rock concert.

"Your class is somewhere to go out of the library," one young man told me.

Not having reached public schooling beyond Grade Twelve, I was fortunate that in Canada as well as the States at that time, a more unrestricted approach to education was encouraged rather than a strict, totally academic methodology. Students were keen to learn from those professionally practiced in the subjects they taught. At McMaster, this news may have encouraged me to apply for the part-time role, but didn't help my nervousness about teaching smart teenagers.

Sheila Geoghan, a friend in Therafields, advised me to coat myself in white light as protection before I stepped into the school's building.

"Imagine the strengthening, healing light surrounding you like a cocoon."

She was into all that. I was more inclined, then, to think it voodoo stuff. Not totally convinced of this idea, to make doubly sure, on arriving at the main office to pick up my mail and nod to the guardians of all knowledge behind the administrative barrier, and despite unseasonably warm weather, I wore not only a gigantic smile within my white light but also a thick, white, faux-fur coat I'd recently bought from Goodwill. For almost three years I taught those classes, directed lunchtime entertainment by my class (part of their curriculum), and learned more about teens than one would ever want to learn.

St. Catharines isn't far from Hamilton, I thought, when the offer from Press Theatre came. The wife in Ira Levin's play *Deathtrap* was too good to pass up. Rather than finding a substitute teacher, one week, I figured this would be an excellent experience to give the class.

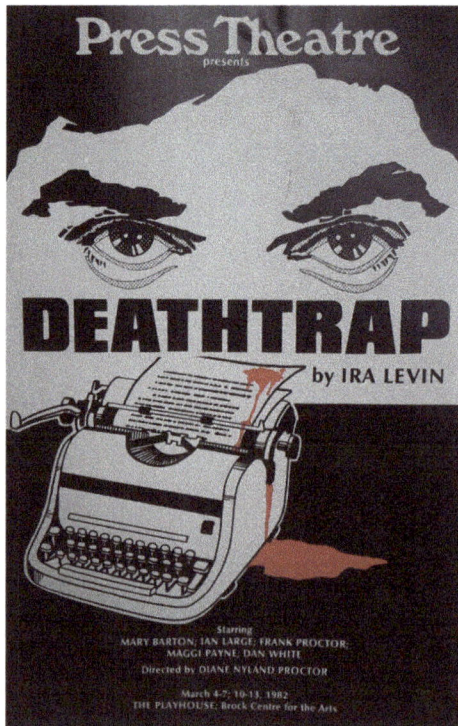

Programme cover for *Deathtrap*

My character, Myra Bruhl, dies on a darkened stage at the end of the play's second act, with a shriek from the audience at her terrorizing death. I count this as one of my most thrilling experiences on stage. When I saw the film version of *Deathtrap* that same year, there was barely a gasp from the full house at that scene. Are movie-goers more sophisticated? I think live theatre is definitely more enlivening.

During class time, my current script was very useful *as* an example to show my students how a voice can transmit emotion.

"How does an actor scream without straining his throat?" I asked. (Most women still used the male pretext.)

"How?" they asked, with hints of interest.

"He screams his laugh!"

I had them all. "The audience believes it hears a cry of pain because that's what it expects," I explained. "Imagine Myra silently crossing a room in moonlight. The buildup is dramatic. She stops. The audience knows she's in danger. They hear something! In the dim light, each person sees a movement. Myra screams. Half the audience screams too. It's a relief to scream because they haven't recognized the actress' elongated cry of *joy!*"

The class experimented.

"I keep tightening my throat and it stops me screaming," a girl said in astonishment.

"Exactly!"

They tried a silent laugh in slow motion, then, the room resounded with exhilarating release of overwrought frustrations. Well, what are drama classes for?

Through the following classes they helped me organize a "field trip," amazing me with their superb thoroughness in every detail of planning: obtaining permission, hiring transportation, ordering tickets, and collecting monies. Even then, I suspected nothing. I knew time away from the school would be popular, but twenty-five arrived *en masse* from McMaster to see a Friday matinee at Brock University Playhouse.

After the show, I'd planned to discuss the play and assign papers on the bus while we returned to McMaster. Silly me. I was the sole passenger, with a driver who'd spent the afternoon sleeping. The teens had disappeared.

Throughout Saturday and Sunday, my slow but anxious mind pictured them walking the streets of St. Catharines that night, all screaming in real fear—and I was responsible! Losing my students gave my stomach a pain far worse than any thriller. While I'd been getting dressed backstage, the whole gang had taken off for where they'd intended in the first place: downtown St. Catharines, or even across the border to the US. They had contrived for weeks how to escape the clutches of culture. I know. I would have done the same in their runners.

One student later explained, "But Miss, we forgot the time. It said in the program: *Scene three: two hours later.*" Such smart kids.

Nothing more was said. No one was injured—for which I am grateful. My classes, not surprisingly, became even more popular.

But over-popularity itself can become a problem. During my second year, the Dean of Humanities called me to his office. Apparently, against my initial instincts, I'd accepted into class a young man who put me over my new maximum of thirty students. He twisted my gut into accepting him and then had become one dick of a troublemaker. So even though the dean smilingly offered me a seat, I expected dismissal.

"Don't let them get you down. They'll sense it and take advantage. Take courage. All you need is to arm yourself more strongly."

Surprised and touched by his support, we parted with a handshake. I ejected the class jackass and continued, armed with faculty cavalry and more respect for Shelagh's calming white light. Later, I was asked to teach the University's first summer drama course. I did, and thoroughly enjoyed that.

* * *

George Brown College gave me the most heartache: I was fired and then rehired, for the third time in my theatrical history. That September, following McMaster's summer course, Joseph Shaw, actor and founder of the school's Drama Department, engaged me to take over first-year speech classes from an escaped instructor (so went the rumour). I taught not only those now in second year but also a much larger class of first years. Great! Three months later, the day before Christmas Eve, I found myself walking the frozen shores of Lake Ontario, crying to the gods to help me understand what was happening.

Shaw had given me no reason for his frequent unexpected, stony-faced visits to my classroom. Eventually I was called to his office, where I stood before his desk.

"There has been a complaint."

"About what?"

"I cannot say."

"How can I defend myself?"

He shrugged. "If I told you what it was, you'd know where it came from."

My contract was terminated.

My mind circled the possibilities of who in my first-year class could be so covertly dissatisfied. These classes were looser, more fun, and more exploratory than I'd ever taught before. Was that the problem? I knew the second-year group were making good progress even though disgruntled with repeating a few vocal exercises they hadn't yet mastered.

To my amazement, before New Year, Joe Shaw phoned me, apologizing profusely, said it had all been a huge misunderstanding.

"However, I've already hired a replacement. So sorry."

He offered me a job teaching diction for the rest of the year. I couldn't afford to tell him to shove it. So with reduced hours, I ended up teaching the very students that had wanted me ousted. Not a nice arrangement, but it settled my finances somewhat. Shaw retired from the college that year-end to return to Stratford to act. We both preferred life on stage.

Chapter 49

Coaching the Stars

By the early 1980s, I was beginning to be seriously go-getting in my coaching career. My most fascinating invitation came from a company filming a television version of George Bernard Shaw's *Pygmalion*. I agreed to coach Margot Kidder, a renowned Canadian film actress, plus two other actors who, I was told, needed assistance with pronunciation of "precise" English. This gig I could handle like a mitt. Or so I thought.

I'll be coaching Lois Lane from the Superman *movies!* I loved Kidder's un-romanticized spirit and her unusual melodic, raspy voice. I could now help guide this exciting young star toward a classical success.

On arrival at the studio, I found my two minor-role charges had no problems with accents. They were theatre trained. I could concentrate on Miss Kidder. Extremely bright and strong-willed, she had delightfully aced the Cockney accent of the lowly flower-girl, Eliza Doolittle, but Kidder's attempts at nobility would have proved challenging even to Shaw's Professor Higgins. In the play and the movie, Eliza successfully convinces the Edwardian aristocracy she is born of their ilk. But unlike her character, the actress-producer had little time for pure vowels. Her classes were arranged in whatever area of the site she happened to be located: on set, the makeup room, wardrobe, hair, or office. I tagged along attempting to have her focus.

When I caught her, I began with the basics.

"Repeat after me, Miss Kidder—"

"Oh, for God's sake, call me Margot."

"Thank you. Now, repeat: Hah-oo nah-oo, brah-oon cah-oo!"

"How now—"

"Listen! And watch my lips." I showed her. "Hahoo! Let the breath open wide the back of the throat," I said. "Smile back there!"

Between tasks Margo valiantly tried her sounds. Protecting her face from hairspray, she would shout, "What?" in answer to a call at the door. "I need to talk with advertising," she'd say, and be out of her seat and out the door.

As a co-producer, Margo had her mind on ten million problems. Although a good mimic, she couldn't repeat what she didn't hear. She had the looks, the stature, the elegance, but her vowels desperately needed "pluming." I wanted her to sound more like a virtuoso artiste than a student violinist.

I pleaded, "Eliza Doolittle practised for months before her big test."

I don't think she even heard me. I saw the star each day for approximately half an hour. She had, unfortunately, memorized her lines backwards and forwards, and heard already in her head how the lines sounded. Could she unlearn, relearn? A film set, with all its competing vibrations, is the last place to focus on something as profound as a change of habit. I was too late to help her reproduce subtle nuances of tone, rhythm, inflection, placement, all spoken in supreme confidence, or so I beleived.

On my second day, I enjoyed reconnecting with a few familiar faces as I wandered through the building toward my duty. In one corner of the huge main studio, all technicalities were being positioned for the significant Drury Lane market scene. I found one of my assigned students, Ron White, and several other Canadian actors already in their makeup and period costumes, waiting near the set. We lazily joked, as one does before the onslaught of intense work.

We were joined by Peter O'Toole, dressed as Professor Higgins, and John Standing, who was also imported for the movie. Standing I recognized as a familiar character actor who invariably appears in films as rather a pompous Englishman. O'Toole we all knew—or presumed we knew. But the famous actor was having no small chit-chat. Suddenly my soft summer cap was grabbed from my head. The tall, majestic imp entertained us, parading around like a fashion model. Then he began a game of catch. He and Standing were like teenage boys high on testosterone, leaping into the air with my hat as their ball. I dusted it and kept it for many years in memory of that outrageous actor. John Standing was another matter.

After the novelty of the ball game, the male stars joined us for a chat.

A young actor turned to me. "What do you do here if you're not crew?"

A discussion on accents began. Ron White, who played Freddie, commented on some difficulties he'd met in the past. Then O'Toole, with a facetious smile on his face, turned to Standing.

"Do you think you have any problems as Colonel Pickering?"

Standing made as though musing, then said with pseudo surprise, "I don't believe I do!" Tilting his head, he eyed me. "What do you think? Do I have any problems?"

I took a breath—and should have kept it held. As I'd watched the filming the previous day, I'd heard something questionable despite all the senior actor's remarkable experience. Here was a challenge to speak my mind. I'd spent years in psychotherapy learning to acknowledge my opinions.

"Yes, I heard a word that you mispronounce."

All eyes turned to me. There was silence. I watched Standing's choppy cheeks turn a cooked beet colour. His eyes stared, ugly, all humour gone.

"Well," I plunged foolishly on, "it's the word 'gal.' You pronounce it 'gail.' You make the word into a diphthong …" I faded out. I'd been utterly sincere. But halfway through my speech, I doubt enveloped me. I couldn't back down. I'd spoken my truth. Standing and I could have simply agreed to disagree on the subject of "gal," but the actor began accusing me of accusing him of errors of speech.

To Peter O'Toole, I have to hand a medal for cool and diplomacy in times of trauma. He quickly assessed the situation and escorted the distraught star toward some other distraction.

The matter, however, worsened for me. Fifteen minutes later, a tall, beefy executive-type, our American producer as it turned out, appeared at my side in the dark of the filming studio. He had me "step aside."

"I'm told you are causing a disturbance on the set," he said, his face several feet above me. "Miss Barton, you were engaged to instruct four actors, and only four."

"He *asked* my *opini*—"

"I must ask you to leave the set immediately."

I acquiesced. Well, one does, doesn't one? For the third time in my professional life, I'd been fired. That weekend was one of my most miserable. One's experience of being dismissed never lightens. But I did a bit of checking. John Standing was really somebody. Born and bred of British theatrical nobility—and later knighted by the Queen for his contribution to English theatre— I'd understood he was originally from Australia. I'd confused him with another well-known actor. I get confused regularly, to the ongoing delight of my friends.

I determined to make this humiliating experience a good lesson. I should have demanded a written contract. I'd been too keen—too flattered.

At dawn Monday morning, after two sleepless nights, I received a call.

"Miss Kidder wants you on set—8:30— SHARP!"

I was there at eight.

Miss Kidder appeared in the hallway of the studios, her eyes fixed on me, her finger pointing. "I want you always present," she called. "You understand? Wherever I am, I want you there!" She was ushered along by an assistant director into another conference room. She disappeared with a donut in one hand and a script in the other. Fortunately, I knew better than to be *always* by her side.

I was called again to continue close to the star, hearing and correcting her speech. Once again, thankfully, I stood in the middle of the tension and intensity of filming. Elated, I was given a captain's chair by a crew member and encouraged to relax near the live set, just within the curve of light, where I could be "in sight."

That day, I sat in the warm company of Frances Hyland, a fine Canadian actress I'd admired for years. We chatted comfortably. Margot joined us for a while. In the semi-darkness, she plunked herself in her private chair beside us. Between sucks on a straw from a can of Diet Coke, she complained how tired she must look.

Frances smiled fondly. "My dear," she said, "with that beautiful bone structure, you'll never look anything but perfect."

The star snuggled deeply into her chair. Such gentleness is rare in this business.

Before the day's work finished, a few minutes of break-time opened up for me. I stepped into a vacant and deserted area of the studios. Breathing deeply in the silence of the furnishings of a forsaken set, I contemplated. Not a word had been spoken in reference to the firing. Filming is a microcosm of life—one knows for certainty only rumours.

Suddenly, I felt another body enter the quiet space. It was John Standing. Like his name, he held himself on his feet, yet half in and half out of the light. I waited.

"I didn't know you graduated from Guildhall in London."

I felt my muscles let go. Was he about to apologize?

"I thought you local, you see—Canadian. I didn't realize you'd studied."

With sudden urgency, I moved away. "I have to get back."

Standing snapped to attention.

"Of course!" he said and stepped aside—like a perfect gentleman.

I guessed I'd proved acceptable. I knew then why I'd left England.

What transpired after my temporary dismissal I like to imagine: Margot furious, exploding with brassy wrath—all in her effective Western Canadian accent? Knowing Margot a little, I doubt Standing's complaints held up very long. As far as Margo's final performance in *Pygmalion*, I consoled myself with the knowledge that most in the audience would hear said exactly what they were told to hear.

* * *

One Friday evening I was flown to North Bay to give a stage vocalization workshop for the Gateway Theatre Guild: the class where I found my most unforgettable student. I cannot finish this book without telling of her.

The dainty, tiny lady arrived punctually on Saturday morning, escorted by a short, slim guy who addressed me. "I'm Richard Howard. My wife, Lila, is already registered. I'll come by to collect her at four."

Unusual care, I remember thinking as he departed, *although his wife certainly looks rather elderly.*

Because of an unexpected delay in opening the rehearsal hall of North Bay's newly renovated Capitol Centre on Saturday morning, I began the full class of twenty without the usual exchange of greetings. Likely the students were all familiar to each other, so I'd catch up. Not until the noon break when several students invited me to join them at a local diner, and we were well into chilli-con-carne, did I discover whose jaw I'd handled with especial care and attention that morning.

"My accent is troubling," Lila had said with genuine appeal.

Her accent was charm itself to me, but I'd sensed an urgency in her and understood the articulation problem. Despite her senior years, she appeared the most earnest student, so I'd taken extra time supporting her head and chin while she practiced vocal exercises.

"Lila's really getting into it, isn't she?" one student in the restaurant whispered, indicating with her head toward the next booth. "You know ... Lila Kedrova!"

My mouth opened. Half-munched chili beans fell onto my plate.

My informer smiled. "Didn't you know?"

Didn't I know my idol from *Zorba the Greek*, the movie—an Academy and Tony Award winner—had literally placed her head in my hands? This luminary figure from my drama-school days, the movie minx of sexual and exotic artistry, had shared herself as though she were a mere human.

I desperately wanted to find her in the next booth, to tell Miss Kedrova I'd sat through *Zorba* "forty times." One needs heroes. I'd once adored Claire Bloom—so elegant, so ... English. But in Kedrova I'd found the pulsating, dangerous spirit I'd secretly dreamed of.

After lunch break, I quickly touched ground, then stood tall before them all, concentrated like a pro, and shared equal time with all students. But I worried. Was I now avoiding this woman because of her fame?

"Marye, are you coming to join us this evening?" Mr. Howard asked, taking Lila by the arm at the appointed hour.

At these events, there is usually a highly anticipated Saturday night party offered for all participants. At eight o'clock, Mr. and Mrs. Howard were waiting for me in the hotel party room, where

370

a crowd was enjoying the free pizza and cold drinks. I longed for something stronger, but as the night wore on, I cared less for alcohol.

I sat by a wall, opposite my idol, more and more spellbound.

Her husband, sitting on the other side of me, said, "Lila tells me she's feeling safe and comfortable and learning plenty of helpful tips from you."

This more than pleased me. I could see my glamorous, aging star was well cared for with this man. I learned later, from research, that Richard Howard was a highly respected producer, director, and award winner. But that night I knew the Howards as a simple tender couple enjoying each other's stories, which they must have heard endless times before.

Lila grew more and more free as the evening progressed. She entranced me with tales of moviemaking and her life before her international fame: her work with the Moscow Art Theatre, that birthplace of modern dramatic art. I told her that in the 1970s I'd played Moscow and St. Petersburg on the Stratford Festival tour. I expected a return of awe but she simply smiled graciously. She was born in Russia, she said. No! I presumed French-born, like Madame Hortense in *Zorba*. Or Greek. I still believed what the moving pictures told me.

Even greater enlightenment came Sunday afternoon. We changed venues from a rehearsal hall to working directly on the grand stage of the new centre. The day went well. After a rousing final chorus of voices, I decided to offer a solo exercise for volunteers. Participants were invited to present a five-minute scene of their own invention, but I allowed them only one spoken word. Through body language and vocal skill, each performer needed to make clear the scene's Who, Where, What, When, and Why with the sole text: "Goodbye."

Sitting as audience on the polished floor of the stage, we guessed the farewell of soldiers leaving for war, or a distraught teen leaving home, a pet lover leaving the vet, funeral goers, and the time-honoured lovers parting. Not all performances were tragic, or clear: a somewhat confusing presentation came from a young man who simply stood in one spot with his arm up. "Goodbye," he shouted. We had no idea.

"I'm sailing off in an air balloon to Paris," he protested.

We laughed and cheered him on.

Lila volunteered last. She took us all to another realm of experience—to a change of breathing. Undeniably magnificent, we saw a divine diva excessively exultant in her farewell gesture, desperately reluctant to leave. After the grand double-handed kiss to "the gods," the actress turned away toward the opening between the back curtains. Turning toward the audience again, she grasped both sides of the blacks, her eyes embraced every-one. Then, hands to heart, lifting her chest, she uttered a brave, lingering, "Good ... bye." With a shaky smile, and a bow she moved to her left to disappear. But one tiny, pink hand, in the light, was seen gripping the edge of the curtain that she drew along with her, just a little. We watched the hand claw at the black fabric, then slowly slide downward. Finally, alone on the stage, the hand lay in the spotlight, jerking slightly before its ultimate stillness.

After the applause, I gave our celebrity a huge hug of gratitude before I flew back to Toronto star-stunned by her passion and skill. Lila taught me about true stardom—reminiscent of those twinkling brightnesses in the sky that stop giving only when they expire!

Lila Kedrova travelled to London, England the following year, at seventy-one, to perform brilliantly in Stephen Sondheim's *A Little Night Music.*

Chapter 50

Will Again

"You surprise me," Alf said. "From the history that I read in your hand you should be a lot weaker than you are."

In my mid-forties, I was visiting a recommended Irish palm reader by the name of Alf Marron.

"Will I be successful?" (My idea of "success" was of no more auditions, no need of endless short periodic gigs.)

"You will have many careers and many successes," was Alf's disarming answer.

If acting won't be primary, what are these other successes? Alf was busy still searching.

"And will I be happy in a relationship?" I asked as casually as possible.

"The man whom you've given your heart to is not what he seems."

I left with many unanswered questions.

I wondered about Alf's words about Will. Was my ex-boyfriend not a Jekyll and Hyde type? How does he really feel about me? By that time Will and I had been non- communicative for almost another year, although both living near each other in the Annex. Then one day he asked me out to dinner.

Do I, or don't I start again this whole damn thing between us?

"Dinner's a good way to renew friendships," Jillian said with practical sense, and was supported by two other women I'd asked. "Just don't drink too much," they laughed.

How could I still want a guy who gave me such grief with his forgetfulness, his lateness, his lack of dependability?

"You're very hard to love," I recalled Will once saying. *Was he any easier?*

My attachment to these dramas was a serious problem. Previously I had tried to describe my difficulty to Grant Goodbrand. "He thinks I'm fantastic no matter what I do." I was furious with Will for ignoring me yet at the same time quietly pursuing me. I forgot how inconsistent I could be, dropping everything if a great offer came. "Will looks up to me. It's awful. He says I'm really important to him."

"Are you not?" Grant asked.

"Nobody's that important."

Really caring was tough to take in. I didn't want to mean that much to *anyone*.

However, Will and I, the next Saturday evening, dined together at a first-class restaurant with candle and flowers as centrepiece on our table, and there, with the splendid food and an endearing face in front of me, all the irritations and rages of the past were forgotten.

On hearing Will's words during coffee, "… we could get married," my heartbeat quickened.

Will stayed staring intently at his cup.

"Was that a proposal?"

He opened his eyes to me. "I guess it was."

I knew. As sure as the quickening felt good, I knew our time had come. I almost shouted, "Why not? We've tried everything else."

He laughed, and we toasted, to us, with clinked coffee cups.

"I hate cooking and ironing and I will refuse to do your laundry," I warned him, although most of that changed after our wedding.

Will had been a true friend who had once spent days repairing the floor of my temporary teaching studio, who checked out my car for safety every time I took off for far away places. He was truly firm ground beneath my storms. The first time I knew I loved him was one chilly winter's day when I suddenly missed his bearlike hug, his deep and gentle lovingness. His presence almost always brought a gloriously feeling of completeness that I'd never known before. But then the feelings would disappear again into times when he seemed to drive me insane. Marriage may not be much different but at least we would be more together.

Chapter 51

Tracks

Before my engagement to Will, the realization that life in Therafields housing was not for me had strengthened. I no longer saw myself as needing all the distractions of community living. I'd joined Ann and Wayne who'd recently rented 183 Arlington Avenue, near St. Clair Avenue West. Everything seemed to come together for me: a huge space to myself on the ground floor with a basement where I held an active Friday night drama club for eager young thespians.

Cast of *Jack* in front of Will's Scenery

The outcome of the club was *Jack*, a musical based on the story of Jack and the Beanstalk, presented for one performance at Doug Saunders Auditorium in the Spring of 1982. One never knows where life will lead. I had great support with *Jack*, having the music especially written and played by John Korcok, the props and costuming designed and created by Kate Delmage, and Will Kennedy, my new fiancé made a great debut as scenic designer. Because I had written the book and lyrics, young Tom Sniders, who played Jack, must have related his enthusiasm to Barrie Nichol who, later, remembered me. However, my strength or interest didn't include producing, and when my energy was spent after one successful presentation, all I wanted was peace and quiet.

While were creating in Arlington Avenue, further northeast of the city, a board, "The Committee for the Development of a Professional Theatre in Cobourg," was having meetings. I was contacted by Jennifer O'Rourke, the administrator, who asked if I would apply to be its paid researcher in finding an artistic director plus a Canadian playwright, both willing and perfectly able. I accepted and presented the committee with applicants. Burton Lancaster was chosen as artistic director and bpNichol as playwright.

Burton Lancaster, director

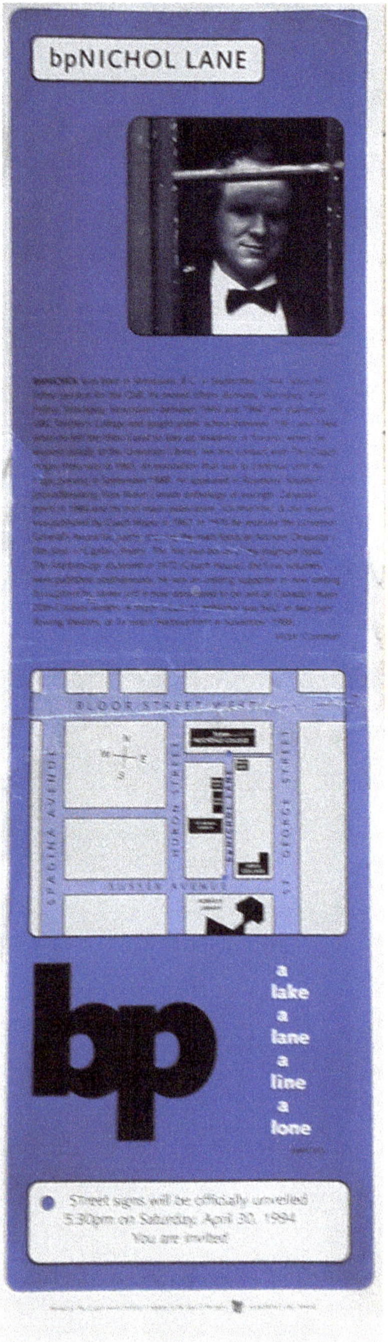

poster bpNichol Lane

detail of poster

"I've always wanted to write a musical," Barrie declared, "but I'd like it if you'd write together with me."

I was non-plussed.

Well, that's how that came about. Then the time came to collaborate. While nourishingly fed by Barrie's artist wife, Ellie, with delicious lunches for us each day as we sat in their comfortable rooms in Toronto's Annex, our long days of penning had superb support. To my surprise, I found the great Barrie Nichol to be extraordinarily ordinary. Without denying his own doubts about storylines, characters, or lyrics, I was able to relax into truly sharing ideas.

As we initially sat musing, amongst stacked bookcases and a jolly poster displayed on the back of Barrie's office door advertising his favourite musical *Singing in the Rain,* he told me, "Archibald Lampman was an inspiration to me when I was in high school. I've always loved that poet. He was from Cobourg."

We thought of maybe incorporating many famous people from that locale but finally zeroed in on the famous story of the Cobourg-Peterborough railroad venture of the early 1830s, Barrie said was built with a structure across Rice Lake to shorten the journey. Tragically the long bridge collapsed during the winter of 1860. (I have since, on a boat, been shown that those old tracks still can be seen, on good sailing days, just below the shallow waters near Harwood.)

Tracks the musical

"I'm into railroads. My father was an administrator for the Canadian National," Barrie proudly claimed.

We created a central family story plus railroad characters both from the 1880s and modern times, and the result was *Tracks,* with music by Philip Schaus, then leader of the Northumberland orchestra in Cobourg, also a professional cast, and chorus of local folk.

I'm happy to say *Tracks,* directed by Canadian theatre pioneer Burton Lancaster, didn't collapse but was claimed by audiences and local critics as "a triumph." (Toronto critics didn't make the trip).

On the first night, as I listened to the love song—there are always love songs in musicals—I recalled how much I dreaded trying to write it. I told Barrie I couldn't, "I only sound too cutesy sentimental," I said. But he suggested we both give it a try. The next day he produced a whole song.

When I presented my four lines, he cried, "Mary, you've found our chorus!"

His positivity as well as his talent was therapy for me, and so many others. It was with terrible sorrow that five years later we heard of his sudden death on a hospital operating table.

Chapter 52

Will and Mary

"You cannot be married in Mother Church unless you're practising Catholics."

We heard this repeatedly as Will and I searched for a priest. If our union was to be witnessed by all our friends from Therafields and elsewhere, followed by a big party, as we hoped, God, our essential ingredient, could not be missing.

Finally, we found Father McCabe, pastor of St. Peter's Church on Bathurst Street, across the street from where once stood the Grail Toronto Centre.

McCabe, a calm, handsome Paulist missionary from the US—and an intelligent student of theology—held the opinion that for the Sacrament of Marriage, all that was necessary were consenting celebrants, live witnesses, and the desire for consecration. The rest, he said, was "earthly tinsel."

"However, you are required to meet with me for six weekly sessions before the ceremony." Father McCabe stared at us under his graying eyebrows. "This, I'm afraid, is obligatory."

Obediently, we convened in his office for pre-marriage instruction.

"Companionship is an admirable reason for marriage," he began. He knew we expected no children. At my advanced age of forty-seven, the forbidden birth control for Catholics set no problem. To our relief, sex wasn't discussed further.

Will surprised me by attending all the meetings with no fuss.

"I've Irish background … was an altar boy for years," my chatty lover told McCabe with genuine enthusiasm.

Don't overdo it, I thought. I'd heard him scoff at God talk. Now he seemed over keen about the tuition, making sure I was on time, taking very seriously his role of protector-husband.

The meetings took enormous effort on my part. My equilibrium dropped with these highly personalized talks. This priest was getting to me with his generosity, his commitment, his speaking as though he cared for the two of us, and not merely as retrieved flock. Toward the end, I broke down in tears.

"You are angry with the Church, Mary. I can tell."

He hit the bullseye. I hated him too. He'd pierced a store of ire that came flooding through my mind. *I'm pissed off with your so-called leaders in holy goodness … you demand blind faith in a doctrine nobody actually understands, are afraid to argue with. How come you have the goods on God?*

Maybe my wanting a church blessing was my way of appeasing the ghostly, power-laden gods of the universe. If so, I readied myself for an earful of propaganda. Reconciliation might be a way out, but definitely no promises of mass every Sunday.

Finally, I sniffed and said, "I think the Church has a lot to answer for."

The Reverend Father quietly answered, "Human frailty is a mystery that will forever haunt us."

Caught between St. Peter's Rock and my own truth, I could only nod my head behind a wet hanky at human frailty.

Father McCabe was too wise a man to demand we submit to his beliefs. He simply wanted to know who we were and if he could help with spiritual foreplay (not his word) before administering the Blessing.

After our final instruction, he shook our hands, adding, "I wish every pre-marriage couple would be as prepared and as committed as you two seem to be."

We passed the test!

* * *

Will's mother was especially proud. She had married Will's father, then deceased, in that very St. Peter's Church. So good to recall, she said. His family were church-going folk. Most of our guests were of the "heathen" type, like Will and I. Many had never entered a church, perhaps with memories of ceremonies in gardens and living rooms, although one declared she'd actually heard of a female priest. I remember Paul Dutton crying, "A church? How novel!"

That chilly September afternoon, the nuptial ceremony almost never began. My brother John and I stood waiting in the church-yard for the signal to enter. Our guests, filling half of the nave, were sitting in pews, chatting, waiting, waiting, while Will's family, in the front row, sat mystified. Ann Young, my maid of honour, told me she stood by herself in front of the altar, flowers in hand, very worried.

Will's sister Joan had bustled around me, that morning, setting my hair and headpiece, my makeup, helping me on with a new white and beige knitted dress that Ann Young had assured me, the previous day was the perfect choice because the store was about to close.

No word from inside St. Peter's. The sounds of traffic from the nearby street were all John and I heard, until, suddenly, I found beside me a small, familiar-looking woman.

As though wanting to touch me, she leaned forward and said, "Is it all right if I go inside? I so love weddings."

My God, Nessa! So tiny and frail I hardly recognized my first therapist.

"Yes, please go in," I said. *Thank God I remembered to invite her.*

John opened one of the front doors, and my mother-figure from the past slipped inside like a lost cat. My heart followed her for a moment as the door closed, but then it reopened a crack. Charlie, a friend and an usher, poked his head around.

"No worries. The guy up front—in the frock— he's telling us this happens sometimes." His head disappeared.

What happens sometimes? I began to shiver.

My darling brother who had crossed the Atlantic with his family to "give away" his middle-aged sister put his arm around me. "*There was I, waiting at the church*," he sang, trying to make happy with an old Musical Hall song. This was worse than waiting in the wings to go on stage.

I smiled. John was a good man. But so was Will. He wouldn't do this to me. No, clearly there was a church problem. Yet I couldn't understand why no news.

Finally, Charlie's face reappeared. "We're good to go!"

The organ began, and we were off. Confident and fulfilled, I walked with my arm linked tightly with John's. Ahead, near the altar rails, I saw my Will waiting with Ben Woolfitt, his best man. Father McCabe stood centre, arrayed in white alb and long flowing, embroidered, green chasuble, holding his Holy Book.

I remember my brother reaching the altar and letting go of my arm. I felt a sudden chill. Then, turning to look for my intended, I swear I saw Ben nudge a startled Will forward. Strangely, both men looked hot and bothered, were breathing heavily, their eyes wider than seemed comfortable. Then, with Will's body tall and warm beside me, his hand firmly grasping mine, I felt us both relax.

As we followed our flower girl, Will's niece, Sarah, back down the aisle, the congregation gave us a standing ovation. We looked about us, saw our families, and Francie, Rod, Jillian, Frank, Barrie, Ellie, Jim, Paul, and so many from our Therafields years. Then Nessa, sitting alone in the back row.

"Please come to the feast," I asked her as guests gathered outside for photographs. But she declined gracefully. I discovered later that the poor woman was suffering from Alzheimer's disease, but nobody then knew.

Wedding group

At the reception, the reason for the delay was spread around. Will and Ben truly had forgotten the rings. Ben that morning had woken the groom from the bachelor's night on the town. He'd walked Will up and down the Toronto streets to ease both of their hangovers. Cleaned up, they had arrived at the church a half hour early to discover empty pockets. They had driven at top speeds to and from Will's place for the golden circles that made the magic happen.

Cutting wedding cake

"Typical," one was heard to say with a laugh. "Will probably forgot what day it was."

Friends and relatives were very forgiving. People laughed again as we all waited for the nuptial dinner—a seated meal for a hundred in a distant church hall in another parish. The activity coordinators at St. Peter's—less universal than our Father MacCabe—had refused use of the adjacent hall. We'd been forced to find another. Unfortunately, the hired caterer-friend found problems with a fused stove. Dinner was delayed at length as we nibbled cold canapés and drank more and more wine. All would be well. Janet, Will's sister, paid the wedding photographer to keep guests distracted with extra pictures while Joan, Janet's twin, acted as Jesus that night by driving out and miraculously returning with more wine.

Entertainment that evening included dancing to recorded music arranged by Jillian Cook, and brother John—a professional jazz musician who sang and self-accompanied on a loaned guitar. Finally, Will's surprise: enter Sharon Leigh Keates and James Carroll with accompanist Dr. Stan Boon! Even Barrie was stunned. The actors had agreed to be smuggled into the hall to sing the love song from *Tracks*, so beautifully performed by them that summer in Cobourg. Will beamed, especially pleased at keeping the secret.

The party lasted for hours. We asked not for gifts but whatever cash people could afford for a honeymoon in New York in December. People were generous. My husband and I left the hall after most guests had gone home. Both too excited to eat dinner all evening, we arrived for a two-day stay at The Harbour

Castle to find room service closed. After finishing a bag of chips from a machine, we fell asleep, laughing in each other's arms.

Each wedding is unusual, but I've never heard of the bride's family joining the couple on their honeymoon.

I said to Will, "I can't possibly enjoy this lavish living knowing they're all squashed into my apartment. They don't know the city—"

"We'll have a pool party," he shouted.

So we did. All afternoon, the pool and hot tub was ours alone. The kids didn't want to leave. Afterwards, on a sight-seeing walk, John and Margaret were beaming. Belinda, the eldest at fourteen, forgot to miss her boyfriend in England. John Junior, barely a teen, and Austin, his younger brother, seemed almost peaceful.

"Are they having a good time?" I asked.

John whispered, "Who can say? But they haven't fought since we left England."

Many years later, Austin sent a book he created from photographs taken during their stay in Toronto. It now sits in Will's hospital room, a treasure to him, too.

Our weekend honeymoon was a perfect dream. The New York visit with theatres and galleries would come later, and then, the settling in to walking a new path.

Epilogue

Will and I celebrated our fortieth wedding anniversary last year, even though I left him and our little East York house after living together for nearly thirty years. His generous sister Pat helped me pack. As I did, she encouraged Will to move with me as I had done, to a building with elevators, but his art studio in our garage was too hard for him to leave, and nobody guessed his health was about to fail completely. Amazingly, after the separation, we grew even closer.

Looking back, I see I gathered many life lessons from the groups and associations I've connected with. From Catholicism, mainly: sacred and evil; from The Grail Movement: the strength of womanhood; from Therafields: personal responsibility; from Ruah Toronto: universality, science, and mythology; and, most recently, the Shambhala community: meditation, humanity, and compassion.

All these communities, even the ones I only touched, such as Spiritual Science, the local indigenous, and the art of dowsing, are in search of healing the world's ills. They are all like a web of learning for whom I am so deeply grateful, as I am for all the "angels" who have help me along our journey together. I say "our" journey because now I know we are all together in this miraculous creation, one in this wondrous Earth.

Regarding my career: as Alf Marron predicted, I did follow more than one path, intrigued to discover whether or not I could dance them. Yet rarely lost my love of acting.

Regarding stars: today, Canada still supports no star system, yet now I live with a whole slew of "stars." By moving to the Performing Arts Lodges, Toronto (PAL), I joined flocks of divas, musicians, and a variety of performing artists and supporters—another group to learn from. Come visit us in our Celebrity Club where we entertain or cheer on our aging yet ever-giving talented community.

During our COVID-19 years, when we all were so very isolated, from my storage area I retrieved my amateur clown outfit—red nose, cute dress, funny shoes.

Mary as clown Joy Fuller

That dark winter evening, after testing my appearance at one neighbour's door—and she warning me to "Go home!"—I set myself up inside P.A.L.'s lobby in one of the red leather armchairs near the entrance. At a side table, my ghetto blaster played Django Reinhardt music while silently (a true clown does not talk) I tossed candy to the occasional incoming or outgoing resident, hailing the delivery folk or PAL people as they passed in and out of the elevators behind me. Unfortunately, after about an hour of this fun (for most people), the superintendent received a complaint about "the intruder" from a male resident of unfortunate wit who also, for a while, stood waiting in the lobby. Our superintendent's assistant was sent to forcibly evict me.

Because I could only smile my resistance, he threatened. "We're calling the police."

As my right arm was being dragged outside the main doorway, the lobby elevator doors opened and Pamela Hyatt, one of our prima divas, appeared and, having attended a workshop with me, quickly sized up the situation.

"Set her free! This instant!" her inimitable voice resounded. "Don't you recognize Marye Barton—the world's funniest female clown?"

Oh Pam! My heroine of far too much hyperbole!

The next morning, I wrote a note of apology to the supers for not asking permission. Carole Pilote of PAL residence posted a blind "Thank You" message on the notice board.

Note on PAL notice board

During my many years in this world I've come to see that I am, as is everyone, a combination of many fluctuating emotions, desires, accomplishments, failures, dreams, hopes, and disappointments. We are all in not on a stage.

Despite its failings, I am proud of the accomplishment of this book, and grateful for the enormous physical, mental and spiritual help on the way.

Acknowledgements

Firstly, my gratitude to my late husband and best friend, Will Kennedy, for his constant encouragement. He didn't care what I wrote as long as I wrote.

To FriesenPress for their patience, help and creativity as publishers, to the management, boards, staff, and especially the valuable volunteers at the Performing Arts Lodges, Toronto, for their space, time, and encouragement that residents creatively continue through their senior years – also, to my talent agent, Elvira Graham who, on several occasions, ignored my attempts to retire. To all, I offer my gratitude.

Throughout the 15 years of learning how to write a book, I have many people to thank for their generous help along the way, too many to recount and I am sorry that I cannot remember all.

For guidance and encouragement from several Toronto writing groups, the late Mick Burrs (poet), Neila Lem, Gary Labovitz (for his Toronto Alexander Technique classes), Cathleen Hoskins (psychotherapist and first adviser that I find more variety in my wording), the multi-talented Dave Wilson, Diana Griffin (for her amazing massage treatments and support), Pat Magosse (artist), Michael Marino (especially for his loan of *Bird by Bird* by Anne Lamott), Nicholas Power (poet, who is in the book), Sharon Marcus, Beth Anne Cole, Sylvia Hughes, Rosetta Raso, Elizabeth Leslie, Maria Sant'Angelo, Norman Hart, Valentina Hurtado Becerra, Agape Mpamira, Toronto Ruah, and the Shambhala Meditation Centre – to you all my deep gratitude.

20% of each book sold will be donated to PAL and GREENPEACE CANADA.